BONNIE DU

· *John Graham of Claverhouse* ·

BONNIE DUNDEE

FOR KING AND CONSCIENCE

॰๑๏

MAGNUS LINKLATER AND
CHRISTIAN HESKETH

CANONGATE

First published by George Weidenfeld & Nicolson Ltd

First published in paperback edition in 1992
by Canongate Press, 14 Frederick Street, Edinburgh

ISBN 086241 371 0

Printed in Great Britain by
Billing & Sons Ltd, Worcester

CONTENTS

Contents

ILLUSTRATIONS

ACKNOWLEDGEMENTS

That the Scots still feel passionately about their own history, and remain remarkably well informed about it, emerged strongly in the course of our research. Time and again we were given willing help by those whose local knowledge or family stories illuminated different aspects of the period we were interested in; those historians on whose territory we trespassed, were universally generous with their time and pointed us in the right direction. We would like to thank especially: Mrs Charles Findlay of Urrard, Mr James Mair of Newmilns; Professor Gordon Donaldson (H.M. Historiographer in Scotland), Dr. Julia Buckroyd, Mr Ronnie Black (Lecturer in Celtic Studies, Edinburgh University), Dr Ian Grimble, Marion Stewart (of the Dumfries Archive Centre), Iain Flett (Archivist at the City of Dundee District Council), Viscount Weir, Captain Alwyne Farquharson of Invercauld, the Revd Ian Anderson, the Revd Ian Hamilton, the Revd James Fraser, the Revd Ian Collins, the Duke of Buccleuch and Queensberry and the staff at Drumlanrig Castle, Major Maclean-Bristol, Miss J. Poyzer, Dr Rosalind Marshall (National Galleries of Scotland), Owen Dudley Edwards, Rosalind Mitchison, Lady Carnegy of Lour, E. Jarron, Lord Rollo, Helen Watson and Julie Murphy (National Gallery of Scotland, Publications Dept), Mary, Countess of Strathmore, and Ian Gow at the Royal Commission on the Ancient and Historical Monuments of Scotland, and Mrs M. Merrington, who compiled the index. The staff of the National Library of Scotland and the London Library were unfailingly courteous and professional. And once again the ability of local libraries in London and Edinburgh to locate and supply books not generally available, was impressive.

FOREWORD

*'Did you ever read about the death of Dundee? Graham
of Claverhouse, you know, who persecuted the Covenanters and had a black horse that could ride straight up a
precipice. Don't you know he could only be shot with a
silver bullet, because he had sold himself to the Devil?
That's one comfort about you; at least you know enough
to believe in the Devil.'*

*'Oh yes,' replied Father Brown, 'I believe in the Devil.
What I don't believe in is the Dundee. I mean the Dundee
of Covenanting legends, with his nightmare of a horse.
John Graham was simply a seventeenth-century professional soldier, rather better than most. If he dragooned
them, it was because he was a dragoon, but not a dragon.
Now my experience is that it's not that sort of swaggering
blade who sells himself to the Devil.'*

G. K. Chesterton, *The Incredulity of Father Brown*

On 27 July 1689, a battle was fought at a place whose name still has the
capacity, in Scotland, to arouse stark images. The name Killiecrankie
speaks of red-coated soldiers with smoking muskets facing wild Highlanders as they charge to death or glory, swinging their broadswords
and breaking the ranks of a terrified enemy. Few of the tourists heading
north along the road which now bisects the battlefield near Pitlochry in
Perthshire know much about the origins of the battle, or even about
the man who fought and won it – John Graham of Claverhouse,
Viscount Dundee. His relative eclipse this century is surprising, for he
was a crucial figure in the religious conflicts that tore Scotland apart
between the Restoration of King Charles II and the Union of the two

kingdoms in 1707. And in the Highland wars that settled the fate of the exiled Stuarts, he was a General to match Montrose.

The strong and vivid legends that surround him are built into the two names by which he is remembered. The first is Graham of Claverhouse, scourge of the Presbyterian Covenanters, still spoken of with bitterness in the west of Scotland, where his reputation is etched in folk memory and on crumbling gravestones throughout the shires of Dumfries, Ayr and Galloway. There he is recalled as a vicious persecutor, the very symbol of religious repression. It was Walter Scott in *Old Mortality* who first elaborated this picture of him, one which was then stamped firmly in the minds of Victorians by Macaulay, who wrote: 'Rapacious and profane, of violent temper and obdurate heart, [he] has left a name which, wherever the Scottish race has settled on the face of the globe, is mentioned with a peculiar hatred.'

But then there is the other man, Viscount Dundee, still remembered, mistily, as 'Bonny Dundee', he who championed the cause of the exiled James VII, led the Highland clans against the army of William III, and was killed in battle, thus robbing the Stuarts of the best chance they had to reclaim the throne they regarded as theirs by right. To them, Dundee was summed up in an elegy written after his death and put into verse by the poet Dryden:

> Oh, last and best of Scots, who didst maintain
> Thy country's freedom from a foreign reign.
> New people fill the land now thou art gone,
> New gods the temples, and new kings the throne.

As with many legends, the truth which lies at the heart of them is more complex and more interesting than the legend itself. Those historians who wrote much about Claverhouse in the last century and the early years of this one felt the need to challenge the image presented by Macaulay, and in doing so presented a Claverhouse so sanitized that he was virtually unrecognizable as a real human being. The great three-volume biography by Mark Napier, completed in 1862, which first revealed the many letters written by Claverhouse, is flawed by its author's fulminations against Presbyterian historians. More balanced works by Professor C. S. Terry and Michael Barrington in the early part of this century nevertheless ignored the political role that Claverhouse played as a close confidant of King James, the influence he had in the formation of policy, and the contribution he made to the stability of the state as a sheriff in the west of Scotland.

For fifty years there has been no reappraisal of John Graham of

Claverhouse. This book does not claim to be a definitive biography, but it does attempt to portray him as a man rather than a symbol, and here lies, in our view, the most intriguing aspect of his life. For Claverhouse, as Father Brown so wisely observed, was, for most of his life, 'a seventeenth-century professional soldier', schooled in the military disciplines of his time, and a determined supporter of law and order. Yet he ended his days as a rebel commander at the head of a ragged clan army in the hills of northern Scotland.

Explaining how and why he did so has been, in the end, our main objective. In doing so, we have been back to original sources, to the many letters written by Claverhouse and his contemporaries, and to the official documents of the period. These we have examined in the light of the many advances made by contemporary historians in reaching an understanding of the period, and the reassessments these have occasioned.

Any modern writer addressing contemporary accounts of life in seventeenth-century Scotland faces certain decisions about the manuscripts and document she or he encounters. The first is spelling. Claverhouse himself was accused by Sir Walter Scott of spelling 'like a chambermaid', but he was by no means unique among his class, and in fact was better than most. Variety, not to say eccentricity, seems to have prevailed amongst letter-writers of the day. We have chosen to use modern spelling to make all quotations straightforward and easy to follow without changing their sense. Likewise, we have made minimal corrections to grammar when that seemed necessary. Here and there, however, when the spelling appeared to us essential to the character of a particular document, we have left it as it was. Claverhouse himself spelt his name 'Grahame', with a final 'e', and Dundee as 'Dundie'. In both cases we have used the modern spelling. This has also been the rule in translating the names of the various Highland clans and their chiefs.

Scottish measurements and money also present problems. The Scots mile was 1,973 statute yards, which makes the distances routinely travelled by Claverhouse's troops in the course of a day even more impressive. Money was scarce in Scotland: £1 Scots was worth one-twelfth of an English £. A Merk was worth two-thirds of a Scots £. Many of the fines levied on recalcitrant Whigs, large as they sound, may well have been paid in kind, as were rents.

More complex has been the task of exploring the character of Claverhouse himself, without imposing modern values inappropriate to the times he lived in. We have sought to place him firmly against the background of his century, and to see him through the eyes of his contemporaries. If, in the course of that, we have succeeded in bringing him to life, then the enterprise will have been worthwhile.

What has emerged is a man driven by twin forces, rare in his time – a fierce sense of loyalty to the King in whom he believed, and a total confidence in himself and the dictates of his own conscience. Neither of these made John Graham of Claverhouse an easy man for his friends or his enemies. But he emerges in the end as one of the more remarkable figures in the history of a country which has not been short of remarkable men.

Magnus Linklater
Christian Hesketh
Edinburgh, 1989

CHAPTER ONE

Assassination

*'They were acted by a spirit of hellish and insatiable
cruelty'*

Privy Council of Scotland, May 1679

The coach which laboured up the rough track towards the ridge-top of
Magus Moor marked its owner out as a man of high rank. It was a
handsome affair, London-built, topped with nine gilt coronets, and
bearing the royal coat of arms. Drawn by a full team of six horses and
manned by a coachman and postilion, with a footman at the rear, it was
accompanied by two outriders, armed with carbine, pistol, and sword.

In the midday sun of an early May day, the coach stood out against
the drab green of the moor which sloped diagonally eastwards along
the Kinness burn, before falling away to the sea and the broad sands of
St Andrews Bay, three miles distant.

It carried two passengers, James Sharp, Archbishop of St Andrews,
and his daughter Isabel, now on the last stage of a two-day journey
from Edinburgh, and approaching their destination, the cathedral city
of St Andrews. The Archbishop, at the age of sixty a grey-haired but
still vigorous figure with a set and tight-lipped look to his face, had
expressed anxiety about these last few miles. He had few friends in this
part of the country, and he knew of at least one man in the neighbourhood who would seize any chance of attacking him. He had already
been the target of a crude assassination attempt in Edinburgh when he
had narrowly escaped with his life, and the incident had left him with
an almost permanent sense of wariness.

As the coach neared the point where the road began to run down
towards the tiny village of Strathkinness, a band of horsemen appeared
on the track behind them to the south. There were nine of them, led by

a small stocky figure, swarthy featured, squint-eyed and bearded, with holster pistols on his saddle, and carrying the long curved sword known as a shable, looped to his right wrist.

Seeing them closing in, the Archbishop urged his coachman to whip up the horses, and the team gathered speed. For a time they made ground, but the pursuers, galloping hard, closed the gap. One of the Archbishop's mounted servants, who had dropped back behind the coach, tried to fend off the attackers, but as he cocked his weapon he was cut down by a sword-blow to the head. The first of the band to pull alongside the coach leant in and fired a pistol through the window. The shot ploughed across the Archbishop's chest and scorched his cloak but left him unhurt. His daughter beat out the smouldering cloth with her hands.

Now others amongst the nine pursuers caught up, and they began slashing at the traces and at the ham-strings of the horses. One of them struck out at the driver, wounding him in the face, and finally the coach lurched to a stop.

The Archbishop was ordered out. At first he refused to do so, sitting back in the coach and trying to talk the men out of their plan. But one of them leant in and stabbed hard at him, wounding him with a sword-thrust to the kidneys. Now surrounded by his attackers, he opened the door of the coach and came out, falling to his knees in front of them. One of the band, a tall figure on a white horse, stood away from the rest. The Archbishop turned to him for help, but he refused to intervene as the rest of the men closed in.

Held back in the coach, his daughter watched in horror as the end came. Her father's hands were cut as he tried to fend off the sword-thrusts, then a massive blow caught him above the left eye and he fell to the ground. Several more blows split open the back of his skull. There was a final deep stab to the stomach, but the Archbishop was already dead.

Turning from the body, the men ordered his daughter out of the coach and began to search through its contents. What they found confirmed the status of its owner. There was a trunk full of fine clothes which they went through and discarded; a magnificent bible, engraved with coloured pictures of the Saviour and the saints; a pair of well-wrought French pistols in a case; and a box of state papers. These the men looked through carefully, together with some other documents they found lying in the coach and which they bundled together to take with them.

They appeared to be in no hurry. Their search completed, they disarmed the servants and rode back down the track, leaving the Archbishop's daughter to tend the body of her dead father. The whole attack had lasted three-quarters of an hour, and though it had taken place in open country, not far from at least one garrisoned village, no one seemed to have heard the shots or acted to intervene.

The murder of James Sharp on Saturday 3 May 1679 was not only a savage and shocking affair, it had profound consequences for the Scottish state. In a turbulent decade it stood out as an act of particular brutality, one that struck at the heart of the King's Government in Scotland and called for immediate retaliation.

It would be used by the Privy Council, acting in the name of Charles II and with his express approval, to usher in extreme measures of suppression, not only against those believed to be supporters of the Archbishop's murderers, but against all who refused to condemn them. The murder itself would become a talisman in the conflict of faith that divided the people of Scotland, cited by both sides as a test of allegiance.

Archbishop Sharp, Primate of all Scotland, had been a key player in the affairs of the nation for more than two decades. As such he had conferred frequently and personally with Oliver Cromwell, then, later, with Charles II, arguing with both about the conduct of religious affairs in Scotland, and the political state of the country. As a bishop and the most Reverend Father in God, he was dedicated to fighting for the independence of the Scottish Church. But as a Privy Councillor, and the last in a long line of political bishops, he was involved in the dangerous art of compromise.

At the time of his death he was, in the eyes of his critics, and even of some of his friends, a discredited figure who was judged to have sacrificed his principles on the altar of secular ambition. He was accused by his enemies of corruption, perjury, and the cynical manipulation of power – and some at least of these charges were justified. But the manner of his death resolved, for the Privy Council at least, all controversy over his public role. 'Let the unjust world say what they will,' commented the Chancellor, Lord Rothes, 'he was not only Lord Primate of this kingdom, but a very faithful subject ... I do not know what to do since he is gone but to revenge myself on all that murdering sect.'

The first news of his murder was brought when his daughter Isabel, with the wounded servants and injured horses, arrived finally in St Andrews with her father's body. A small band, including one of the footmen who had been with the Archbishop when he died, set out for Edinburgh. Their horrifying account of the attack was delivered to a full meeting of the Privy Council, which met all day at Rothes's lodgings to hear first-hand evidence of the assassination.

A proclamation was drawn up on the afternoon of Sunday 4 May, and was sent out to be posted on the market crosses of Edinburgh, Fife, and Kinross. It left no doubt about the seriousness with which the killing was viewed. The 'late horrid and bloody murder' was an act of open treason, said the proclamation, and the Privy Council linked the murder directly with the many outdoor services, or 'conventicles', which were being held up and down the country by Presbyterian dissidents in defiance of the orders of the Council.

These dissidents were the Covenanters, so called after the document which stood as an article of faith for them – the National Covenant, drawn up in 1638 to proclaim the Scottish Church's defiance of Charles I's hated innovations to their traditional forms of worship. Now, under Charles II, they were outlaws, their ministers driven out of churches to hold their illegal conventicles on windswept fields and hills. These acts of worship were denounced as 'rendezvouses of rebellion, and forges of bloody and jesuitical principles'.

But it was the brazen nature of the attack on the Archbishop which most offended the Council:

> ... which murder is, as far as is possible, rendered yet more detestable by the unmasked boldness of such as durst openly with bare faces, in the midst of our kingdom, at mid-day, assemble themselves together, to kill in our highway the primate of our kingdom, and one of our privy council, by so many strokes and shots, as left his body, as it were, but one wound, and many of which being given after they knew he was dead, were remarkable proofs they were acted by a spirit of hellish and insatiable cruelty.

The people of Fife were ordered to assemble on specific days to be questioned by the sheriff-deputes in each town. A reward of 10,000 merks was posted for information leading to the arrest of the murderers, and an indemnity was offered to any of those involved who would turn king's evidence.

Within days, the identity of most of the attackers had been established, and their names issued as wanted men. Chief among them were the two who had led the attack, both lairds, the thickset John Balfour of Kinloch, who had laid on the first blow, and the enigmatic David Hackston of Rathillet, who had stood back from the killing but had failed to intervene to save the Archbishop's life. The others were tenant farmers: James Russell in Kettle, George Fleming in Balbuthie, Alexander and Andrew Henderson in Kilbrachmont, William Dingwall in Caddam, and George Balfour in Gilston. Finally, there was a Dundee weaver called Andrew Guillam.

But it was Balfour of Kinloch and Hackston of Rathillet who would become, in the next few weeks, the chief names to be quoted as symbols of the fierce opposition in Scotland to the Government and the King.

One hundred miles from the place where Sharp had been hacked to death, and on the morning after his murder, a man whose name would become every bit as notorious, though for very different reasons, was riding hard through thick fog with sixty troopers and a hundred dragoons at his back.

Captain John Graham of Claverhouse, one of King Charles II's officers in Scotland, had set out early that day from his garrison at Dumfries with the aim of reaching the Lowther Hills by mid-morning. His objective was a patch of windswept moorland somewhere beyond the headwaters of the River Ae where he hoped to come upon a handful of rebel preachers and their scattered congregations. Finding anyone when he arrived there was a matter of chance, since his intelligence was a week old and his information at best imprecise. But his mission was to help maintain the peace of the nation, and, as always, he was carrying it out with the professionalism of an experienced officer.

He had pushed his men as fast as the mist would allow, riding without a break over rough country where paths were non-existent and the marshland treacherous. The troopers, on their big English horses, were fresher to the task than the dragoons, who under their Captain, John Inglis, had been summoned at short notice the previous day from their headquarters at Kirkcudbright, forty miles away, and had been given barely half the night to rest. Some of them were riding two to a horse, since Claverhouse had ordered them to mount the foot-soldiers behind them. But they were less heavily armed than the troopers, and the smaller cobs they rode took the uneven ground better.

Claverhouse himself, aged thirty-one, short and slightly built, with delicate, almost feminine, good looks, was the best-mounted amongst them. He rode a big sorrel stallion and was lightly armed with a sword and a pair of fourteen-inch pistols. There was no doubting the authority he bore. He had sensed that morning an eagerness for action amongst his men, and he had given them a brisk warning before they set out that they must either 'fight in good earnest or be judged as cowards by a Council of War'. He was fully aware that some of those they were pursuing that day were armed and would be prepared to fight, and, as a soldier he was far from being dismayed at the prospect. But he was not over-confident about the information on which he was working. He had been told that on the previous Sunday three or four notorious preachers had held illegal conventicles in Glenae, around Queensberry Hill, then further north towards Crawford Moor. But whether they would be there again that day was a matter for conjecture. He had complained about the meagre resources he had been given for his military operations, and in particular about the lack of money to pay spies. But nothing extra had been forthcoming. And the fog was not helping.

Those whom he hoped to track down were far from conventional rebels. That they were men of God was not in doubt, but their refusal to conform to the new laws had driven them from their churches out on to windswept hills or into draughty barns, where they preached with all the passion of their convictions.

For Claverhouse and his lieutenants, they were troublemakers whose names figured on a list of wanted men published by the Privy Council. One of them, Richard Cameron, who was to become an almost mythical figure in the years ahead, figured high on the list, together with his brother Michael, who was on the run after a scuffle in a dark Edinburgh close which had left a soldier of the City Guard close to death. Both faced the possibility of execution if they were caught.

For King Charles in London and his Secretary of State for Scotland, John Maitland, Earl of Lauderdale, men like these, with their 'fanatical principles', were not so much religious dissenters as part of a mounting political problem. It was one they were determined to confront and deal with by force before it grew into civil war. A succession of royal bonds and indulgences held out to the expelled or 'outed' preachers to lure them back to the Church had not only been rejected, but fed their determination, driving them from one conventicle to the next. Their reputations as eloquent exponents of their faith spread steadily across the country.

Some of them were now drawing congregations of thousands – tenant and laird, women and children alike – and had armed guards to protect them, and well-posted lookouts to warn of approaching troops. 'Their meeting places are most commonly at the side of a moss or the side of a river', wrote Rothes to Lauderdale, and they have their spies at a distance on all hands who give warning if any party appears ... the cause of most of this trouble is occasioned by some outed ministers against whom both council and commission have proceeded. They have put themselves in disguise so as when they preach they are in grey clothes ... and it is alleged some of them preaches in masks and these rogues stir up the women so they are worse than devils.

Soldiers who had attempted to intervene had been attacked, robbed, beaten, and in some cases killed. The view from Edinburgh and London was that parts of Scotland were in a virtual state of civil war. The murder of Archbishop Sharp confirmed them in that belief.

Claverhouse, though he knew nothing as yet of the events on Magus Moor, was well acquainted with Sharp, who had been Professor of Divinity at St Andrews University in his third year there, and was now, as a Privy Councillor, one of his political masters. The news, when it reached him, confirmed the reports which he and his fellow-commanders had been sending back to Edinburgh, reports which painted a picture of growing disorder in the country. They described the weekly conventicles as 'seeds of rebellion' and listed incidents, small in themselves, which showed how volatile the situation had become.

Only that week, eight soldiers had been thrown into irons by their officers after a running brawl which ended with them trying to burn their way into a farmhouse. And a trooper in one of the neighbouring companies was on the point of death after being stabbed with a pitchfork in the course of a drunken fight. As Claverhouse and his men rode north through Nithsdale, they were prepared at any moment to face trouble.

But they found nothing. The trail was cold. People they questioned on the way either affected ignorance or were deliberately vague. They followed the steep course of the Water of Ae towards the head of the glen, and then crossed over towards the hill of Queensberry. It was deserted. They swung west to join the main track beyond Thornhill, and headed for the bleak expanse of Crawford Moor.

This time they came unwittingly within three miles of a great congregation of worshippers. But they saw and heard nothing of it, and only learnt about it later when they stumbled on, and took prisoner three startled men who were on their way back from the service. With this the sole prize of a dispiriting military expedition, they turned around and marched next day back to Dumfries. Two parties of troopers, sent ahead to spy out the land, got lost and failed to return until the next day. By the time they were back in the barracks, they had covered all of fifty miles to no very good effect.

This was far from the kind of soldiering for which Captain Graham had been trained. In his time he had served under Marshal Turenne, along with officers like John Churchill, later Duke of Marlborough. He had faced Condé's cavalry at the murderous Battle of Seneffe, and had been at the siege of Maastricht with William of Orange. What he was engaged in now was little more than police-work. But it was hazardous nonetheless. 'This may prove in a sudden dangerous', he had warned his Commander-in-Chief, the Earl of Linlithgow. The south-west of Scotland was, in his opinion, 'the most irregular place of the kingdom'.

When, therefore, he sat down on 6 May 1679, two days after his abortive expedition, to pen a report from his headquarters at Dumfries Castle, his letter was a catalogue of restrained complaint. It reflected his dissatisfaction with the conditions in which he was expected to control the area: the poor supplies, the lack of support from his superiors, and the paltry funds from those who were meant to be paying his troops. Although he had held his command for less than a year, he did not hesitate to single out by name those whom he believed to have fallen short of their responsibilities. They were powerful men: the Earl of Queensberry, who, as heritable sheriff of the area, was his immediate overlord, and Sir William Sharp, the late Archbishop's brother, who was cash-keeper to the King, and thus his paymaster.

It was the letter of a man with a clear and unquestioning sense of obligation, but an equally clear view of what others owed him; an awkward man, it would appear, with high standards and the expectation of a similar rectitude in others; a conventional military man, trained to a strict code of discipline, but by no means subservient; a hard commander, but self-evidently a humane one, whose letter ended not only with the understatement characteristic of his class, but on a note of compassion:

> My Lord, I hope your Lordship will pardon me, that I have not sent in the prisoners that I have here. There is one of them that has been so tortured with the gravel [gallstones] it was impossible to transport him. Besides, expecting considerable orders, I had no mind to part with thirty or forty horses. And then, Sunday's journey has a little jaded our horses. No appearance here of any stir . . . .

The confidence expressed in that report was now about to face its strongest test. Within a month, Claverhouse was to have the confrontation which he and his men had long been expecting. Under the steep crest of Loudoun Hill, forty miles to the north of Dumfries, at a place called Drumclog, he would encounter a ragged but determined army, which would turn from prayers and hymns to do battle with pitchforks and pikes. Among its ranks would be Hackston of Rathillet, Balfour of Kinloch, and James Russell, three of the murderers of Archbishop Sharp, still uncaptured and now joining forces with those who applauded their deed as a blow for freedom.

The resulting combat would be more a bloody skirmish than a true battle, but its significance would reach far beyond the little stretch of moorland on which it was fought, to become a landmark in the history of the Church in Scotland. It would be one of only two battles in the course of Claverhouse's life in which he commanded.

It would also be his first and last defeat.

CHAPTER TWO
A Soldier's Tale

I saw the man who at St. Neff did sie
His conduct, prowess, martiall gallantrie.
Anon

On 5 October 1675, James Graham, chamberlain to the Claverhouse family, wrote to acknowledge the receipt of some family jewels from David, Earl of Northesk. They had belonged to John Graham of Claverhouse's mother, Lady Magdalene, who had just died. Her son, then aged twenty-seven, had asked for them back, and now they had arrived, though not all of them:

> ... ane embroidered purs, quhairin ther is ane pear of gold bracelleitts, an gold ring, in it a litel diamond, another smal ring of litell worth, ane litell hinger sett about with stons and sum rubies, wherof it leaks on ston, and hath an litell pearl; which things did belong to the leat Lady of Clawerhous, and was given to the Earl of Ethie [later Northesk] in custody, with the consent of the sed Laird of Clawerhous his freinds; which particollars abowe names I obleidge me, my airs, execotoris, and sukcessors to preserw and keip for the behow of the sed John Graham of Clawerhous, his airs or assignais. Butt it is to be remembred, that there is yitt in the custody of the sed noble Earll an portugall dowcott, ane ear whoop, with ane peic of monij wyghting thrie six dollors, which was leikways delywert up to the sed Earll of Ethie, with the affoirsed particollars.
>
> In witness wherof I haw wreitin and subscraywed thes presentis with my hand, at Errol, the fyft day of October, JmVIc and seventie ffyw yeirs, befoir this witnesses . . . .

There is no record of whether Claverhouse ever retrieved his 'portugall dowcott' or his 'ear whoop', but the Grahams were thorough people, and he would certainly have pursued the matter if they had not been found and delivered.

The history of great Scottish families is usually marked by the milestones of their stirring accomplishments, from battles, victories, and deeds of valour or treachery, to the seizure or surrender of territory. The record of the 'proud' Grahams has no lack of these. But closer scrutiny of the 400 years, from the thirteenth to the seventeenth century, in which their fortunes fell and rose shows that the kind of careful accounting which James Graham demonstrated as he listed the family's modest collection of jewels was every bit as characteristic of them as their participation in great events. This was particularly true of the Claverhouse branch, whose calculated marriages, civic responsibility, and husbandry of their lands around Dundee show that they succeeded in avoiding to a remarkable extent the military and religious conflicts that shook and divided Scotland in the sixteenth and seventeenth centuries.

It is, of course, the exception that commands most attention, and the military exploits of James Graham, first Marquis of Montrose, on behalf of Charles I, stand out to this day as spectacular feats of arms, and generalship of a high order. His devotion to the Stuart cause and the way in which he rallied the clans to its support have usually been held up as formative influences on his kinsman, John Graham of Claverhouse. But Claverhouse himself rarely referred to Montrose, and his many letters reveal far more of Graham prudence than any sense that he wished to emulate his kinsman's achievements. Not until his own Highland campaign did the parallels between their two careers come close.

The Grahams traced their origins back to the Anglo-Norman aristocracy, and the lordship of an English manor, recorded in the Domesday book as Graegham or 'grey home'. The first Graham of note in Scotland was William de Graham, who came north with the Earl of Huntingdon, later King David I, and witnessed the royal charter which founded the Abbey of Holyroodhouse in 1128. By the following century the family had acquired land in central Scotland: Sir Patrick de Graham, who was killed at the Battle of Dunbar against the English in 1296 – 'lamented and applauded even by his enemies' – married into the powerful house of the Earls of Strathearn, and was granted an estate on the banks of Loch Lomond. That wild and beautiful territory was passed by Sir Patrick's son, David, to King Robert Bruce, by royal request, in exchange for estates at Montrose in Angus, thus establishing the family's long connections with the east coast of Scotland.

In the early fifteenth century, Sir William Graham of Kincardine cemented the family's royal connections by marrying, as his second wife, Lady Mary Stewart, daughter of King Robert III. The eldest son of this union, Sir Robert Graham of Fintry and Strathcarron, was the direct ancestor of the Grahams of Claverhouse, who thus acquired a trace of royal blood.

The first Graham of Claverhouse, recorded in the fifteenth century, was John, the elder son of Sir Robert Graham of Fintry and Strathcarron and Matilda, daughter of Sir James Scrymgeour of Dudhope. The Claverhouse branch therefore brought together royal blood and strong links with the City and title of Dundee. For Robert was the grandson of King Robert III, and Matilda's family, the Scrymgeours, were not only Scotland's hereditary standard-bearers, but also Constables of Dundee, and owners of Dudhope Castle on the outskirts of the city. Later on, in the seventeenth century, they became Earls of Dundee.

In his time, John Graham of Claverhouse would acquire both the Dudhope property and the title of Dundee.

The lands owned by the Claverhouse Grahams lay in Angus and in Perthshire. Over the years, in steady but unspectacular fashion, the family added estate to estate, until, by the seventeenth century, they were substantial landowners, their property stretching from Dundee north and west towards Kirriemuir and the Sidlaw Hills and east to a line between Forfar and Broughty Ferry. The first recorded lands were those of Ballargus in the regality of Kirriemuir, obtained under charter by John, grandson of Sir William. By 1530, his son, another John, had acquired Claverhouse, itself an estate some three miles north-east of Dundee, alongside the Dighty Water. It first appears in the records in 1534 as belonging to John Graham's son another John. For the next hundred years this was to be the family's main abode, but apart from a name on the map there is now no trace of the 'Barns of Claverhouse' as it is now called.

It was John Graham of Claverhouse's great-grandfather, Sir William, who was the most successful and acquisitive of his forebears. William Graham was a member of Parliament in 1633, was knighted, and was twice married. In 1620 he bought Claypotts Castle, a mile north-west of Broughty Ferry, a small sixteenth-century keep, now surrounded by urban dwellings. Twenty years later, he acquired the lands and barony of Glen Ogilvie, eight miles to the north, in the parish of Glamis. Henceforth, Glenogilvie, known locally as 'Glen', became the family home. Until John Graham of Claverhouse acquired something better, the family divided its time between Claypotts Castle and the 'house, biggings, yards and orchards' which surrounded the 'tower, fortalice and manor place of Glen', as it was described in Claverhouse's marriage contract.

Sir William was born into a turbulent century. Given the family's brave history and royal connections, it is surprising that it was not sucked into the upheavals of the Civil War and the campaigns of its chief, the Marquis of Montrose. The more so because the ties linking Sir William to the House of Montrose were particularly close. Montrose, who was the fifth Earl and later the first Marquis, was only fourteen when his father died. Curators were therefore appointed to manage his affairs until he attained his majority, and amongst them was Sir William Graham of Claverhouse. He is recorded as taking a close and solicitous interest in the young Earl's affairs, pointing out at one stage, in typical Claverhouse manner, that there should be a proper accounting of the rentals from the Montrose properties at Mugdock, north of Glasgow, and insisting that he would pay for his own horses when he travelled to Kincardine on Montrose business. He was, therefore, a close friend of the family, a neighbour, and trusted as a reliable adviser.

But Sir William died in 1642, two years before the young Montrose embarked on his spectacular Highland war, and his son George, a Justice of the Peace who married into a respectable local family, the Fotheringhams of Powrie, died only three years later, in 1645, without showing any warlike tendencies. George Graham's heir, William, was Claverhouse's father. He inherited the property at a critical period in Montrose's campaign, but, despite his connections with the Montrose branch, he neatly avoided answering the Graham call to arms, while not noticeably losing face with the rest of the clan, almost all of whom came out in Montrose's support.

He did so by judiciously supporting both sides – advancing money to the Government when asked, and serving on one of their local war-committees, while remaining a supporter of the King at heart. His generosity clearly had its limits – in March 1649, he was named as one of those who had failed to lend 'any money to the public in the time of the Troubles'. But he managed – just – to avoid reprisals, and that in itself was a remarkable achievement, for the great religious divisions of the time touched virtually everyone – lords, lairds, and commoners.

It was the King's Scottish subjects who first instigated the developments which led to the Civil War. The Scottish passion for the Reformation, the unquenchable belief of its supporters in the rigorous principles of Calvin, led to a growing conviction among some that Presbyterianism should not only be the religion of Scotland but the established faith of England and Ireland as well. These feelings were matched in intensity by a deep-seated fear that the moderate Episcopacy imposed on the Kirk by King James might bring about a return of Popery under his son. At his accession, Charles I inherited an ageing Privy Council, suspicious of change. He could not understand its opposition to his proposed reforms, the most radical of which, as he saw it, stemmed from his father's policies. The difference lay in their implementation. James VI always maintained a balance between the sharply-defined views he held, and a wary avoidance of dangerous confrontations. His son shared only the first characteristic.

When he came north, with the future Archbishop Laud, to be crowned at Holyrood in 1633, he insisted on the full Anglican rites, with candles, crucifix, and the already contentious bishops officiating. In 1635, he appointed an Archbishop, John Spottiswoode, as Chancellor. He then set up a commission to revise the prayer book, thus challenging the validity of the Scottish ritual, with its emphasis on extemporary prayers and an absence of ceremony. By doing so, he was judged by many to aim at the Anglicanization of an independant church and the promotion of political bishops. As Robert Baillie, one of his critics, wrote: 'Are we so modest spirits and are we so towardly handled that there is appearance we shall embrace in a clap such a mass of novelties?'

And when, on Sunday 23 July 1637, the new prayer book, derided as the 'Popish-English-Scottish-Mass-Service Book' was read for the first time at St Giles in Edinburgh, it was heard by a congregation 'in the white heat of indignation'. The service broke up in disorder when some of the women among the worshippers hurled their stools at the pulpit in a planned demonstration. Before long, the wrath of the mob had reached such a pitch that the Privy Council had to retreat down the Royal Mile to find sanctuary in the Palace of Holyroodhouse, and the Bishop of Brechin took to conducting his services with a pair of loaded pistols in front of him.

Protests continued and grew all that year, but the King refused to back down. Instead he issued a proclamation, ordering all the nobles of Edinburgh who had opposed the prayer book, to conform or leave town. This proved unacceptable and led finally to the signing, in 1638, of the National Covenant. As a document it was carefully designed to appeal to as wide an audience as possible, yet passionate in its commitment to the true religion.

The National Covenant was a symbol of Scotland's rejection of the Divine Right of Kings in favour of man's duty to God, and much of it was a closely argued denunciation of Roman Catholic doctrine. It was attractive to nationalists, for it contained a defence 'against our poor country being made an English province', but, in a key and carefully worded passage, it acknowledged the authority of the King:

> We promise and swear that we shall, to the utmost of our power, with our means and lives, stand to the defence of our dread sovereign the King's Majesty, his person and authority, in the defence and preservation of the aforesaid true religion, liberties and laws of the Kingdom.

Close reading of the passage in question shows that the acknowledgement was conditional. It could be, and was, argued that if the King did not himself defend the faith, then his authority was empty, and in this it echoed the famous Declaration of Arbroath of 1320: 'But after all if this prince shall leave these principles he hath so nobly pursued . . . we will immediately endeavour to expel him as an enemy . . . and make another King.'

Finally, the document contained a promise that was to be regarded by its subscribers as unbreakable:

> . . . we promise and swear, by the great name of the Lord our God, to continue in the profession and obedience of the foresaid religion; and that we shall defend the same, and resist all those contrary errors and corruptions, according to our vocation, and to the uttermost of that power that God hath put into our hands, all the days of our life.

On 28 February 1638, a crowd of several hundred, drawn from the nobility, the burgesses, and the clergy, assembled at Greyfriars Kirk in Edinburgh to hear the Covenant read, and to celebrate what was called 'The great marriage day of this nation with God'. Then everyone signed it. At the top were the signatures of the Earl of Rothes and the young Earl of Montrose, at this point an enthusiast for the cause. The process took all day, with the sheepskin parchment spread out on a flat stone in the kirkyard, some people adding phrases like 'Until death' after their signatures, others signing, or attempting to sign, in their own blood.

The Covenant became as much a declaration of Scottish independence as of religious faith, and the reverberations of that day at Greyfriars were to echo through the rest of the century. But from the start the movement attracted extremists, whose narrowness and bigotry alienated many of its original supporters. As the Covenant bandwagon picked up speed, moderates moved away from it, and, in the Civil War, Montrose and other members of the Graham family took the King's side.

For the Covenanters the Civil War and its aftermath confirmed a deep unease about the Stuart dynasty. They accused both Charles I and Charles II in their time of betraying the terms of the National Covenant, and its successor, the 1643 Solemn League and Covenant, which sought to spread the Presbyterian discipline beyond the borders of Scotland. With Lauderdale as one of the Scottish Commissioners, the terms of the League were agreed at Westminster between the Scottish administration and Parliament. Subsequently a Covenanting army helped to ensure Charles I's defeat in the Civil War.

By 1648, however, the allies were at odds, and a powerful body in Scotland was prepared to fight for the King's release. This led to the so-called Engagement and the overthrow of a Scottish army by Cromwell at Preston.

In 1649 the King was beheaded and his son looked to Scotland for support. Montrose and his followers offered it unreservedly, but the Covenanters would accept only a Covenanted king. In attempting to play off one side against the other, Charles II sacrificed Montrose and made a deal with his enemies which neither side saw in the same light. When in the summer of 1650 the young king reached Scotland and was persuaded – much against his will – to sign the Covenant, the Scots who pressed him to do so genuinely expected him to fulfil its terms.

But they had pressed him too hard. Charles never forgot the humiliation he had been forced to undergo in Scotland. He had been obliged to state his desire 'to be deeply humbled and afflicted in spirit before God' because of his father's opposition to the Covenant, and for the 'idolatry' of his mother. After his restoration, he never came north of the border again.

John Graham of Claverhouse was just two years old in 1650 when Charles II signed the Covenant. It was a year which saw, too, his kinsman Montrose's final campaign in Scotland, his defeat, betrayal and execution in Edinburgh, where he was hanged, and quartered, with his head set up on the Tolbooth and his dismembered limbs distributed to the cities of Stirling, Perth, Aberdeen and Dundee (though that city refused the offer).

Montrose's sense of loyalty was one that Claverhouse himself would echo, though never so eloquently as the Marquis himself who, in his death cell, told the ministers who threatened him with excommunication if he did not recant:

> I would with all my heart be reconciled to the same, but since I cannot obtain it on any other terms – unless I call that my sin which I account to have been my duty – I cannot, for all the reason and conscience in the world.

In the autumn of 1650 the Covenanting army of the Scots was defeated by Cromwell at Dunbar, despite outnumbering the English by more than two to one and being better positioned. The Presbyterian clergy had insisted that it should be purged of all 'Malignants', as they termed all those who had fought under Montrose or supported the Engagement. Not for the first or last time the zealotry of the Covenanters proved to be their own undoing.

Within a year Scotland was in Cromwell's hands, with Dundee one of the last strongholds to fall. There was terrible slaughter in the city when it eventually surrendered. General Monck gave no quarter till he reached the market square. Among the dead, according to one source, were two hundred women and children. The governor, Lumsden of Montquanie, was shot after receiving quarter.

But the Claverhouse family, who lived barely ten miles from Dundee, was spared. A personal instruction from Monck gave 'Lady Carnigges of the Glen' an order of Protection on 30 August 1651, thus ensuring the safety of the Graham children as well as of their mother. Lady Magdalene Carnegie had married William Graham of Claverhouse five years earlier and John, their eldest son, was born during 1648, some time in the summer. There were two sisters as well as a younger brother.

John Graham's childhood on the Glenogilvie estates was shielded from the worst troubles of the times, but it was not untouched by them. Montrose's execution and Monck's bloody revenge on the city for its resistance showed how close disaster could come even to those, like the Grahams, who chose a neutral path. The period of the Commonwealth was for them, as for most landowning families in Scotland, one of great hardship. As Robert Baillie wrote in 1658:

> The country lies very quiet; it is exceedingly poor; trade is naught; the English have all the money. Our noble families are almost gone. Lennox has little in Scotland unsold; Hamilton's estate, except Arran and the barony of Hamilton is sold; Argyll can pay little annual rent for 700,000 or 800,000 merks, and he is no more drowned in debt than in public hatred, almost of all, both Scots and English. The Gordons are gone; the

Douglasses are little better; Eglinton and Glencairn on the brink of breaking; many of our chief families estates are cracking, nor is there any appearance of any human relief for the time.

In 1653, the Claverhouse family suffered a further blow when John's father, William Graham, died, leaving his widow Lady Magdalene with four children to bring up. Her son John, then only four years old, was officially declared heir on 3 February, but his mother acted as guardian or 'tutrix' until the end of his 'pupillage' at the age of fourteen. Support came from both sides of the family: from William's brother, who had an estate at Potento in Perthshire; and from Lady Magdalene's brother, Lord Lour, to whom his nephew's wardship was granted in July 1662. In 1656, two Grahams and a Fotheringham were recorded as discharging a debt 'on certain bolls of meal' outstanding from William Graham's time, a transaction which suggests both that money for unpaid bills was not always available and that there were relatives around to help meet them.

The standing of the Graham family remained high in the neighbourhood, and its position was recognized by the City of Dundee when, on 22 September 1660, both John Graham, who was only twelve, and his brother David, who was younger, were admitted as 'burgesses and brethren of the guild of Dundee, by reason of their father's privilege'.

By that date, John Graham had already been at university for two years. The normal age for a student to begin his undergraduate education was ten, at which age he was expected to undertake a full course in the liberal arts, philosophy and mathematics. It is likely therefore that Graham was admitted to St Salvator's College at Montrose's old university, St Andrews in 1658.

It was no longer quite as easygoing a place as it had been when Montrose was there; he had filled his hours by hunting, hawking, horse-racing, playing golf, and winning the silver medal for archery. Intellectually, St Andrews was not considered particularly distinguished at the time, certainly not when compared to Aberdeen. Things had changed, however, by the time John Graham arrived at the university. St Andrews, which had held out against the National Covenant, finally backed down and subscribed it. In 1641, the Covenanters appointed a commission to visit and reform the university. As a result, there was a greater emphasis on students' morals, and any criticism of the regime was discouraged. The three categories of student – noblemen's sons, called 'primars', lairds' sons, who were, 'secondars', and tradesmen's and farmers' sons, who were 'ternars' – were required to observe strict discipline, working a full session, with restricted holidays. The 'primars' were allowed to go 'to Cowper races for a day or two', but this was not a privilege accorded to the others. Prayers took place in the morning and evening during weekdays, and on Sundays the members of each college walked in procession to church wearing their scarlet gowns.

John Graham was a student of the liberal arts, mathematics, and philosophy. One account claims that one of his favourite subjects was Gaelic poetry, but there is no evidence that he ever acquired a command of the language. According to the memoirs of Sir Ewen Cameron of Lochiel, compiled by his grandson:

> He had made considerable progress in the mathematics, especially in those parts of it that related to his military capacity; and there was no part of the Belles Lettres which he had not studied with great care and exactness. He was much master in the epistolary way of writing; for he not only expressed himself with great ease and plainness, but argued well, and had a great art in giving his thoughts in few words.

That judgment is certainly borne out by the many letters he wrote later as an officer, which are precise, frequently witty, and sprinkled with the occasional classical allusion. His spelling, however, was always idiosyncratic, though in this respect he was no different from others of his generation.

In his final year, there arrived at the university a man whose standing in the country was already considerable, and on whom much of the religious controversy of the time was to be centred. On 16 January 1661, James Sharp, then minister of Crail in Fife and the King's chaplain in Scotland, was transferred to St Andrews to be third master at St Mary's College. At the end of February he was formally admitted as Professor of Divinity. In December that year, he was consecrated Archbishop of St Andrews. For Presbyterians this was the ultimate endorsement of episcopacy, and it earned Sharp the hatred of those who saw him as a betrayer of the Covenant. A satire composed to mark his elevation ran:

> Judas I am, what ever Court may say
> Arch traitour false: for Christ I do betray.

Sharp was not at the same college as Claverhouse, who had enrolled for a third-year philosophy course at St Salvator's on 29 February 1660, nor did he teach the subjects that Claverhouse was studying. But he got to know the young student and liked him. A contemporary, the Revd Thomas Morer, wrote later that Claverhouse 'was admired for his parts and respects to churchmen, which made him dear to the Archbishop [of St Andrews], who ever after honoured and loved him.'

Until the Restoration, Sharp had consistently argued the Presbyterian case, though always as a moderate, an exponent of the art of compromise, and a firm believer in the authority of the King. As time went on, however, he became so steeped in politics that his principles became subordinate to the exercise of power. Cromwell referred to him as 'Sharp of that Ilk'. With the Restoration of Charles II, he decided, along with other colleagues, to take the bishop's mitre in order to steer the Church in the direction of moderation.

The sermon that he gave at St Andrews in 1661, on his return from his consecration in London, to explain and defend his decision is a model of pragmatism. It would be instantly recognizable to any skilled politician of today, and, though what he had to say enraged those who still adhered to the Covenant, it is as good a reflection of John Graham's own views as he ever delivered himself.

> I say that I have entered on that office not out of any ambition or any covetous disposition and desire of worldly honour, gain and greatness, but out of obedience to the will of God and the King's Majesty whom I own to be supreme in all causes ecclesiastic and over all persons and the original of external exercise of all church power.

The reinstatement of episcopacy, he argued, was a better method of church government than Presbyterianism, and was 'that which is most convenient and necessary for Scotland as it now stands'. He recognized that some members of the Church might disagree with him, but in the end, he said, they owed 'their duty and submission to the will and determination of his Majesty'.

Claverhouse himself would later use very similar language to express his own belief in the King's authority. He was to be conventionally religious himself, and he believed implicitly in the King as the head of the Church on earth. His later opposition to the Covenanters came not so much because he disputed their principles but because they challenged the authority of the Crown. To him, episcopalianism, and the authority of the bishops, gave the King a natural hierarchy through which to exercise control, not just of the Church, but of the country. His firm views on these matters were very much the same as those enunciated at St Andrews by James Sharp.

His teenage years after university were spent at Glenogilvie, where he and his brother David ran the family estate and filled the civic role which would have been their father's had he lived. On the eve of his twenty-first birthday, in February 1669, John was appointed a commissioner of excise and a justice of the peace for Forfarshire, only to have to surrender the office when it was found that he had not quite attained his majority. The post was not to be restored until September, a few months after his birthday. Bureaucracy, it appears, is by no means a twentieth-century phenomenon. Claverhouse could well have continued a modest career on the land, much as his immediate forebears had done. Instead, in 1672, he volunteered for military service abroad.

The attraction of a soldier's life for a young man of twenty-four was not simply the chance of adventure, but the prospect of considerable rewards. For more than 400 years, the sons of noble families from Scotland had seen a military career abroad as offering advancement of a kind they could never have contemplated had they stayed at home. When Archibald, fourth Earl of Douglas, went to the aid of the Dauphin in 1422, 10,000 knights and soldiers accompanied him, and he went on to become Lieutenant-General of Charles VII's forces and Duke of Touraine. Families like the Hamiltons and Lennox Stewarts won titles, lands, marriages, and an established place in French society. And in the seventeenth century a man could still start in the most junior rank and end up with a Field Marshal's baton in his knapsack, as John Spalding, whose memorials chronicled the times, recorded:

> 'Ther cam out of Germany fra the warrs home to Scotland ane gentleman of basse birth borne in Balveny, who had servit long and fortunatly in the Germane warres and callit to his name Felt Marshall Leslie his Excellence.'

The commander whose regiment of foot Claverhouse joined, as a junior lieutenant, on 25 July 1672, was just such a man. Sir William Lockhart had run away from school to join a Scottish regiment abroad, and had put his military experience to good effect in the Civil War, before being appointed ambassador to France, first under Cromwell, then under Charles II. The regiment that he raised in 1672 formed part of the British forces commanded by the Duke of Monmouth, who brought 6,000 men to join the standard of the great Marshal Turenne. Charles had secretly agreed the Treaty of Dover with Louis XIV, and had promised military assistance to help France in its long wars against the Dutch.

Among Claverhouse's fellow-officers at this time was John Churchill, later Duke of Marlborough, who was two years younger but already a captain, having seen service in Tangier. And leading the Dutch army was another young man, William of Orange.

William, then only twenty-two, had that year been swept into power as Captain General and Stadtholder of the Dutch United Provinces, and had proved himself, with no military experience, an able strategist who exploited Louis XIV's incompetence as a commander and succeeded in pushing his invading army back across the Dutch border. William, whose mother, Mary Henrietta, was Charles I's daughter, was to spend most of his life caught up in a seemingly endless war across the plains of Flanders. But from a young age he was aware of his strong links with England, and his potential claim to the English throne. From as early as 1672, when he visited England, he encouraged anti-French support among influential friends at court, and in February 1674, when Austria and Spain formed an alliance with Holland and it became clear that the war would be a long one, he was able to persuade Charles II to agree terms by which Monmouth's forces were withdrawn from France in return for recognition of English naval supremacy from Norway to Cape Finisterre.

At this point, Lockhart's regiment came back to England, John Churchill returned home to become a Colonel of Foot, while Claverhouse, 'wishing', as his contemporary Sir John Dalrymple later tactfully put it, 'to know the services of different nations', switched sides and joined William's army. There was no automatic commission for him, as there had been under Lockhart, and Claverhouse, like the 'many gentlemen of talent and family' who are recorded as offering their swords to William, volunteered his services as John Graham of Claverhouse Esquire, and became a cornet in the Prince's own company of Guards.

He did not remain anonymous for long. During his time in the Dutch service, he impressed William sufficiently to win promotion, and later to be recommended directly to the English court when he returned home. What almost certainly happened was that, at some point during the long campaign, Claverhouse saved William's life. Quite where and when the rescue took place is uncertain, but the story itself is consistent in its detail. In the course of one of his battles, William was knocked from his saddle. Claverhouse rode to his aid, pulled him on to his own horse, and carried him away from danger. Cameron of Lochiel, who saw a great deal of Claverhouse in later life, recalled that it was at the battle of Seneffe – the first and most bitter of William's encounters with the Prince de Condé – when the French caught the last of the three Dutch columns as they marched through a defile, and fell on their exposed baggage-train:

[The Prince] being, in the year 1674, dismounted by the enemy at the battle of Seneffe, and in the greatest danger of being either killed or made prisoner, the gallant Mr Grahame rescued him out of their hands, mounted him upon his own horse and carried him safely off.

It is true that William, somewhat unwisely in the view of his officers, did ride to the aid of the baggage-train, but there is no evidence that he was ever in direct danger. The rescue almost certainly took place later. Another contemporary, James Philip of Almericlose, who was Claverhouse's second cousin and who wrote an epic poem about his Highland exploits, has Claverhouse recounting the episode in his own words, but makes no mention of Seneffe:

> Did not I when thou [William] fleddest on wearied steed through Belgic marsh from the conquering troops of lily-bearing France – did not I myself snatch thee from the enemy, and mount thee on the back of my fresh steed, and restore thee safe to the camp?

And an anonymous writer who picked up the story ten years later, wrote:

> I saw the man who at St. Neff did sie
> His conduct, prowess, martiall gallantrie.
> He wore a white plumash that day, not one
> Of Belgians wore white but him alone.

Seneffe or not, it is clear that Claverhouse performed a signal service for William, and there was certainly no lack of opportunity for gallantry in the course of that long campaign.

Claverhouse acquired military expertise in the course of a war in which his compatriots played a significant part. The Scottish regiments of the Anglo-Scots Brigade, which had been in the Dutch service for over a hundred years, were considered to be amongst the best in the army, and William depended heavily on their bravery and discipline. Well-equipped with the latest muskets, and dressed in scarlet uniforms, they had recently become part of the 'National' Dutch army. The Highlanders among them had a reputation for flamboyance on the battlefield, and William later attempted to recruit them in large numbers. But most of the Brigade came from the southern part of Scotland, carrying names like Balfour or Ballantine. They marched to an air known as the 'Lowlands o' Holland', and in the course of their campaigns in the Netherlands they acquired a skill and reputation which later prompted James VII to comment that if his English regiments could be as good as the Scots Brigade he would be 'doubly pleased ... they do truly look like old regiments'.

In the early 1670s, the officers of the Scots Brigade included a dour Highlander called Hugh Mackay of Scourie, who was eight years older than Claverhouse and senior in rank. As General Mackay, fourteen years later, he would command the Government forces against Claverhouse in his final battle. Mackay became almost more Dutch than Scotch when, in 1672, he proposed marriage to a Dutch heiress, Clare de Bie, whose family strongly disapproved of her marrying a mercenary soldier in French pay. He therefore shifted allegiance and espoused the Dutch cause, becoming one of William's military advisers. He won promotion, first as a Captain, then as a Colonel of one of the three regiments that made up the Brigade.

Claverhouse's own advancement was slower. It was not until November 1676 that he received a commission as ritmeester, or captain of Horse, in a regiment where he was recorded as the 'baron de Claverhous'. By this time he had learnt the stern military lessons of a continental war, much of it a succession of sieges, which required patience, good supply-lines, and a strong artillery train rather than bravura on the field. As a cavalry officer, he was skilled in the use of carbine and pistol, and he may well have witnessed the last of the old-fashioned horse-arquebusiers, mounted soldiers carrying heavy guns which acted as a kind of portable artillery, much favoured for their weighty, if inaccurate, firepower. The arquebus, however, was a clumsy weapon, and by the 1670s had been largely replaced by the lighter musket.

In 1675, Claverhouse's mother, Magdalene Graham, died and he returned to Scotland for a few months to tidy up the family's affairs. Early in March 1676 he was in Edinburgh, where he wrote a letter to a friend in Perthshire, Sir Thomas Steuart of Grandtully, chiding him for being mean over a horse. The tone was cheerful and bantering:

> Sir, – I think no wonder that a poor lad like you should prig thus for five pounds with your good friend, who will maybe never have the occasion to ask another favour of you. Send but your horse here, and if he be whole and sound, it shall not be so little a business shall keep us from a bargain. Give orders to John Steuart or Colin, to receive my obligation. If there be anything wherein I can serve you, either here or elsewhere, you know how freely you may command me. I have always been, and shall still be, as much as I really am,
>
> Dear Sir, your most humble servant, J. Grahame.
>
> I have got four of the best greyhounds of Scotland now, and you be a good fellow you will send me a setting dog, and then I would be a prince.

Claverhouse got both his horse and his dog. He wrote a brief letter of thanks before sailing for Holland, where, as James Graham, his estate manager, wrote to Grandtully, he went 'a little in haste'. The horse 'gives him good satisfaction at present, and I hope the longer he keeps him the better'. The time in Scotland had not been wasted, for Claverhouse used it also as a recruiting exercise. In the same letter, James Graham added: 'Sir, Claverhouse commanded me to entreat you if you could help Colonel Graham with any men who would go to Holland with him willingly, he would take it as a favour done to himself. He [Colonel Graham] is here for the present.'

The 'Colonel' was Henry Graham, who commanded one of the Scots regiments, and Claverhouse may possibly have had ambitions for promotion under him. But Hugh Mackay was ahead of him. When Colonel Graham was killed during the grim siege of Maastricht, in the summer of 1677, William gave the command of his regiment to Mackay. It was gazetted on 17 August.

The rivalry between Claverhouse and Mackay is said to have been heightened by this promotion, but Claverhouse himself, who had been a captain for less than a year, would have been very junior for such a post, and hardly a contender.

There is evidence, however, that Claverhouse did have ambitions for a command under William, and believed that he had been promised one. At some point he appears to have had a public row with a rival officer, David Colyear, later the first Earl of Portmore, whom he accused of intriguing behind his back for a promotion that was rightfully his. Lochiel claims that Claverhouse gave Colyear 'some blows with his cane' and that he was seized by the guards and brought before William for the crime of striking a fellow-officer – a crime for which the punishment could sometimes be the loss of the striking arm. Claverhouse apologized, but went on to bring up the question of his promised promotion, to which William responded: 'I make you full reparation for I bestow on you what is more valuable than a regiment – I give you your right arm.'

In the memoirs of Hugh Mackay it is said that he, Mackay, was the rival, and that, when Claverhouse failed to get the command, he left the Dutch service in disgust. But this too is improbable, for Mackay had long since won promotion. Claverhouse did not, in fact, leave William's service until four months after Mackay had been given his regiment – hardly the act of a hasty man.

But there is one element in these differing accounts that does ring true. Claverhouse did have a quick temper and a strong sense of injustice, especially as far as his own affairs were concerned. He had no hesitation in complaining to his superiors if he felt he had been dealt with unfairly, and he seems never to have been particularly concerned about the possible consequences.

Whatever the circumstances of his departure, Claverhouse appears to have left on reasonable terms with the Prince. Indeed, William was instrumental in bringing him to the attention of King Charles II and his brother James, Duke of York, later James VII.

In the autumn of 1677, William left his army camped at Enghien and sailed for England, where, in November of that year, he married the Princess Mary, James's daughter. At about the same time, Claverhouse returned to Scotland. There he was to find that, despite his junior rank, his reputation had preceded him. Word had been given by the King's brother, James, that John Graham of Claverhouse was a man to watch – and he could only have known that from William of Orange.

A close link with the House of Stuart had thus been established, thanks to the man whom he would one day battle to depose.

CHAPTER THREE
The Western Whigs

*'No. We cannot receive your Accomodation. It is a cloak
under which tyranny will pursue its way unsuspected. It is
a drug to bewitch our own vigilance into sleep.'*
Presbyterian response to Robert Leighton, Bishop of
Dunblane

Claverhouse came back with no immediate prospects of a military
career ahead of him. The army was highly unpopular both north and
south of the border in a land still recovering from the iron rule of
Cromwell, and an officer enjoyed little of the status which was natural
in Flanders. In England, such was the prejudice against the military
that in 1678 Parliament voted the standing army illegal and forced the
King to disband all forces raised the previous year. In Scotland, where
the army consisted only of the King's Horse and Foot Guards, an
infantry regiment, two companies of Highlanders, and three companies of dragoons, amounting to little more than 1,000 men, there
seemed only limited opportunities for a man with his experience.

For a time, Claverhouse appears to have contemplated renewing his
career on the Continent, and, in February 1678, he was granted leave
by the Privy Council to 'go off the Kingdom', a licence that anyone
contemplating a trip abroad had to seek. But William's recommendation had not been without effect.

On 19 February his kinsman, the third Marquis of Montrose, was in
London offering to raise a troop of horse at his own expense for the
Duke of York, who was assembling a regiment for service in Flanders.
Montrose discussed the matter personally with the Duke, who gave
him Claverhouse's name as a likely recruit. There was only one
problem: Montrose was looking for a lieutenant, and Claverhouse was

a captain. Montrose did all he could, in the letter that he wrote to Claverhouse that day, to present the matter in as favourable a light as possible:

> Sir, You cannot imagine how overjoyed I should be to have any employment at my disposal that were worthy of your acceptance; nor how much I am ashamed to offer you anything so far below your merit as that of being my Lieutenant; though I be fully persuaded that it will be a step to a much more considerable employment, and will give you occasion to confirm the Duke in the just and good opinion which I do assure you he has of you. . . .

Montrose assured Claverhouse that it would be the 'first troop of the Duke of York's regiment' and that 'none but gentlemen should ride in it', but there was no disguising the fact that Montrose was proposing a demotion, and to Claverhouse, with his Graham pride already dented by failure to win command of a regiment, the offer was hardly flattering. Besides, something better was now available.

The growing ferment in south-west Scotland had persuaded Charles II, on the recommendation of his Secretary of State, the Earl of Lauderdale, to increase the size of his forces in Scotland, thus offering Claverhouse an opportunity for the command he felt he deserved.

The possibility of a rebellion had been there from the early years of Charles II's reign. When the King decided to restore episcopacy in Scotland there were powerful reasons behind his choice. Under the Cromwellian occupation, with General Assemblies abolished and political preaching banned, religious discord was temporarily shelved. It returned with the monarchy. To Charles the restoration of Presbyterianism in Scotland meant the ascendancy of all he most disliked in that country; above all, a strident theocratic body demanding a Covenanted King and the right to impose its religious views on England. His views had the support of the Earl of Middleton, his first Commissioner in Scotland, and most of the nobility, bankrupted by the Civil War, who also dreaded the revival of a powerful church.

Among his advisers only Lauderdale saw the danger of revoking all the legislation passed since 1633. Unlike Middleton, who was not a politician and cared little for theology, he understood the power of the Covenant. He also appreciated the yearning felt by many for a General Assembly and a moderate Presbyterian settlement. Unfortunately moderation was lacking.

The King and his English court were determined that the days of the Covenant should not return. All Covenanters to them seemed rebels, and the one thing they expected of the Scottish administration was that it should impose and maintain order. Within less than a year of the Restoration, laws to restrain religious dissidents were being introduced. Ministers of the kirk who refused to accept episcopacy were 'outed' from their churches, often taking their flocks with them to worship elsewhere. And in order to demonstrate the supremacy of the King, the date of his birthday and his Restoration, 29 May 1660, was designated an anniversary to be celebrated – by order.

The Seventeenth Act of Parliament, passed in 1661, laid down that: 'the 29th day of May be for ever set apart as an holy day unto the Lord, and to be employed in prayer, preaching, thanksgiving and praises to God. All servile work is discharged, and the remaining part of the day is to be spent in lawful divertissements suitable to so solemn an occasion.' The 'divertissements' envisaged were probably more staid than those which had greeted the King's restoration. On that occasion in Edinburgh cannon boomed from the Castle, claret flowed from 'all the spouts', and after all was over, 300 dozen broken glasses were left to litter the streets of the 'braw toun'.

But for the Covenanters, 29 May became an anniversary of despair. They preferred to look back to a brief but golden period of freedom, between the tyranny of the 'papist' Stuarts and the repression of Oliver Cromwell, when the Church had spoken directly to its congregations, unencumbered by bishops, in the true spirit of the Reformation, through General Assembly, Synod, Presbytery and the Parish, a very complete, self-contained and powerful organization.

It was a period described by James Kirkton, one of the Church's most eloquent sons, as 'the best years that Scotland ever saw'. 'Then was Scotland a heap of wheat set about with lilies, one form, or a palace of silver beautifully proportioned; and this seems to me to have been Scotland's high noon.'

That high noon was turned, in the eyes of the Presbyterians, to darkness on the return of Charles II. Within two years of his Restoration, the glorious Covenants, their articles of faith, were declared unlawful, despite the fact that the King had signed them. His promises broken, the holding of conventicles was declared illegal, and the 'sole and only power and jurisdiction' of the Kirk, a writ which had been an article of faith since 1592, was unceremoniously scrapped. Three years later, more than 300 ministers had resigned their callings or been forced from their churches rather than accept a form of moderate episcopacy to which most of the nation had subscribed under James VI. It was not the re-imposition of bishops so much as the revival of lay patronage

and the banning of the Covenants which provoked dissent. Conventicles were an inevitable consequence.

The Government added one final indignity by ordering, in 1661,
that the Covenants should be publicly burned in the streets. It was not
surprising, therefore, that the line between religious and political
dissent should have become first blurred, and then obliterated. 'The
opposition of a grieved oppressed people', wrote Kirkton, was set
against 'the cruel severities of a persecuting power'.

The Covenanters' only consolation was 'the hearty smack of the
sweetness of the gospel'. The size of the congregations which gathered
illegally to hear it grew steadily, partly because there was safety in
numbers from the harassment of the soldiers, partly because the
reputation of a handful of preachers grew steadily over the years, and
people travelled many miles to hear them.

The backbone of the Covenanting movement was in the farmlands
of Galloway and Ayrshire, whose ties were often closer to Northern
Ireland than they were to Edinburgh. From there, the great Presbyterian traditions were nourished. Generations of articulate farm labourers
whose education owed more to the pulpit than the village school found
it a faith both simple and satisfying. There was also a solid class of lairds
who drank in the word of God as it was preached every Sunday by
ministers who were usually university graduates, wholly committed to
the Covenant. And finally there were the lords, like Loudoun, Cassilis
and Eglinton, who supported them, and whose activities became a
matter of increasing concern to the Privy Council.

They became known as 'Whigs', after the so-called 'Whiggamore
Raid' of 1648, when a force supporting Cromwell marched on Edinburgh after the Battle of Preston. But the name went back further, to
the cry of 'Whiggam', used by the ploughboys of the west to urge on
their horses. The word stuck, and became a term of derision or pride,
depending on which side of the religious divide one stood.

The great figureheads of the Covenanting movement were those
who had been evicted from their ministries in the years immediately
following the Restoration, and who had held their services illegally
ever since, criss-crossing the country, protected wherever they went
by their faithful supporters, evading their pursuers in a series of close
escapes which added to the mythology that surrounded them.

They were men like Donald Cargill, from the parish of Barony in
Glasgow, a naturally shy man, but of tough constitution and fiery
eloquence, and later notorious for publicly excommunicating the
King, his brother, and most of his Scottish hierarchy; or like John

Welsh of Irongray, perhaps the most celebrated of them all, and great grandson of John Knox. There was a price of £500 on Welsh's head, but he had always eluded the Government's troops, including those of Claverhouse, because of the loyalty he inspired amongst his people, and because of the astonishing stamina which allowed him to stay long hours in the saddle as he moved about the country. Guarded, it was said, by twelve gentlemen in scarlet, Welsh was a romantic figure who had once held a conventicle standing on the frozen waters of the Tweed so that his voice would carry to the faithful gathered on either bank.

It was in Welsh's parish of Irongray that the Pentland Rising of 1666 began, and he personally recruited more than a hundred horse and foot for the ill-fated enterprise, which was as much a gesture of protest against the financial hardships imposed by a rough soldiery as an act of rebellion. Defeated at the battle of Rullion Green by an army headed by Sir Thomas Dalyell of the Binns, the rebels dispersed. But vengeance, in the form of a regime of torture, trials, and executions, was swift and brutal. A failed assassination attempt against Archbishop Sharp further increased tension in 1668, though it was not until ten years later that the would-be murderer, James Mitchell, a 'lean, hollow-cheeked man of a truculent countenance', was caught and hanged.

In the late 1660s and early 1670s, a different approach to the militant Presbyterians was tried. Acts of Indulgence were introduced, whereby ministers who had been banished from their churches were allowed to return provided they accepted certain conditions, which included a ban on preaching. Nearly half of those who had been deprived of their livings – 136 out of just over 300 – accepted, giving rise to great bitterness amongst those who held out. The attitude of those who rejected the Indulgences was summed up in a famous non-conformist statement made when Robert Leighton, Bishop of Dunblane, offered the Presbyterians an olive branch: 'No. We cannot receive your Accomodation. It is a cloak under which tyranny will pursue its way unsuspected. It is a drug to bewitch our own vigilance into sleep.'

By the late 1670s, the holding of conventicles was once again widespread, to the fury of the Earl of Lauderdale, Secretary of State for Scotland, who wished that he had a proper rebellion on his hands 'that so I might bring over an army of Irish papists to cut all their throats'. Instead, he backed a scheme which was every bit as extraordinary – the 'Highland Host' – an enterprise whereby 6,000 Highlanders were brought down from the north to be settled on ordinary households in the western shires. The arrival of these clan mobs, who stole, pillaged and lived off the meagre resources of the land, caused enormous suffering and resentment – though there was no killing. A young soldier-poet called William Cleland wrote a scathing poem about the 'gipsy' habits of the Highlanders:

> Nought like Religion they retain
> Of Moral Honesty they're clean
> In nothing they're accounted sharp
> Except in Bagpipe, and in Harp.

In the immediate aftermath of the Host, more conventional military methods were again adopted. Two companies of dragoons to add to the existing one were raised by royal warrant in May 1678, and a new regiment of foot, containing eight companies of a hundred men each, which was eventually to become the Royal Scots Fusiliers, was levied by the Earl of Mar. Finally, three independent troops of Horse were commissioned by the King. As commanders of two of them, Lauderdale's recommendations were accepted: the Earl of Airlie for one; the Earl of Home for the other. Both were the heads of distinguished Scottish families, both had long military records – in the case of Lord Airlie, stretching back to Montrose's campaign. The command of the third troop was given, on the Duke of York's personal recommendation, and at the King's command, to Captain John Graham of Claverhouse, whose status in Scotland was negligible.

It was a signal favour. The contrast in background between Claverhouse and his fellow-commanders was reflected in the class of officers chosen by each. Both Airlie and Home had sons of the nobility beneath them. Claverhouse appointed a laird, Andrew Bruce of Earlshall, as his lieutenant, and two Grahams, Robert and James, as his cornet and quartermaster. Later, his brother David took the place of James Graham. But if Claverhouse felt outranked by his more senior colleagues, he never showed it. And round his small band of trusted and reliable officers, he built a troop which was to stay together throughout his service in Scotland.

The three independent troops were commissioned on 23 September 1678. Claverhouse was now thirty, a captain on a captain's pay of fourteen shillings a day, with an allowance of four shillings for two horses, enough to keep them fed, but only just. That, of course, was not his only source of income, since that summer he had officially succeeded to his father's estates at Glenogilvie, and to the remainder of his grandfather's and great great-grandfather's lands in Forfar, which brought in £600 a year. But he was by no means well off, and the problem of finding provisions for his men and their horses was to be a constant theme in his letters over the next few years.

His brief was to patrol the extreme south-west area of Dumfriesshire and Annandale, to break up the field conventicles being regularly held there by Covenanting ministers, and to maintain law and order. The Privy Council in Edinburgh had become steadily more alarmed at the size of these meetings, and at the armed bands which tended to accompany them. They were by no means restricted to the west. One, in Fife, drew 16,000 people, and a three-day conventicle in East Nisbet in Berwickshire in 1677 was attended by squadrons of horse to protect the congregation. Not surprisingly, the Council reported to the King in May 1678 that troops were urgently needed 'for dissipating and interrupting these rendezvouses of rebellion'.

Claverhouse's headquarters was the castle at Dumfries, whence he was expected to control the whole of Dumfriesshire and Annandale, a wild and independent territory some 200 square miles in area that considered itself only loosely tied to the Government in Edinburgh. His troop consisted of sixty rank-and-file soldiers, three corporals, two trumpeters, a lieutenant, a cornet and a quartermaster. He also had on call one of the dragoon companies, commanded by Captain John Inglis. From the start he found his role of policing the area as much political as military, dealing with local parishes divided in their loyalties between an 'outed' minister and his frequently unpopular substitute, or deprived of regular clergy altogether.

His commanding officer, the Earl of Linlithgow, an elderly Major-General nearing the end of his career, was not much interested in the operational detail of a captain's job, and Claverhouse rapidly discovered that his commander had little time for the earnest detail and administrative problems that Claverhouse regularly dispatched to Edinburgh. An early report to Linlithgow, written at nine o'clock on the evening of 28 December 1678, contains all the unnecessary precision of a junior officer determined not to put a foot wrong:

> ... my Lord, they tell me that the one end of the bridge in Dumfries is in Galloway and that they may hold conventicles at our nose, we do not dare to dissipate them seeing our orders confines us to Dumfries and Annandale. Such an insult as that would not please me and on the other hand I am unwilling to exceed orders. So that I expect from your lordship orders how to carry in such uses?

Linlithgow plainly found such fussiness irritating, and described Claverhouse's misgivings as 'frivolous', which elicited a pained response

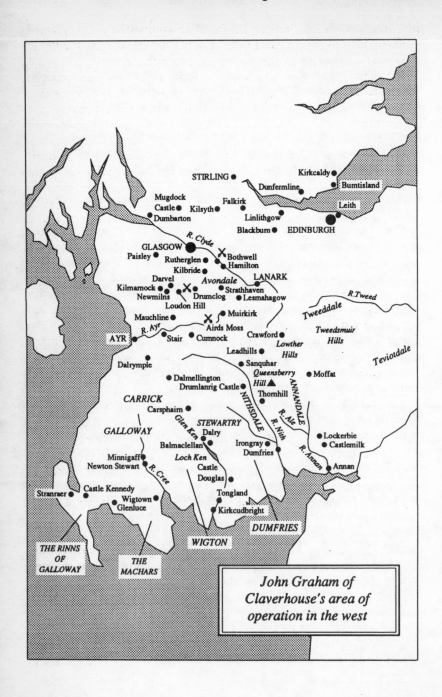

John Graham of Claverhouse's area of operation in the west

in Claverhouse's next report, in which he apologized and explained that: 'till now in any service I have been in I never enquired further in the laws than the orders of my superior officers.'

But in the meantime there had been some action. At Castlemilk in Annandale he had discovered a building masquerading as a byre which was in fact purpose-built for conventicles 'upon the expense of the common purse of the disaffected'. He ordered the local deputy, with eighty reluctant people from the neighbourhood, to pull it down. They argued strenuously that it really was a byre, but Claverhouse pointed out that the hooks and manger had been only recently added in a vain attempt to disguise its real purpose, and insisted that the place be destroyed. The deputy duly 'performed his part punctually, the walls were thrown down and timber burnt, so perished the charity of many ladies.'

He also dealt with a serious lapse in discipline amongst the dragoons guarding the castle at Dumfries, an incident which he handled with typical diligence. A shot had been fired from the castle into the street, killing a horse. The guard denied hotly that his men had fired it, but witnesses round about insisted that they had seen the shot from the guard hall and the horse then falling down. Claverhouse ordered the bullet to be dug out of the horse's head, and found it to be of a calibre which matched that of the dragoons' muskets. He arrested the acting commander of the guard, found the owner of the horse, and insisted that reparation be made. 'It is an ugly business, for besides the wrong the poor man has got in losing his horse, it is extremely against military discipline to fire out of a guard', he reported.

By the beginning of 1679, the Privy Council's Committee for Public Affairs was taking measures to control the spread of illegal services and the 'dangerous and pernicious principles instilled into the minds of unwary people, by seditious preachers in their scandalous con-- venticles'. To impose discipline, it proposed giving the local commanders civil powers.

One of those who drew up the rules was a close friend of Claverhouse's, Sir George Mackenzie of Rosehaugh, the King's Advocate, who had been born and brought up in Dundee, and who was married to the daughter of a close neighbour of Claverhouse's, Sir James Halyburton of Pitcur. Mackenzie had been amongst the first to welcome Claverhouse back from Holland, describing him as 'our generous friend', and he was now on hand to offer some useful legal advice. An Act of Parliament had been passed, appointing deputy sheriffs, and on 27 February 1679, John Graham of Claverhouse and his lieutenant, Andrew Bruce of Earlshall, were nominated Sheriffs-Depute of Dumfries, Annandale, Wigtown and Kirkcudbright, 'to put the laws into execution'. Amongst others in the area given similar responsibility was Sir Robert Grierson of Lag, a young man whose name was to become as notorious as that of Claverhouse himself.

The sanctions they were given were remarkably detailed, and some of them peculiar. The Committee proposed that, since they would probably be unable to arrest everyone attending a conventicle, they should remove their upper garments as a means of identification later. Any scholars, merchants or tradesmen – 'the chief persons who are ordinarily poisoned with factious and schismatic principles' – should be deprived of the right to continue to further education or apprenticeship until they agreed to go to church. Soldiers were to have virtual immunity in carrying out their duties. And a reward of £500 was offered to anyone who would turn in John Welsh, the minister of Irongray. They were also given the power to impound possessions, excluding 'labouring oxen or horse from the last of October to the last of May for labouring', and they could prosecute anyone who failed to attend the services in his local church. Fines extracted were to be used to finance the exercise, and courts would be held 'once on every week at least, and oftener as you think fit'.

It is not surprising that the new Sheriffs-Depute were widely resented, and not only by the local people. Claverhouse's new status was to bring him into direct conflict with the irascible Earl of Queensberry, known as 'the De'il o' Drumlanrig', who was the Sheriff of Dumfriesshire, and a hard man to get on with. A tyrant to his wife, whom he kept scandalously short of money, he had fallen out (rather like a subsequent Queensberry), with his son, Lord Drumlanrig. He was also involved in a feud with his wife's sister, Lady Anne. The family was somewhat eccentric. A popular story was that the Earl's sister, Lady Margaret Jardine, who was extremely rich, nevertheless used to ferry people across the River Annan for a halfpenny a time to earn extra money. She sat on the banks to ply for custom whenever there was a local fair.

Queensberry was less than helpful in providing Claverhouse's men with the provisions they needed. He was supposed to be responsible for the commissioners who supervised the 'locality', as the system of exacting hay and straw from local inhabitants was known. But he failed to exercise it properly. Claverhouse described one frustrating day when he turned up at the village of Thornhill, expecting to meet the commissioners, only to find Queensberry and a friend who knew nothing about the provisions, and said there was little they could do about them. They pointed out helpfully that Claverhouse was paying over the odds for his hay, and, as he said:

> They found it strange that we who have the honour to serve the King should be ordered by the Council to pay more for hay and straw than will be asked for any stranger; that if it had been recommended to them they would have given us a better bargain.

Claverhouse was outraged by Queensberry's attitude, and did not hesitate to complain to Linlithgow, despite Queensberry's seniority and influence:

> My Lord, I hope your Lordship will not suffer those under your command to be thus used nor the Council suffer such a peremptory order of theirs that was to be thus neglected.... What prejudice the King's service may receive by this I know not.

Free quartering of soldiers – lodging without pay – was against all custom in the army. But he was also being kept short of money by Sir William Sharp, the King's cash-keeper, and there was no alternative: 'If we march I must take free quarters, for I cannot pay money if I get none; Sir William Sharp is short of paying us near six hundred pounds sterling.' This was another reason for Claverhouse's anger, since he always insisted on playing by the rules.

Claverhouse soon clashed again with Queensberry, who clearly resented the way he had assumed powers he regarded as his own, and the arrogance with which he carried out his duties. On 22 April, Queensberry wrote to one of his factors (agents):

> Since I came home I have seen some very peremptory, and, as I conceive, illegal orders from Claverhouse anent his locality; in which I have very freely written to him, and if he resolve to delay troubling the country till the Commissioners meet, I shall labour to get a quorum of them together sometime next week.'

The meeting duly took place on 1 May, but Claverhouse decided not to go himself, sending instead his lieutenant, Andrew Bruce. Lengthy negotiations took place, and an offer was made to provide 158 horses with hay and straw for fifteen days. Each horse was estimated to need two stone of straw and six stone of hay, paid for at a rate of 'two shilling per stone of straw and two shillings and sixpence per stone of hay'.

The deal was reasonably generous, but, to Queensberry's fury, Claverhouse rejected it. He wanted another fortnight's worth of feed, and insisted that it be provided. It was a measure of the authority he now had, vested in him directly by the Privy Council, that Queensberry was forced to agree, though he did so under protest: 'If Claverhouse act warrantably and legally, there is no ground for complaint; otherwise he may assure himself, we who have interest in this shire will do what we can for redress. . . .'

At one point he threatened to go directly to the Council, but Claverhouse knew that he was in the right, and Queensberry was forced to back down. The point was won, though at the expense of an angry Earl. It was hardly consummate diplomacy.

Claverhouse was just as concerned about the lack of intelligence as he was about provisions. Like most troops operating in hostile country, his men were given as little help as possible by the local people. Claverhouse complained about it vigorously to Linlithgow: 'My Lord, good intelligence is the thing we want most here. Mr Welsh and others preach securely within twenty or thirty miles of us, but we can do nothing for want of spies.'

By contrast, the other side knew well in advance whenever Claverhouse's troop was approaching. On one occasion, having received an order to arrest some suspects in Galloway, he and his men rode forty miles through the night, only to find their quarry had flown:

> . . . their wives [were] lying above the clothes in their bed and great candles lighted waiting for the coming of the party and told them they knew of their coming and had as good intelligence as they themselves . . . and the truth is they had time enough to be advertised for the order was dated the 15 and came not to my hands till the 20 . . . There is almost nobody lies in their bed that know themselves in any way guilty within forty miles of us.

From one group of wives he learned that families regularly paid for advance intelligence about approaching Government troops, and they talked derisively about one local household which had been caught because it was too mean to provide the money.

The fact was, he concluded, that the territory he was being asked to secure was far too large for the tiny band he had at his command. 'I hope your Lordship will consider', he wrote to Linlithgow, 'how hard it is to keep so vast a country as this with so few forces. . . .'

Events were now beginning to grow more serious. In March 1679, a dragoon lieutenant, John Dalyell, had been killed at Lesmahagow when he and a party of soldiers twenty strong confronted an armed prayer-meeting and found themselves outnumbered. Claverhouse himself reported the capture of a dragoon by enraged townspeople in Stranraer after the murder of the Provost there. And on 21 April he wrote a letter to Linlithgow from Dumfries warning that the signs of armed rebellion were now everywhere apparent:

> I find Mr Welsh is accustoming the back ends of the country to face the King's forces and certainly intends to break out in an open rebellion. I expect him here next. ... My Lord, I think it my duty to put your Lordship in mind that the arms of the militia in this shire as well as that of Wigton and Annandale are in the hands of the country people ... this may prove in a sudden dangerous.

He decided to garrison the town of Kirkcudbright with Inglis's dragoons, and to equip them for the battle he expected at any moment.

CHAPTER FOUR
Defeat

*'The ruffle of an inconsiderable party of the King's troops
will raise a formidable rebellion'*
Lt.-Gen. Thomas Dalyell of the Binns

Amongst the Whig 'fanatiks', as they were derisively known in Edinburgh, there were some who had grown impatient to exploit the armed potential they now possessed. Sir Robert Hamilton of Preston, whose father had signed the original Covenant, was one of a small but determined faction which believed there was a moral obligation to use force to restore the true religion. These were the extremists, by no means representative of the majority of peaceful Presbyterians, but threatening nevertheless, as all activists can be in times of repression. They subscribed to the views set out in a manifesto published ten years earlier, 'Jus Populi Vindicatum', which argued that the killing of all deserters from Presbyterianism should be not only lawful, but a duty, and they singled out the Archbishop of St Andrews for special revenge.

Hamilton was also, according to his tutor, Gilbert Burnet, a 'crack-brained enthusiast'. Still only in his twenties, he had been arguing for more than a year to his fellow Whigs, that 'somewhat further should be done by them as a testimony against the iniquity of the times'. In May 1679, Hamilton was joined in the west by others who shared his enthusiasm. The assassins of Archbishop Sharp, including Hackston, Balfour and Russell, had all eluded capture, despite the Government's Hue and Cry and the rewards offered. Lingering first in Fife, they had later gone north to Perth, then Dunblane, passing themselves off as militiamen and professing sorrow at Sharp's death. Then they crossed the country to the west.

On Sunday 25 May, after attending a large conventicle at Avondale, to the south of Glasgow, Hamilton, Hackston and Balfour met in the little town of Strathaven, then rode north to see the old preacher Donald Cargill and the town-clerk of Glasgow, John Spreul. There they drew up a manifesto which suggests that Claverhouse's suspicions of a rebellion were justified.

Claiming grievances dating back to 1648, they listed seven categories of Acts passed against them, including:

> that presumptuous act for imposing an holy anniversary day, as they call it, to be kept yearly upon the 29th of May, as a day of rejoicing and thanksgiving for the King's birth and restoration, whereby the appointers have intruded upon the Lord's prerogative.

They had intended to fix their testimony to the market cross in Glasgow. But troops stationed there under Lord Ross made that too hazardous, so instead, on 29 May 1679, the King's birthday, backed by a band of eighty horsemen, they clattered into the narrow streets of Rutherglen, two miles outside the city.

In Rutherglen, as in other Scottish towns, bonfires were blazing on the streets to mark the royal birthday as the Covenanters rode in. Under Hamilton's orders, they ceremoniously doused the fires, rounded up the town's magistrates, and then proceeded to the market cross. There, Thomas Douglas, a rebel minister who had been with them since the previous Sunday, prayed in front of the crowd which had rapidly gathered. Psalms were sung, and Douglas delivered an address. Then Hamilton unfurled his declaration and read it through, listing the hated Acts one by one:

> ... for confirmation of this our testimony, we do this day, being the 29th of May 1679, publicly at the cross of Rutherglen, most justly burn the above mentioned acts, to evidence our dislike and testimony against the same, as they have unjustly, perfidiously, and presumptuously burned our sacred covenants.

He then produced a bundle of papers representing the Acts and set them alight.

It was a very public gesture, and it made a 'mighty noise' as one Covenanting historian put it. At about the time it happened, Claverhouse was in Falkirk, writing a report for Linlithgow. He had received word of a massive conventicle, to be attended by the congregations of eighteen parishes the following Sunday at Kilbride Moor, about four miles outside Glasgow, and he had decided to ride west to join Lord Ross, who had four companies of foot and a troop of horse stationed in

Glasgow. He then planned to proceed to Kilbride to break up the conventicle.

'They say they are to part no more but keep in a body', he wrote, and he was right.

Some of the townspeople of Falkirk were in mutinous mood as his men prepared to ride out. Three troopers, finishing their morning meal, were fired at from across the street by a local shoemaker who put two bullets within a foot of them, before fleeing. They caught him a quarter of a mile outside the town, questioned him roughly, and took him prisoner. Then they set off for Glasgow, half-a-day's march away, approaching it from the north by way of Mugdock Castle, seat of the Marquis of Montrose. It was here that Claverhouse first learned about the Rutherglen declaration. He detached a party of troopers to chase Hamilton's men, which they did, with no great success, for most of the night. By Friday he was in Glasgow.

The city's garrison was not large, Ross's numbers came to around 240 soldiers and a troop of Montrose's Life Guards brought the total to little more than 300 officers and men. With Claverhouse's arrival at the head of his mounted foot and a company of dragoons, the complement was still below 500. That does not seem to have concerned either officer. On Saturday night, 31 May, Claverhouse left Ross to man the garrison in Glasgow, and took his men south-east of the city in pursuit of the rebels. He left behind a company of dragoons, whose lieutenant, John Crichton, would in later years give a highly coloured account of the ensuing events to the satirist Swift. Even with Captain John Inglis and his dragoons, his force could not have numbered more than 150 men. Both Ross and Claverhouse wrote dispatches that weekend to their headquarters. It is clear from reading them that neither had been expecting anything more than a mopping-up exercise. It had, after all, been like that for the best part of nine months.

Claverhouse went first to Rutherglen to make inquiries about the events of the previous Thursday. There he was given the names of some of those who had taken part, and at Hamilton, eight miles away, he caught three suspects as well as an outlawed minister called John King. More important, he learned that a large conventicle was due to take place next day near Loudoun Hill, a spectacular outcrop, 1,000 feet high, famous as the site where Robert Bruce in 1307 broke Lord Pembroke's army and sent it, shattered, back to England.

By six o'clock on the morning of Sunday 1 June, Claverhouse was in the little town of Strathaven, some six miles south of Hamilton. 'I thought we might make a little tour, to see if we could fall upon a conventicle; which we did, little to our advantage . . .', he wrote drily in his report that night. It was something of an understatement.

Claverhouse took his morning meal at the Tower Inn in Strathaven, and then set off at the head of his mounted troop and the dragoons over gently rising country towards Loudoun Hill, some five miles distant, approaching it from the east. The sight that met his eyes as he breasted a long sweep of hill north-east of Stobieside, a small scattering of houses and farms, showed that at last he had made the kind of encounter he had so often missed before.

The congregation which had gathered that day was later numbered in thousands, but, by the time Claverhouse saw it, most of the women and other non-combatants, warned of his approach, had been withdrawn. Claverhouse later calculated the rebels as four battalions of foot and three squadrons of horse. The best estimate, made later by the Covenanters themselves, put that at about 250 men. Though other accounts exaggerated their numbers wildly, they certainly outnumbered Claverhouse, perhaps by as much as two to one. They were a strange army.

Assembled on a green slope, under the lee of Loudoun Hill, they had begun their service, conducted by the preacher, James Douglas, whose weighty theme was tyranny and its evils. Hamilton was there, with his mounted bodyguard of some sixty men, having appointed himself commanding officer. He had been joined by Hackston, Balfour, and Russell along with their followers, and these were reasonably well armed, with pistols, carbines, and swords. The 'infantry', however, formed a more motley collection, most of them ordinary worshippers, with little or no fighting experience. Barely half of them were armed with muskets. The rest carried pikes, halberds, and even pitchforks.

Their commander, however, was a remarkable young man. William Cleland, just nineteen, was the son of the Marquis of Douglas's gamekeeper, and a poet as well as a soldier, already confident enough of his ability to be given command of this rough but zealous band of amateurs. Cleland had taken part in the skirmish at Lesmahagow in which Lieutenant Dalyell had been killed.

Douglas was nearing the end of his sermon when a warning shot fired by a lookout on a nearby hill, announced that soldiers were nearing the area. The story goes that the congregation looked to the minister, who announced: 'I have done. You have got the theory. Now for the practice. You know your duty. Self-defence is always lawful. But the enemy approaches. . . .'

The old men, the children, and some, but not all, of the women were shepherded back to the rising ground behind them, while the Covenanters marched forwards to take up a position under High Drumclog on firm, sloping ground looking north over marshy ground to a hilly platform half a mile in front of them where Claverhouse and his men now appeared. They formed into ranks and advanced to a defensive position singing one of their best-loved psalms 'In Judah's land' to the tune known as 'Martyrs'. Above them, the King's troopers watched.

For the first time since his service abroad, Claverhouse found himself confronting a military force rather than a sprawling mob. The distinction was clear at once: 'We found them drawn up in battle, upon a most advantageous ground, to which there was no coming but through mosses and lakes', said his report. 'They were not preaching, and had got away all their women and children. They consisted of four battalions of foot, and all well armed with fusils and pitchforks, and three squadrons of horse.' Claverhouse was on the higher ground, but the key to both positions lay in the 'mosses and lakes' in front of him, described by James Russell on the Covenanting side as 'a great gutter like a stank [ditch]', full of water, which ran diagonally west to east between the two sides.

There is every indication that Claverhouse took seriously the threat posed to his men by the little army that now faced him. He ordered his prisoners back, under guard, to a nearby farm at North Drumclog, and dispatched a messenger to Glasgow asking Ross to come with reinforcements. Observing military protocol, he sent forward a flag of truce and offered the rebels terms for surrender – terms which were brusquely rejected.

At the same time, there is little evidence of the caution that a commander facing larger odds and treacherous ground might have been expected to employ. There was to be no waiting for reinforcements – the rider to Glasgow had barely covered a few miles before the first action was taken.

The battle began with a gambit that would have been well recognized on the plains of Flanders – despite its miniature scale on an Ayrshire hillock. Claverhouse detached a small party of dragoons and sent them forward, down the slope to the edge of the marsh, inviting a skirmish. They prepared their muskets for fire. William Cleland answered with an equal number of foot-soldiers, who advanced a short distance in front of the main body, and exchanged the first shots of the day before retreating. There were no casualties.

Now a larger force of about forty men from the Covenanting side approached the boggy ground, facing Claverhouse's sixty dragoons, who dismounted to fire. The distance between them was still too great for the shots to be effective. The muskets used by the dragoons were the new firelocks, made in England and faster to prime, but, though their range was around fifty yards, they were rarely accurate beyond that distance. The few volleys that were exchanged did little damage. One dragoon was wounded, but it was the other side which scattered first, running back to rejoin the ranks.

Claverhouse now pushed forward more of his men to the edge of the swamp. His firepower was greater, and, though the shots loosed off by his dragoons had caused no casualties, there were signs of confusion amongst his opponents.

So far Claverhouse had controlled the day. The rebels, he said, had 'run again shamefully'. But now the disadvantage of the ground and the determination of the Covenanters began to count against him. The waterlogged marsh offered no opportunity for the cavalry charge that might have scattered the enemy. And the ragged army opposite him seized the advantage in a way that he had simply not foreseen:

> In the end, (they perceiving that we had the better of them in skirmish), they resolved a general engagement, and immediately advanced with their foot, the horse following [he wrote]. They came through the loch, and the greatest body of all made up against my troop. We kept our fire until they were within ten pace of us: they received our fire and advanced to shock.

The move for hand-to-hand fighting amongst the Covenanters had become irresistible. William Cleland, exercising remarkable discipline, took his men across the marsh towards Claverhouse's left flank, threading through the water, finding firm ground on the run. The main body pressed forward in the centre, those on foot charging through the bog, the horses coming up behind them.

The sight of this fierce, yelling mob, waving pikes and pitchforks, pouring over the wet ground towards them, must have been suddenly daunting to the waiting troops. There is evidence that some of the dragoons had advanced through the marsh and become bogged down in the mud, which would have added to the confusion. Claverhouse's claim that his men held fire until 'they were within ten pace[s]' is contradicted by Russell's more colourful description of the advance:

> Presently Clavers advanced all in a body to the stank brae, when he was within shot of the honest party, and fired desperately; and the honest party having but few guns, was not able to stand, and being very confused in the coming off of the last party, cried all out, For the Lord's

sake go on! and immediately they ran violently forward, and Clavers was tooming the shot all the time on them.

The firing seems to have been ineffective, which suggests that it was too early. One account says that the Covenanters threw themselves to the ground at the first volley, then picked themselves up and ran on. Certainly the casualties at this point were negligible, though Claverhouse said he saw several of the enemy fall. The smoke, the unevenness of the charge, and the sheer drive of the rebels as they strove to get at the waiting soldiers gave them the initiative. As they came to close combat, two of Claverhouse's men, Corporal Crawford and Captain Blythe, were brought down, and then his cornet, Robert Graham, was killed and trampled underfoot.

It is clear from James Russell's account, that some of the women on the Covenanters' side had joined their men. He himself was on the right flank, and later described being with a small group of mounted men, including his friend William Dingwall. They loosed off three volleys at the enemy, then galloped across the open ground towards them. As they did so, Dingwall was shot and wounded. His horse fell over and knocked Russell to the ground. Seeing Dingwall badly hurt, Russell called to one of the women to help him back to safety, which she did. 'The women', he said, 'ran as fast as the men.' Russell himself remounted and charged back into the action. He saw another friend, Thomas Weir, ride into the middle of the troopers' ranks and seize the King's standard, only to be knocked to the ground and killed.

Claverhouse himself was attacked with a pitchfork which 'made such an opening in my sorrel horse's belly, that his guts hung out half an ell.' Maddened by the wound, the horse bolted, and took Claverhouse from the field at a crucial point. Instead of standing firm to the charge, with bayonets plugged into the muzzles of their firearms, his troops began to fall back, then broke into a retreat which quickly became headlong. Claverhouse wrote:

> Their horse took the occasion of this, and pursued us so hotly that we got no time to rally. I saved the standards; but lost on the place about eight or ten men, besides wounded. But the dragoons lost many more ... I made the best retreat the confusion of our people would suffer.

Despite its terrible wound, his horse took him three miles back to the village of Hillhead, where it collapsed. Here he mounted his trumpeter's horse and rode on towards Strathaven with a party of dragoons. (One account, written later by one of his own officers, claims that he dismounted the trumpeter, which sounds unchivalrous.

But another report, from a Covenanting source, says that the trumpeter was killed. A well, still there, is known as the Trumpeter's Well.)

The pursuit was not as hot as it might have been if the 'jaded' horses of the rebels had been stronger, and the discipline tighter. At Strathaven, the townspeople tried to cut off the retreat of Claverhouse and his fleeing men. There was a fierce hand-to-hand tussle, and about a dozen Covenanters were killed before the dragoons charged through and galloped on.

It was nine o'clock in the evening by the time Claverhouse and his dragoon captain, John Inglis, with what remained of their beaten and dispirited force met Ross and the reinforcements, who were now many hours too late, at Catkin north of East Kilbride. Ross had only set out at five o'clock in the afternoon, by which time the battle was long over. The party turned back towards the city.

On the field of Drumclog, the Covenanters were triumphant. As always, the stories of heroism and pathos on the winning side outstripped anything that was later heard of the defeated. Young Cleland was clearly the hero of the day, having held the foot together as they charged. He was said at one point to have got to Claverhouse himself and to have seized the bridle of his horse before he escaped. John Nisbet of Hardhill claimed to have killed seven troopers.

Amongst the casualties was William Dingwall, who was one of the band that had taken part in the murder of Archbishop Sharp. He was mortally wounded but survived for some days, and spoke before his death of the ravishing vision he had of heaven, 'knowing that his place in Paradise was assured'.

Hamilton, whose bravery was also spoken of, had ordered 'no quarter', and fulfilled it by pistolling one prisoner. He would have killed others if he had not been stopped. He later claimed that

> there was five more that without knowledge got quarters, whom notwithstanding I desired might have been sent the same way that their neighbours were, and it's not being done I reckoned ever amongst our first stepping aside.

It had been, for the Covenanters, a complete victory, though the numbers on both sides barely qualified the action as a battle. Casualties amongst the Government's soldiers were put by Russell at thirty-six. A contemporary account records three officers killed on the field, with about eight troopers and twenty dragoons. On the Covenanting side, the dead were numbered as no more than six, with one estimate as low as three.

Apart from Hamilton's execution of a prisoner, there seems to have been no vindictiveness on the winning side. The pursuit was only carried through as far as Calder Water, less than four miles from the battleground, most of the victors preferring to return to celebrate their success. Stirred by their achievement, and urged on by Hamilton, they resolved to stay together. With all the confidence of a seasoned army, they fell into line and marched the thirteen miles to Hamilton, where they bivouacked. Next day, they intended to take the City of Glasgow.

CHAPTER FIVE
Storming the Bridge

'Like stump orators, the perfervid demagogues carried their pulpits with them'

J. King Hewison

The news of Drumclog was brought to Edinburgh by a galloping post-boy, who roused the Earl of Linlithgow in the early hours of 2 June 1679. Thereupon a summons was sent to the Privy Council, whose members met within an hour at the Tolbooth. It was decided to call together troops scattered across the country from Fife to Teviotdale, and a proclamation was issued calling the rising 'an open, manifest and horrid rebellion, and high treason', and demanding that the rebels lay down their arms and surrender in person to the army. Linlithgow announced that he intended to march west on 4 June. But before any action could be taken, another dispatch arrived from Ross.

The Covenanters had now reached Glasgow. After celebrating their victory, they had spent the night at Hamilton, where a debate had taken place about their future action. They had decided to 'continue and abide together in arms'. Despite the fact that the city was held by Ross's Life Guards as well as all three of the independent troops, commanded by Airlie, Claverhouse and the Earl of Home, who had joined them, they had pressed on towards Glasgow, reaching it at ten o'clock the next day.

Barricades had been placed across the streets, and the soldiers had withdrawn to the centre of the town ready for an attack. The rebels divided into two groups. One group, under Hamilton, stormed up the Gallowgate, the other attacked from the direction of the University. But this was a very different battle from Drumclog. The Covenanters' horses stumbled on the cobbled streets, and the firepower pouring down the narrow wynds [alleys] was ferocious. After losing half a dozen men, they pulled back to the Gallowgate port. Finally, they decided to retreat in two parties, one to Hamilton, the other to Tollcross Moor. Ross's dispatch reported the action:

> This morning these rogues had the confidence to assault us about eleven o'clock. The first attempt was up the Gallowgate, their next was down that street which comes from the head of the town; but I barricaded all the four streets ... and lined them with musketeers, and placed dragoons behind them for a relief, keeping Earl Home's troop and Claverhouse's entire in a body.

He said it was impossible to estimate how many of the rebels had been killed, since the townspeople had pulled some of the dead bodies off the street, but he reckoned that only two of his soldiers might die from their wounds. 'I know not what judgment to give of this affair', he concluded, 'but I am sure this was the warmest day I saw the year.'

Linlithgow now decided that the rebellion was more serious than he had thought, and sent word to Ross, Claverhouse and Home to evacuate Glasgow and rendezvous with him at Stirling. On 3 June they marched out of the city, leaving it to the mercy of the rebels. Two days later they had joined Linlithgow's horse and foot at Bonnybridge, the combined force amounting to about 1,800 men. Early in the afternoon of 6 June, Linlithgow gave orders to retreat to Stirling. On the same day the Privy Council sent him orders that he was to return to Edinburgh forthwith.

The Government was convinced that they had a full-scale revolution on their hands, and next day a proclamation was issued for a general mobilization of local militia up and down the country. A bonus of half a crown was offered to every foot-soldier as an inducement to join up, and such hackney carriages as existed in Edinburgh were pressed into service to and carry provisions for the army.

The orders looked impressive on paper, but in the end the militia numbered less than 5,000, drawn mainly from Fife and the Lothians. They were ill-equipped, and very soon hungry. Gathered in pouring rain on the outskirts of Edinburgh, they were desperately short of provisions. 'I hope all of us here will do our duty in our stations', said Linlithgow gloomily, 'but men must eat.'

By now the King himself had been stirred into action. Flying packets, sent daily to London, had painted such an alarming picture of seething revolt, that he decided to appoint James, Duke of Monmouth, his illegitimate son, as commander-in-chief of his forces in Scotland. A letter from Lauderdale in London to Chancellor Rothes, dispatched on 11 June, announced that two regiments of foot and horse were to be raised, together with three regiments of horse, 800 dragoons, and three troops of grenadiers. The whole expedition, Lauderdale calculated, would cost £500 sterling a day and that, he concluded dramatically, if imprecisely, would come to £150,000 a year.

In fact, Charles II had neither the inclination nor the resources to spend anything like that. Monmouth duly arrived in Edinburgh on 18 June after a three-day journey, with his secretary and his master of horse, and joined Linlithgow at Blackburn next day. But the promised forces were slower in coming. In the end, only two English troops arrived to supplement the Scottish army. The artillery consisted of 'four pieces of cannon', and there was great difficulty in finding a competent gunner. In the end, only one experienced man was located, together with 'three men that were pressed from Leith, who proved very unfit for service'.

But if the army was smaller in numbers than everyone, from the Privy Council to the King, had promised, it was strong in generalship. Monmouth, whose star was at its height, had fought in Flanders; General Dalyell, who was proposed by the Privy Council as his lieutenant-general – though he refused the post – had seen service under the Czar in Russia; and the three English dragoon officers, the splendidly named Major Theophilus Oglethorpe, Major Edmund Maine, and Captain Henry Cornewall, were seasoned and experienced officers of cavalry. With Claverhouse, Home, and Airlie commanding their separate troops, and the Marquis of Montrose in charge of the Life Guards, there was no lack of skill and discipline.

Amongst the Covenanters, however, there was neither command nor control. Instead there was a fatal confusion of purpose. Time which might have been spent on forming and training an army was taken up instead on the kind of religious debate which was endemic within the Covenanting movement.

'Instead of entrenching, gathering munitions, appointing officers, the leaders turned the camp into a general assembly of the hottest heads. Like stump orators, the perfervid demagogues carried their pulpits with them', wrote one of the Covenanters' later historians, J. King Hewison, who estimated that there were probably as many as four distinct factions within the ranks of the disorganized band which marched into Glasgow on 6 June, following Claverhouse, Home, and Ross's retreat.

In the city, where they burned down the house of the Archbishop and one which was said to belong to Lauderdale, the debate was joined in earnest, headed by the preacher John Welsh, now counted a moderate, who argued, sensibly, that they should forget religious differences until they had formed a proper army. Others, under their commander, Robert Hamilton, and the fiery Donald Cargill, insisted on a new declaration which would take a pure line on the nature of the Covenant.

The debate dragged on for almost a week, until a fractious Council of war on 12 June. At this point, however, outposts at Bothwell, a small village on the Clyde some eleven miles south-east of Glasgow, reported some signs of enemy troop movements. The news sent a shiver of alarm through the ranks of the Covenanters, and Welsh, seizing on it, proposed a compromise declaration which, while still viewed as inadequate 'in all save its condemnation of prelacy', was hurriedly fixed to the market cross at Hamilton. It ended with a stirring plea to the opposing forces to change sides, 'seeing we fight under his banner who is the Lord of Hosts.'

That Sunday, despite desperate attempts by the Hamilton faction to silence him, Welsh preached a rousing sermon, urging all those who listened to unite and prepare for the conflict ahead. But his words fell on deaf ears, and the arguments continued right up to the moment of battle.

On the evening of 21 June, Monmouth, with the dragoons and Lord Home's troop in the van, followed by the rest of the cavalry, including Claverhouse's troop, and 300 foot-soldiers, moved down to Bothwell, and at three o'clock on the morning of Sunday 22 June his advance guard skirted Bothwell Church and approached the bridge, just south of the village, the only place where an army could cross the Clyde without dragging its cannon through deep fords.

The defending army, on the other side, was ill-prepared either for attack or defence. The wrangling amongst the Covenanters had continued unabated, with the argument, unbelievably at this late stage, revolving round the question of who had or had not accepted the Government's Indulgences. Hackston of Rathillet went so far as to draw his sword and declare himself 'equally ready against the indulged men and curates'. Military preparations were minimal, as one Covenanter, James Ure of Shargarton, recalled:

> We were not concerned with an enemy, as if there had not been one within 1000 miles of us. There were none went through the army to see if we wanted powder or ball. I do really think there were few or none that had both powder and ball in all the army to shoot twice.

On the eve of the battle, Ure watched apprehensively the distant flares from the Government's lines as the soldiers kindled the 'matches' they would use for their muskets the next day.

On the morning of 22 June, some of Monmouth's troops advanced to the bridge and shots were exchanged across the river. The sound of gunfire finally persuaded Hamilton that a petition, prepared by Welsh, should be sent over, and two of the moderate party went forward with a written request for 'liberty, under safe conduct, to some of our number'. Monmouth, who seems to have wanted to extend clemency if at all possible, nevertheless insisted that the rebels lay down their arms, a request that drew the brief response from Hamilton: 'And hang next'.

Little time was allowed for discussion: Monmouth gave them half an hour to make up their minds. At the end of this interval, he ordered his cannon up to the bridge. The Covenanters' forces amounted to perhaps 6,000 men. James Ure put the numbers at '4000 foot and 2000 horse', though he added bitterly that 'if we had agreed [it] would have been the triple'. Even so, they had certainly more than double the numbers opposing them. Their men were now divided in two, with the main body, under Hamilton, drawn up about half a mile back from the bridge, on higher ground at a place called Little Park. The remainder, two companies of foot and three troops of horse, with one small cannon – a 'brazen piece' Russell called it – held the bridge they had barricaded.

The first fire, exchanged across the bridge, drove Monmouth's gunners back from their artillery, and, if the bridge had not been barricaded, the rebel musketeers might have been able to storm across and capture or spike the guns. Since these were to have a devastating effect later in the battle, it was an opportunity missed. Then Monmouth's army rallied, and Major Oglethorpe, with his dragoons, laid down sufficient fire to force the Covenanters back from the barricades. The bridge, however, was disputed for upwards of two hours. James Ure, along with Hackston of Rathillet, was amongst those defending it, but, finally, they were forced to retire.

The accuracy of the musket-fire on the Government's side cannot have been very great, for Ure described how he regrouped his men on some flat ground on his side of the bridge and faced the first red coats who came over without losing more than three of his men:

The enemy faced and fired at me from the other side, and from the bridge, upwards of 500 shot; and likewise their cannon played. With the first shot they killed two men to me, and there was another killed with a musket; and I saw none coming to assist. I was forced to retire to the moor to the rest.

Oglethorpe, driven back initially to some houses at the foot of the bridge, was soon reinforced from the other side, and pressed forward again. Finally, Monmouth himself crossed the bridge at the head of Linlithgow's Guards and his own troop to face the main body of the Covenanters, 'but two carabines shot asunder', as Russell described it. More important were the cannon, which now opened up against the Covenanters, throwing Hamilton's left wing into confusion.

Suddenly there was a stampede amongst the rebel troops. It began on the left amongst the cavalry, then spread to the right, with foot-soldiers joining the horse in headlong retreat. Ure, despairing, watched it happen:

> My men fired on the dragoons, and they at them, and their cannons played; the foot, hearing this, and being troubled a little with the horse, fled; and so they all fled, and not a man was standing on all the left hand. I cried to my men to make away. The right hand stood a little, but not so long as to put on a pair of gloves; so they all fled, and I turned with all my speed. Indeed, I was beholden to my horse.

The chaos on the left wing spread to the right where Cleland was in command. His men too threw away their arms and began to flee.

The pursuit was deadly. Monmouth sent part of his cavalry, under Oglethorpe, Maine and Claverhouse, galloping after the rebels, who were streaming back towards Hamilton and south to Strathaven. It seems clear that most of the killing took place in the final stages of the battle and in the course of the pursuit. Claverhouse is said to have been particularly harsh, giving no quarter to captured men. Some of his men seem to have seized on the opportunity to take revenge for the defeat at Drumclog.

Inevitably, tales of brutality later emerged amongst the Covenanters. Unarmed men were said to have been cut down after surrendering; innocent villagers along the road were shot; prisoners were stripped naked and kept lying face down all night. Many such incidents undoubtedly took place, and later on Claverhouse's name was attached to some of the more lurid of them.

It is significant, however, that none of the contemporary accounts from the Covenanting side mentions him. He was, after all, only a captain at the time, with barely eight months' service behind him. Although the number of casualties amongst the Covenanters was high, so was the number of prisoners taken. The report to the Privy Council gave an estimate of 800 dead, with 1,100 prisoners taken, and this seems to have been a reasonably accurate figure, if too low in the eyes of some people, for Monmouth was chided later at court for his clemency. And old General Dalyell, who had refused to serve under Monmouth, is said to have remarked: 'Had I come a day sooner, these rogues should never have troubled his Majesty or the kingdom any more.'

The Covenanters were scattered. Most of their leaders escaped, though some were badly wounded, including Donald Cargill, who was left for dead on the battlefield, but miraculously survived. Hamilton later fled to Holland; Welsh resumed his charmed life as an outlawed preacher; while the Archbishop's murderers, Balfour of Kinloch, wounded in the thigh, Hackston, and Russell, went on the run again.

Three days later, his mopping-up operation in the west completed, Monmouth dismissed the militia, and returned to Edinburgh. The city's populace turned out to jeer at his prisoners as they were led in, roped in pairs, some of them hooded. Because there was not enough room in the prisons, they were penned in a walled-in lot – part of what is now Greyfriars' churchyard – occupying ground that had once been used to sign their Covenant. There was no shelter, little food, and hostility from their guards. Many of them were later ordered to be transported to the plantations, or incarcerated in the stinking dungeons of Dunnottar Castle on the Stonehaven cliffs.

Monmouth, meanwhile, was given a vote of thanks by the Council 'for his great pains in suppressing the late Rebellion'. They threw a banquet for him – 'a very noble Collation of Meats and Fruits' – and presented him with a parchment scroll in a gold box conferring on him the freedom of the city. Three days later, on 6 July, he took his leave and departed for London.

Claverhouse remained in the west, rounding up those rebels who were still carrying arms, and trying to track down their leaders. A proclamation from the Council, dated 26 June and published on market crosses throughout the south of Scotland, named the most wanted men – a list of sixty-five in all. Claverhouse and his troop made their presence felt from Ayr down to Nithsdale and Galloway, while the English troopers criss-crossed the country to the east. The rebels had some astonishing escapes, and at one point Claverhouse was within a mile of Balfour of Kinloch and Welsh. But he never caught up with them.

Then, some time in mid-July, Claverhouse was recalled to Edinburgh for a mission of the greatest importance. It was to take him to

London, where he would form a close association with James, Duke of York – an association which was to last until his death. His absence relieved the pressure on the rebels in the west at a crucial juncture.

On 25 July, with the permission of the Privy Council, Claverhouse left Edinburgh for London, along with his commander-in-chief, the Earl of Linlithgow, and closely followed by the Chancellor, the Earl of Rothes, en route to court. For a young captain, he was in illustrious company.

CHAPTER SIX
The Isles of Menteith

'*I always laid the saddle on the right horse*'
John Graham of Claverhouse

Claverhouse was thirty-two, and unmarried. His military duties had not offered him many opportunities for meeting, far less for courting, eligible women, and he was not noted for his interest in the opposite sex. Even his enemies, who were prepared later to ascribe all manner of vices to him, conceded that lechery was not amongst them. A vicious piece of Covenanting lore, written much later, ran: 'The hell wicked-witted, bloodthirsty Graham of Claverhouse, who hated to spend his time with wine and women, which made him more active in violent unheard of persecution.' And though that can probably take its place along with some of the other Claverhouse myths there was, throughout his long periods at the English court, no hint of gossip concerning affairs of the heart, save for an intriguing piece of doggerel called 'Mitchell's Ghost', written about the attempted assassination of Archbishop Sharp, which ran:

> That crooked Vulcan will the bellows blow
> Till he'll set all on fire, and then he'll go
> A packing to his Highland hills to hide him
> And loves not Mars for Venus sake, beside him.

The poet carefully explained that 'Vulcan' was Sir George Mackenzie, the King's Advocate, that 'Mars' was Claverhouse, and that the reference to Venus implied an affair with Mackenzie's second wife, Margaret Halyburton. Nothing, however, emerges from the correspondence of either man to sustain the suggestion.

Early in 1679, however, the young Captain Graham began a long and protracted campaign to gain for himself a wife, a title, and a useful inheritance. Whether in his own mind they necessarily ran in that order was never entirely clear, not even, on occasions, to Claverhouse himself.

The title he sought was the Earldom of Menteith, which was facing extinction. The eighth Earl, William Graham, was in poor health, separated from his wife, and with no direct heir, while the estate, which had once been a rich one, was now so burdened with debt that the Earl at one point had to ask his cousin if he could borrow his ceremonial robes for a sitting of Parliament.

The Earl's nearest relation was his uncle, Sir James Graham, who lived in Ireland with an unmarried daughter, Helen. She was heiress to the Menteith estates, and if a suitable husband emerged, he would be in a position to claim the title, for it could only pass to a male inheritor. Some time in early 1679, the name of John Graham of Claverhouse was mentioned as a possible suitor for Helen Graham, and he seized enthusiastically on the idea.

By February 1679, he had begun an exchange of letters with Menteith, putting his case as suitor, saviour of the estate, and future Earl. Much of the correspondence was written from London, where, over the next three years, Claverhouse was to spend many months at court. But it opened with a letter, written in Scotland in mid-campaign, in which he put his case formally to Menteith:

> My Lord, as your friend and servant, I do take the liberty to give you one advice, which is that there can be nothing so advantageous for you as to settle your affairs, and establish your successor in time, for it can do you no prejudice if you come to have any children of your own body, and will be much for your quiet and comfort if you have none; for who ever you make choice of will be in place of a son.
>
> You know that Julius Caesar had no need to regret the want of issue, having adopted Augustus, for he knew certainly that he had secured to himself a thankful and useful friend, as well as a wise successor, neither of which he could have promised himself by having children; for nobody knows whether they beget wise men or fools, besides that the ties of gratitude and friendship are stronger in generous minds than those of nature ... I may say without vanity that I will do your family no dishonour, seeing there is nobody you could make choice of has toiled so much for honour as I have done, though it has been my misfortune to attain but a small share.

Menteith was impressed. He wrote to his uncle, Sir James Graham, in Ireland, describing Claverhouse as 'a person exceeding well accomplished as any I know, with natural gifts, for all that's noble and virtuous may be seen in him.' More to the point, 'he has a free estate upwards of six hundred pound sterling yearly of good payable rent, near by Dundee.' So enthusiastic was Menteith by the end of his letter, that he said he would not hear of anyone's being considered as a suitor, 'unless it be Claverhouse, whom I say again is the only person of all I know fittest and most proper to marry your daughter.'

But, despite this enthusiasm, there was no positive response from across the water in Ireland. Claverhouse's formal proposal of marriage met with a long silence, and when Sir James finally replied he was non-committal. Claverhouse's prospects were not helped by teasing letters from his kinsman, the Marquis of Montrose, who first wrote warning him that 'an Irish gentleman has carried away the Lady', then emerged as a rival suitor himself.

To his chagrin, Claverhouse learned that Montrose appeared to be preferred by Helen's formidable mother, Lady Graham – 'a very cunning woman', Claverhouse called her – who was quite determined that her daughter was not going to marry into a branch of the family that had not done particularly well in Scotland, without some financial guarantees. As far as Lady Graham could see, the Menteith estate was virtually bankrupt, and she did not relish the idea of a match 'where she would be a daily spectator of the ruins of that noble family she came from'.

Montrose's proposal, however, finally foundered on the refusal of King Charles II to sign a document allowing the title, with the lands and possessions that made up the potentially profitable part of the estate, to be passed on without approval from all parties. Montrose began courting elsewhere. But, over the next two years, Claverhouse continued to lay dogged siege to Menteith, who had an irritating habit of not replying to letters, and to Sir James and Lady Graham, who were never wholly convinced of the desirability of the match. Helen Graham herself does not appear to have been consulted.

During all this time Claverhouse was at court and enjoying the friendship and trust of the Duke of York, whose name he did not hesitate to use on his own behalf. But he retained a sense of honour in the matter: he refused to take part in a devious plot, proposed by Montrose, whereby the two of them would mount a combined operation on the Graham family, with Montrose doing the wooing, and Claverhouse using his influence at court to get the King's approval. When the deal went through, said Montrose, he would pass the title on to Claverhouse, who could marry Helen into the bargain. Angrily rejecting the scheme, Claverhouse told Lady Graham exactly what Montrose had been up to, and protested his innocence in the matter.

It was clear to most participants in this long-distance wooing that Claverhouse's interests lay in securing a title rather than in Helen Graham herself. But he himself indignantly denied it. 'I need nothing to persuade me to take that young lady', he told Menteith at one point. 'I would take her in her smock.' And as to whether his enthusiasm about the Earl's estate was in doubt, he declared that he was 'in love with the Isles of Menteith'.

Suggestions that he was intriguing at court behind the backs of others drew an equally vehement response. He assured Menteith that 'I never spoke to any of you but as I ought to do, with all the respect and esteem imagineable. I always laid my saddle on the right horse.'

At no stage, however, did he receive much in the way of encouragement from the Grahams themselves, a fact which he recorded philosophically, in a letter to Menteith: 'When my affairs go wrong', he wrote, 'I remember that saying of Lucan, *Tam mala Pompeii quam prospera mundus adoret*. One has occasion to show their vigour after a wrong step to make a nimble recovery ...'.

His letters show that he was, throughout the summer of 1680, a constant visitor at court, both in London and at Windsor, and that he had built up a particular friendship with James, Duke of York. He went with the royal party on a state visit to Dunkirk for eight days to attend the court in France, and he discussed the Helen Graham affair with James on many occasions. Although nothing was to come of the match, Claverhouse used his influence with James successfully to secure a small estate at Freuch in Galloway on the Wigtonshire coast which had been forfeited after its owner was found to be a frequenter of conventicles. As a property, it was not a very grand affair, and there was no suitable house on it, but it gave him a base in the west, where he was to spend so much time.

Towards the end of 1681, even he began to realize that his prospects of marrying Helen Graham were less than rosy. On 11 December, he wrote to Menteith:

> My Lord, you see by this and many other things, how prejudicial it is for you not to come to some settlement in your affairs, either one way or the other, and in the meantime my age slips away, and I lose other occasions, as I suppose the young lady does.

The young lady had not, however, lost her 'occasion', and early in the new year of 1682, Claverhouse learned that Helen Graham was to marry Arthur Rawdon, nephew and heir to the Earl of Conway (and perhaps the 'Irish gentleman' Montrose had warned him about). It was a thoroughly suitable match. Claverhouse made one last desperate effort to persuade her family to change their minds, but he was too late. The marriage took place that spring.

Throughout the long, if prosaic, wooing of Helen Graham by Claverhouse, there was no word that has survived of how she herself felt about him, or his rival, Montrose. But there is one piece of evidence that suggests that she knew nothing at the time of the arguments about the settlement of the estate: a letter from her to Menteith survives, written two years after her marriage, saying that, if she had known about the proposals for the title and the estate at the time, she would have liked to have done something to save them:

> I am so well a wisher to the family, that sooner than the ashes of my ancestors should rudely be trampled on by strangers, I would willingly purchase those two islands [of Menteith] with much more than any other body would give.

Perhaps, if Claverhouse had been allowed to put his arguments directly to her, things might have gone differently.

The Earl of Menteith never did resolve the question of his debt-ridden estate, despite 'frugal and virtuous living'. He died childless in 1694, having conveyed his remaining property to the Montrose branch of the family. With him perished the title. Interestingly, Helen's father, Sir James Graham, blamed Claverhouse for the failure of the negotiations with Montrose. Marriage to Montrose might, in his view, have saved the estate. He wrote to Menteith that: 'the hand of Claverhouse has been in all these contrivances, whose ambitious thoughts to make himself the head of our ancient family brought all the trouble of my Lord Montrose business upon you.'

Claverhouse would have been appalled had he known of that view. In one of his last letters to Menteith, he insisted: 'My Lord, I have both at home and abroad sustained the character of an honest and frank man and defies the world to reproach me of anything.'

CHAPTER SEVEN
Settling the West

*'It fares with heretics as with tops, which, so soon as they
are scourged, keep foot and run pleasantly, but fall so soon
as they are neglected and left by themselves'*
Sir George Mackenzie of Rosehaugh, King's Advocate

By the spring of 1682, Claverhouse's days at court were ending, and he
was eager to resume his career as a soldier. 'I begin to think it time for
me to set a work again', he wrote. Much had happened since he first
came to London. The political climate, both north and south of the
border, had changed radically, and with it his own fortunes.

He had first arrived in London at a time when the influence of John
Maitland, now Duke of Lauderdale, the Secretary of State for Scotland,
and a man of great intelligence and power and even greater corruption,
was coming to an end. 'That famous bird Lauderdale', as he had been
described when he was in exile with Charles II in Holland, was now
out of favour at court. Once cordially dubbed 'the King's buffoon',
delighting Charles by dressing up in lady's petticoats and performing a
skirt-dance, Lauderdale now bored him. His humour was laborious,
and the King was disgusted by his habit of taking huge pinches of snuff
from the royal snuff-box. His skill in political intrigue had grown dull
and irrelevant; his memory was failing; he was dominated by his
rapacious wife, Lady Dysart; and the enemies he and his wife had made
were beginning to outnumber their supporters.

His fall from power, however, left a considerable void, for he had
been a dominating figure in England as well as in Scotland for twenty
years. Lauderdale had seen the rise and fall of parliamentary rule in
Scotland. As Commissioner to the Scottish parliament from 1669 as
well as Secretary of State, he had been charged with forging a union

with England, establishing royal supremacy over the Church, and founding an effective militia. Opposition to his measures had been strong, centring on a powerful 'club' run by the Duke of Hamilton and including Queensberry, Rothes, and Sir George Mackenzie. Although, earlier in his career, he had urged conciliation in dealing with the Whigs in the west, and had understood their concerns better than most politicians in London, he had gradually become an oppressor, and acquired a growing reputation for ruthlessness, even though the power he had once enjoyed was fading. In the end, his main aim was simply to maintain stability north of the border, whatever the cost. But his manner, his greed, and his failure to maintain good relations with vested interests in Scotland, had steadily undermined the foundations of his authority. By the end of 1679, his influence with the King, with the English court and with Scottish nobles was at an end. In November 1680, he resigned as Secretary of State. Two years later he was dead. Into the void stepped James, Duke of York, the King's brother, and Claverhouse's patron, whose star was rising again after a year in eclipse.

In the summer of 1679, James was still in exile in Holland, where he had been forced to retire in the aftermath of the Titus Oates affair, in which a Catholic plot to kill the King had been revealed. The public hysteria aroused by that extraordinary exercise in black propaganda was still poisoning the atmosphere in London, and James, as a known and practising Roman Catholic, was the target of much of it. Claverhouse wrote about the constant attacks being made at the time on 'the honest Duke'. But towards the end of August, the King, who was at Windsor, developed a fever, and James was summoned back from exile in case the worst happened. Within a fortnight of James's return, Monmouth, James's rival, had surrendered his commission as General, and was himself on the way to Holland, his brief ascendancy over.

In Scotland, Lieutenant-General Thomas Dalyell was appointed Commander-in-Chief of the army, and in October, with the King now fully recovered, James was appointed High Commissioner, to act as Charles II's representative in Edinburgh. He travelled slowly north, and with him went John Graham of Claverhouse, who was at the head of his old cavalry troop when James arrived in Edinburgh on 24 November, to be received 'by the whole Council, by the King's troop of horse, and by 2000 other nobility and gentry of several shires', as one witness, Charles Whytford, wrote to a friend in Paris:

When [James] came to Leith 15 companies of the train bands with several pieces of cannon saluted him. At Leith he took horse and received all the forces; towards three of the clock the Provost and the Bailies in their robes met him at the water-gate, then the cannons of the castle went off for a considerable time, and bonfires were made throughout all the town, and the ringing of bells continued until ten o'clock at night.

'Truly,' wrote James on 28 November, 'I have had as handsome a reception here as I could desire, and have great reason to be satisfied with it.'

On 4 December 1679, James took his seat on the Privy Council. He arrived as the Council was attempting to tighten the noose around the Government's opponents in Scotland. The indemnity offered in July to any rebel Covenanters who would promise not to bear arms again had not been particularly successful, and a bond for ministers who would agree to 'live peaceably', or face substantial fines, had met with predictable resistance. On 13 November, a proclamation had been issued threatening with imprisonment all those 'vain and giddy preachers' who had failed to take the bond, as well as those who were still in rebellion despite the 'gentle and easy terms' offered in the indemnity. The Government's troops were ordered by the Privy Council in the name of the King to seize any minister who had not accepted the bond by 1 January 1680, and were instructed to apply to such persons 'all the severity that the law can allow, as enemies to us and their native country'.

In the west of Scotland, on 6 January 1680, new instructions were issued to Claverhouse to identify and round up those ministers in Dumfries, Wigton, Kirkcudbright, and Annandale who had failed to report in, and to procure evidence against them. But by the following month he was en route back to London, accompanying the Duke of York when he returned to England on 16 February.

Claverhouse left his troop under the command of Andrew Bruce of Earlshall, now a captain, while his brother David acted as quartermaster and managed the family's affairs. Why Claverhouse should have been adopted as a member of James's retinue is unclear. He had gone south originally to give his advice on the military situation in the west of Scotland, but he had stayed on far longer than could possibly have been justified by that. The only conclusion is that James liked him and enjoyed his company. Indeed, everything points to their having interests in common.

James, who is usually portrayed as a weak and irresolute monarch, had, at the time Claverhouse met him, lived an active and adventurous life, and had had the kind of military experience that matched Claver-house's own. He had served in the French King's army in France and in Flanders, where he had acquired a reputation for gallantry. After the Restoration, he had helped in the development of colonial trade in the East and West Indies and on the west coast of Africa (the expedition he had sent to America, which took Long Island from the Dutch without a shot being fired, resulted in the main town in the area being renamed 'New York' in his honour). It was James who, along with Samuel Pepys at the Admiralty, rebuilt the navy, in which he also served. In 1665 and again in 1672, he commanded the fleet against the Dutch with courage and skill. At the age of forty-six, he was a man whom Claverhouse, fifteen years younger, could look up to and admire.

That James was a Roman Catholic, unwilling either to disguise or surrender his religious beliefs, was not a matter of concern to Claver-house, who may even have respected James's decision to make his views known and resign his post of Lord High Admiral rather than disguise the nature of his faith. Being at court in 1680 and 1681, Claverhouse was a witness of the Exclusion debates, framed to deprive James of the succession, and he plainly saw nothing to alter his view of the man to whom he would always thereafter pledge his loyalty. The Exclusion Bill was finally rejected by the Lords, and, when James returned to Scotland in the summer of 1681, his succession to the throne had been assured by Act of Parliament.

By the time Claverhouse resumed his duties in Scotland in the autumn of 1681, he was able to bring more than just military experi-ence to the job. He was now a practised courtier with close experience of the political realities of the day, and with direct access to the King's viceroy in Scotland. The country recognized his new status. On 7 October 1681, he was granted the freedom of the burgh of Stirling, along with his brother, David Graham, and his second-in-command, Captain Bruce of Earlshall. With a new estate at Freuch in Galloway, he had, as he wrote to Menteith, 'good hopes not only to command the forces there, but to be Sheriff of Galloway', a hope that was soon to be realized, and which would give him civil as well as military powers.

Then, in November 1681, he was summoned to Edinburgh to serve on the jury in the most spectacular judicial case of the period, the trial, on charges of treason, of the Earl of Argyll.

The case followed a period of sustained repression against those who still held out for the Covenant. Although the number of illegal con-venticles had dwindled, there were two preachers at least who con-tinued to attract large and enthusiastic congregations, and to spread a message which was, if anything, more extreme than any heard before. One was Richard Cameron, later known as 'the Lion of the Covenant', aged only thirty-two, who had returned from a period of study in Holland, vowing that he would rather die than 'outlive the glory of God departing entirely from these lands'. The other was Cameron's colleague and mentor Donald Cargill, who had been left for dead on the field at Bothwell Bridge, but was now, at sixty-one, as resolute as ever in the cause.

These two, whose faction became known as the 'Cameronians', were extremists in the Covenanting movement: while others were prepared to consider reaching some form of accommodation with the Government, they were not. The moderates, still led by John Welsh, refused to go along with them, but their voice was drowned in Cameronian fervour.

Cargill's message was no less ferocious than Cameron's. He dubbed the Duke of York 'a sworn vassal of Antichrist', and referred to Roman Catholicism and episcopacy as 'the kingdom of darkness'. There was no doubting his rebellious intent, for, in June 1680, a friend of Cargill's, Henry Hall, was captured at Queensferry and found to have papers on him which set out a new manifesto, drawn up by Cargill and later named 'The Fanatics' New Covenant'. It called for the removal of 'those who had forfeited authority' – including the royal family – and the setting up of a new republic.

The principles set out in the Queensferry papers were included in a Declaration of Independence which was to become a charter for the most implacable wing of the Covenanting movement. On 22 June 1680, the first anniversary of Bothwell Bridge, Richard Cameron and his brother Michael, accompanied by twenty horsemen 'with drawn swords and pistols in their hands', had ridden into the little town of Sanquhar in Nithsdale, twenty-five miles north of Dumfries, and fixed the Declaration to the market cross. It stated formally that the Covenanters intended to 'disown Charles Stuart, who hath been reigning, or rather (we may say) tyrannising on the Throne of Scotland'.

The response from the Government was inevitable. Eight days later, a proclamation was issued offering 5,000 merks for Cameron, dead or alive, 3,000 each for Cargill and Michael Cameron, and 1,000 for each of their comrades. On Thursday 22 July, Cameron and forty followers, who had now been joined by the fugitive Hackston of Rathillet, were found by Captain Bruce, of Claverhouse's troop, on a bleak stretch of moorland at Airds Moss, heading east for the little village of Muirkirk in Ayrshire. Cameron led his followers into battle with the call: 'Lord, spare the green and take the ripe.' The odds against them were, perhaps, three to one. Hackston was badly wounded and captured. Both Richard Cameron and his brother Michael were killed, along with about seven others, while the rest of Cameron's followers fled across the moor.

Bruce cut Cameron's head and arms from his body, and, using it as evidence, claimed a reward. He was given £500 sterling. The prisoners, including the bloodstained Hackston, were marched to Lanark, where Hackston was interrogated by General Dalyell, who threatened, according to Hackston, to 'roast' him for his unsatisfactory answers. He was then sent on, with the other prisoners, to Edinburgh.

At last, the Council had one of the ringleaders of the Sharp assassination in their hands, and they took fearsome revenge. Hackston was brought into Edinburgh by the Watergate, on a white barebacked horse, his face to its tail, feet roped beneath its belly, hands tied behind his back. In front of him Cameron's head and hands were mounted on a halberd, and behind him, three prisoners, bound to a bar of iron, were tied to the horse's tail.

Placed on trial on 29 July, Hackston refused to recognize the court, but drew up a long statement, giving not only a résumé of his own beliefs, but a full account of the Covenanters' military encounters. There was never any doubt about the verdict, and the manner of his death was specified in gruesome detail by the Council:

> That his body be drawn backward on a hurdle to the cross of Edinburgh; that here be an high scaffold erected a little above the cross, where in the first place, his right hand is to be struck off, and after some time, his left hand: then he is to be hanged up, and cut down alive, his bowels to be taken out, and his heart shown to the people by the hangman; then his heart and bowels to be burned in a fire prepared for that purpose on the scaffold: that afterwards his head be cut off, and his body divided into four quarters: his head to be fixed on the Netherbow, one of his quarters, with both his hands, to be affixed at St Andrews, another quarters at Glasgow, a third at Leith, a fourth at Burntisland.

This kind of brutality was new. Scotland had never, like England, gone in for the prescribed violence of hanging, drawing and quartering, and it was an indication of the fear with which a rebellion was viewed, that such methods were now used against the state's enemies. The same went for torture. Though civilized citizens, like Sir George Mackenzie, could argue that it was only used in extreme cases, it was sanctioned at the highest level, despite the disgust felt by those members of the Privy

Council who were forced to watch, and who made any excuse to try and avoid doing so.

Of the extremists, only Cargill was now left. It was not until July 1681 that he was captured, near Lanark, and brought to Edinburgh for trial. Questioned before the Council, he refused to discuss the excommunications he had pronounced publicly against the King and his ministers. These he said were a religious matter not to be debated in a civil court. He was careful not to commit himself on the question of the King's authority. For a time it seemed possible that these arguments might gain him a reprieve. But there were witnesses to say he had been at Bothwell Bridge, and there was little doubt that what he had said publicly amounted to treason. He was hanged on 27 July at the market cross in Edinburgh, along with four others, his last words drowned by the rolling of drums. Above the noise, however, could be heard the words of the 118th Psalm: 'I shall not die, but live, and shall the works of God discover.'

That same day, Parliament reassembled with much pomp, to hear James, Duke of York, its new Commissioner talk of the 'great honour and happiness' he had in being in Scotland, and pledge himself, on behalf of the King, for the Protestant religion, for episcopacy, and for the suppression of conventicles. One month later Parliament had approved one of the worst Acts ever drafted north or south of the border.

The Test Act of 31 August 1681 was devised as a means of excluding papists from public office by requiring them to swear an oath of loyalty. But it was directed against extremists of the other side as well, thus covering Roman Catholic and Covenanter alike. Members of the royal family were specifically excepted.

As a piece of legislation it was self-contradictory and tendentious, and so restrictive that to swear the oath was to accept the virtual surrender of independent thought. It included as part of the oath, John Knox's lengthy Confession of Faith of 1567, with which many Presbyterians, let alone Roman Catholics, were now unfamiliar. The Confession made Christ the head of the Church; the oath, however, also proclaimed that it was the King who held that position. Despite this contradiction, the oath had to be sworn 'in the plain genuine sense and meaning of the words, without any equivocation, mental reservation, or any manner of evasion whatsoever.' It was, as one critic saw it, 'a confession of slavery'.

Its main drafter was the Earl of Stair, President of the Court of Session, who was said to have introduced the 1567 Confession into the oath simply to make trouble, expecting that it would be thrown out in the course of debate. But the Act was passed so rapidly that few people understood the contradictions, and not many bothered to go and look up the Confession. Stair himself later refused to take the Test which he had himself devised.

Amongst the many who found great difficulty with the oath was the Earl of Argyll, a Protestant and chief of Clan Campbell, but also a staunch supporter of the Government. Skilled politician though he was, Argyll could not bring himself to swear the oath as it stood. Before the Council, he mumbled his responses, finally agreeing to the oath only 'in so far as it is consistent with itself and the protestant religion'. This would never have been enough for a charge of treason, had Argyll not made enemies, both inside and outside Parliament. And even they would not have succeeded without the tacit support of the Duke of York. James pretended to stand aside, and even offered Argyll encouragement, but in the end he was content to see him charged, perhaps because he too wished to see cut back the great power-base Argyll had built up in the west. He wrote later that there was nothing he could have done to help Argyll, since Parliament was so determined to pursue him; but he well knew that he could have rescued him.

Despite James's attitude, the vote in favour of committing Argyll for trial on charges of treason was a very narrow one. It required the presence of the infirm old Lord Nairn who was in bed and asleep. He was persuaded to get up and come into the court, where he promptly fell asleep again. Even with his eyes closed, however, 'he knew how to vote', and the charge was read.

Claverhouse was one of the assize (jury) when the case opened on 12 December 1681. There is no record of how he himself felt about this travesty of justice, but Argyll, offered the chance of challenging the assize, glanced up at them and shook his head. He knew that he had no friends among them, and that, as loyal servants to the King, there was little chance of their bringing in a verdict other than guilty. In the end, the assize did not need much time to reach their decision, and on 13 December they found unanimously 'that the Earl of Argyll hath proven against him the crimes of treason'.

Condemned to death, the Earl managed to escape from Edinburgh Castle on 20 December, the day before he was due to be taken to the Tolbooth. He dressed up as a page and walked out, holding up the train of his step-daughter Lady Sophia Lindsay, a disguise so unconvincing that there is little doubt he was helped by some at least of his guards. Adopting the appropriate name of 'Mr Hope', he travelled south to

London and escaped to Holland. 'It was easy for him to do it', wrote James later to Prince William of Orange, 'since he was not kept a close prisoner ... his life was in no danger, which he and his friends knew very well.'

For the Covenanters, Argyll's case was seen as evidence of a new campaign of persecution, and the Test became the most hated of all the Acts passed against them. In the country, those who refused to take it could be fined, imprisoned, or have their lands and titles taken away. Magistrates were given three weeks to remove from their churches ministers who had 'undutifully refused' to swear the oath, and to find 'fit and qualified persons' to replace them. Nobles and lairds who would not swear were forced to surrender their public offices, and a list of them was published.

For Claverhouse, these forfeitures were a welcome bonus, since in early January 1682, he was granted the Heritable Sheriffdom of Wigtown, forfeited by Sir Andrew Agnew, and the Heritable Regality of Tongland, north of Kirkcudbright, forfeited by Viscount Kenmure and passed by order of the Privy Council to 'the Laird of Claverhouse'. His commission as a sheriff empowered him to summon anyone suspected of joining conventicles. There had been stories of marriages and baptisms held in the fields instead of in the churches of accepted ministers, and Claverhouse was instructed to impose fines, 'and to do and perform everything requisite and necessary for putting the same to due and vigorous execution.' He was also allowed to offer fourteen days' safe conduct to any suspect while he questioned him about his possible involvement in the rebellion, though he was limited to fining and imprisoning, the brief of a magistrate rather than a judge.

His territory, however, was far wider than before, for he was also commissioned to act as Sheriff-Depute in the neighbouring districts of Dumfries, Annandale, and Kirkcudbright, so long as he did not intrude on the jurisdiction of the Sheriff of Dumfries himself, William Douglas, third Earl of Queensberry.

It was to Queensberry, as his civil superior, that Claverhouse now reported. This was the year of the Earl's rise to power, after a period in the shadows when he had been associated with the aristocratic 'club' which had opposed Lauderdale. He was now Lord Justice-General, a title held previously by Argyll, and he was shortly to become Treasurer and be made a Marquis. All this he achieved despite a marked reluctance to take the Test. In the end he had sworn a modified version and had got away with it, thanks to an important ally, the future Earl of Aberdeen, whom he helped to become Chancellor.

Queensberry combined great wealth with notorious meanness. A note written on the Queensberry accounts reads: 'Deil pike oot the een o' him wha looks herein.' On his estates in the west, on the site of the House of Hassock in mid-Nithsdale, he was building the magnificent pile of Drumlanrig, which would thereafter, and up to the present day, be the family seat. He had, however, made as many enemies as friends, and the Earl of Melfort would later tell James VII that Queensberry was 'an atheist in religion, a villain in friendship, a knave in business, and a traitor in his carriage to [the King]'.

When Claverhouse took up his new commission as Sheriff, Queensberry was determined to maintain law and order amongst the dissenters in the west, and on 2 January 1682 he wrote to his ally, Haddo:

> In the heads of Galloway some of the Rebels meet; but their number is not considerable, not exceeding 12 or 16, and their business is only to drink and quarrel: so neither Church nor State (in my judgment) need fear them. However, I'm still of the opinion the sooner the garrisons be placed, and a competent party sent with Claverhouse for scouring that part of the country the better. Besides, I'm told field conventicles continue in Annandale and Galloway, but all [he ended acidly] will certainly vanish upon Claverhouse's arrival, as I have often been told.

On 12 January, a rebel party of forty horsemen and twenty foot, all of them armed, gathered round the market cross at Lanark, defaced it with hammers, burned copies of various statutes, including the Test, then fixed a declaration to the cross, repudiating all the Acts passed against them and, in particular, those approved by Parliament under the 'professedly Popish' Duke of York.

Four days later, Claverhouse wrote the first of many reports he was to send to Queensberry. He said that he had visited the estate of Lord Kenmure, whose sheriffdom he had been granted, and had talked to his wife. He was certain that Kenmure was consorting with the rebels, and was causing trouble by stealing letters from the King's messengers, 'a high misdemeanour'. He told Lady Kenmure that it was only thanks to Queensberry that their moated castle at Loch Ken north of Kirkcudbright, standing high above the marshes, had not been turned into a garrison. He did think, however, that it would be a better place for his soldiers than Dumfries, and he had proposed to her that he should take it over. Lady Kenmure had agreed, providing the crown paid her two or three hundred pounds to repair the place.

So far, he said, things were reasonably calm in the area:

> The rebels have lived, I find, peaceably here till now, and their wives are

still in their houses .... The country hereabouts is in great dread. Upon
our march yesterday most men were fled, not knowing against whom
we designed; but the act of council about the safe conduct amuses many,
and will be of use to make them more unexcusable in the eyes of the
people if they make not use of it, which I am feared few will do.

His priorities were first to seek out active supporters of the rebellion, then to pursue those harbouring rebels, and finally to break up
field conventicles. He intended, however, to be lenient to begin with:

For what remains of the laws against the fanatics, I will threaten much,
but forebear severe executions for a while, for fear people should grow
desperate and increase too much the number of our enemies.

But, as before, there was a shortage of money, and he asked Queensberry to intercede with the Duke of York and the Treasury to secure
any funds likely to come from those whose properties were to be
forfeited. If he could be given those, and three months' back pay owed
to his soldiers, he could pay for the maintenance of prisoners, witnesses, spies, 'and all other expense necessary in this country.' The
proposals, however, came to nothing.

He found himself combining the duties of soldier and sheriff with
that of counter-propagandist. But he seems to have received little help
from his superiors. The Duke of Hamilton, for instance, had said he
would clear all the Whigs from his part of the west, but 'by what I see, I
send more in than he does'.

There were other powerful figures in the area who had no cause to
love him, amongst them Sir John Dalrymple, like his father an advocate, whose house in Ayrshire had, by order of the Privy Council, been
made available to Claverhouse as a garrison, and Sir Robert Maxwell,
in Kirkcudbright, who was also obliged to give him shelter and
accommodation.

All in all, Claverhouse found great difficulty in securing provisions
for his troops. It was a hard winter, and hay was scarce. He decided to
quarter his men in different parts of Galloway until the spring came
and the grass began to grow again. The effect of lodging soldiers in
households which had little enough food to sustain them through the
winter, could be devastating for the reluctant hosts, but Claverhouse
saw it as deliberate policy. When the house of a rebel who had fled was
visited, he ordered the soldiers to seize any goods they found therein,
to the point that 'their wives and children were brought to starving'.
That on its own was not sufficient guarantee of supplies, so he stored

magazines of corn and straw in various locations, thus allowing his troops to move around knowing that there would always be provisions ahead. He also proposed to reduce the Dumfries garrison from sixty to twenty, thus making the hay there last three months instead of one. He hoped that Queensberry would approve, because if he did not, 'the general will be mad'.

This last was a reference to General Sir Thomas Dalyell of the Binns, his commander-in-chief, who was, at the best of times, a difficult man to deal with. Dalyell, who remembered Drumclog, was not impressed by Claverhouse's military record, and it was important for Claverhouse not to annoy him since he enjoyed the friendship of the King. Indeed, Dalyell was said to be so deeply loyal to the Stuarts that when he heard of the execution of Charles I he swore never to shave his beard again. As a result, he was by now an extraordinary-looking figure, bald on top, with a long flowing beard which reached down to his belt. He never wore a wig, only a beaver hat with a narrow brim, and he favoured a close-fitting jockey's coat.

One of his contemporaries, Captain John Creichton, recalled that when he went to London to visit the King, he attracted crowds of little boys who would follow him from his house to court, shouting huzzas. Dalyell, always courteous, would thank them for their attention, but the King was less pleased since, whenever they went for a walk in the park, the crowds around Dalyell made it almost impossible to move. Why, asked the King, could Dalyell not shave and dress 'like other Christians'? But when the General did, on one occasion, abandon his strange clothes and go to court dressed in the latest fashion, the sight was so unusual that the King and the entire court burst out laughing.

Dalyell had told Lord Ross that he was 'very averse' to Claverhouse's returning to the west, and now that he was there he met him as infrequently as possible. Claverhouse, for his part, enjoyed teasing Dalyell behind his back. But he was careful to stay in his good books.

He was just as careful with Queensberry, who was now a powerful political figure. On 22 February, word reached him that Queensberry had been made a Marquis, and he immediately wrote congratulating him, and at the same time asking him to tell the Duke of York he was sorry not to have written more often to him. The explanation, he said, was that he had been too busy – he had not even been able to visit his property at Freuch, 'though I passed in sight of it'.

Part of his time had been spent concocting an ambitious scheme which would 'secure the peace both of the west and this country'. He was obviously delighted with it:

I am persuaded [it] will seem reasonable to your Lordship, and I wonder nobody has thought on it yet; but I will say nothing till I have put things to some order here, and I will beg leave for three or four days to come to Edinburgh and give you an account of it.

A week later he committed the idea to paper. The problem that he and his fellow-sheriffs faced, he said, was trying to impose the Privy Council's laws evenly on a large and disaffected population. To attempt to prosecute 'great and small' alike was not only inefficient, but tended to 'exasperate and alienate the hearts of the whole people; for it renders three desperate where it gains one.'

What he proposed instead was a plan 'to pardon the multitude and punish the ringleaders'. He had already begun to put it into effect by summoning two or three parishes together in one church and telling them exactly what the legal position was. He had explained the powers he had, what the laws against rebels were, and how much they owed to the King's favour. He warned them that there was to be no let-up in the campaign against conventiclers, and indeed that fines had recently been doubled.

However, he added, the King had no desire to inflict unnecessary suffering on his people, and he, Claverhouse, had no personal interest in raising money from fines. If, therefore, they cared to turn up peacefully at their regular church and obey the law, he would see to it that no reprisals were taken against them. But that did not, he emphasized, include the ringleaders amongst them nor those who harboured rebels. The following Sunday, he was gratified to see about 300 people at Kirkcudbright church, amongst them some who had not been there for many years. At that rate, he reckoned, he would very soon have about two-thirds of the congregation back in church.

That on its own, however, would not be enough, 'for we will be no sooner gone but in come their ministers, and all repent and fall back to their own ways.' What was needed was a permanent garrison. He proposed, therefore, that a hundred dragoons should be raised for service in Galloway which he would supervise without pay, leaving immediate command to another officer 'who is to be the drudge'. He gave precise details as to how the new company would be manned and paid for, and he allowed himself a passing joke by suggesting that, to raise money, the Privy Council might withdraw the officer who guarded the prison on the Bass Rock island off the east coast where by tradition Covenanting prisoners were held. There was, said Claverhouse, no need for him, 'seeing he has nobody to guard but Solen geese [gannets] and ministers; the first will not flee away and the others would be as well in Blackness or Dumbarton [prisons].' The twenty-four remaining guards on the rock could be drafted into the new company.

Despite the lighter touches in his letter, Claverhouse was demonstrating a keen awareness of the political realities of the day. He knew that Government policies lacked popular support and could not be made to work without the relentless efforts of soldiers like himself. He knew, too, that the stumbling block of any new scheme was the finance required. The response to his proposals cannot therefore have surprised him. He received approval for his suggestion of local amnesties, but never got his dragoons. And although he followed up his request with a letter to Queensberry, who had gone south with the Duke of York to see the King at Newmarket, in which he wrote that 'it were no great business for the King to send as much money as would maintain five or six hundred more dragoons', he does not seem to have expected anything of the kind. The Bass Rock remained guarded.

He was nevertheless pleased with the way that his scheme for policing the west was working. He had arranged a meeting of all the landowners of the area to persuade them to bring in their own people to church, and was hopeful about the outcome. At the same time, however, he was also beginning to think of harsher measures against those who were convicted offenders. At Stranraer, he captured a known rebel, and recommended that he should be executed. The man was called M'Clorg, and was a blacksmith from Minnigaff, who had been manufacturing 'clickys', sharp instruments used for cutting the bridles of cavalry. Claverhouse had been after him for some time: 'It cost me both pains and money to know how to find him. I am resolved to hang him, for it is necessary I make some example of severity, lest rebellion be thought cheap here. There cannot be alive a more wicked fellow.' Nevertheless M'Clorg was sent for trial.

Clearly Claverhouse believed that he had sufficient authority to impose the death sentence, though he had never contemplated it before. His commission as sheriff empowered him to 'cause justice to be administered ... according to the laws and acts of parliament in this realm', which would certainly have included execution. But the threat was more a gesture than reality. He had been careful to brief himself on the law by taking advice from Sir George Mackenzie, and he knew the limits of a sheriff's jurisdiction.

Not that Mackenzie was always reliable. One letter he wrote to Claverhouse failed to answer any of the questions he had put to him, and, as Claverhouse reported, 'he ordinarily loses the letter and forgets the business before he has the time to make any return.' But on the extent of Claverhouse's commission Mackenzie was quite clear. Suspects were to be questioned, cautioned, and, if the evidence against them was strong, taken before the Council in Edinburgh. The harshest punishment to be inflicted was fining and imprisonment. But Claverhouse added a clever stratagem. If suspects agreed to submit, he would ask for a bond filled out for a blank sum of money and signed. He would then release them, taking a twentieth part of what they would have to pay if they misbehaved. The sanction was that, if they committed any subsequent misdemeanour, the bond would be filled in for the full amount and cashed. So effective did he find this that there is no record of a bond having to be paid in.

Claverhouse could do no more than threaten M'Clorg with execution, and in the event the blacksmith was neither tried nor hanged. Instead Claverhouse brought him, along with some other prisoners, to Edinburgh, where he appears at some point to have escaped, perhaps by using his skills on the prison bars.

A more important prisoner was Robert M'Lellan of Barscobe, who had fought at Bothwell Bridge, was on the wanted list, and had already been forfeited. Barscobe had been captured without a struggle by Cornet William Graham of Claverhouse's troop and was later tried by the Privy Council. Sentenced to death, he was reprieved on the personal recommendation of the Duke of York after acknowledging his guilt and promising to make reparation.

In Edinburgh, Claverhouse was keen to find out whether his new scheme had met with approval, particularly from Dalyell, who was almost certain to be critical. He was concerned that with Queensberry away in the south, 'some people might take the occasion to misrepresent me.' Fortunately that had not happened, and he was able to report to Queensberry that there had been praise all round: 'I have informed them fully of all my measures, and I am so happy as that they all seem satisfied, and particularly the General. How long it will be so, God knows.'

On 1 April 1682, he was back in the west, and painting a glowing picture to Queensberry from Kirkcudbright:

> ... this country is now in perfect peace; all who were in rebellion are either seized, gone out of the country, or treating their peace; and they have already conformed, as going to the Church, that is beyond my expectation. In Dumfries, not only almost all the men are come, but the women have given obedience; and Irongray, Welsh's own parish, have for the most part conformed; and so it is over all the country. So that if I

be suffered to stay any time here, I do expect to see this the best settled part of the Kingdom on this side the Tay.

He ventured to say that things would be even better if he had the dragoons he had asked for, but he had achieved everything so far 'without having received a farthing money, either in Nithsdale, Annandale, or Kirkudbright; or imprisoned anybody.' What is more, he believed he had become quite 'acceptable' in the district.

After signing the letter, he went to church himself, and was delighted to find that only about ten men and thirty women were absent from the congregation. Where recently there had been barely ten worshippers, he counted 600 or 700, including at least one notorious rebel to whom Claverhouse had given safe conduct to discuss terms. And a fortnight later, he wrote to Queensberry: 'I must say, I never saw people go from one extremity to another more cavalierly than this people does. We are now come to read lists every Sunday after sermon, of men and women, and we find few absent.'

Claverhouse's achievements were recognized officially by the Privy Council: on 15 May 1682, he was summoned before it to be given thanks for his 'diligence' in fulfilling his commission in Galloway. He even appears to have persuaded General Dalyell, whose prevailing view about rebels was that the only way to deal with them was to string them up. Claverhouse argued that a softer approach might be more effective. On 20 May, the Council instructed Dalyell to prepare a report on the situation in Ayr and Lanark, which he did with Claverhouse's assistance. The result was a strong recommendation to the Council that safe conduct be offered to those rebels willing to submit, and that a deadline of 15 August be offered to them if they agreed to do so. It was a proposal that had Claverhouse's hand clearly on it.

Claverhouse also presented a full report of his stewardship to the Chancellor, which stressed the changes that had taken place in Galloway since he had been there. The area had, in his view, been 'almost in a state of war', and was thought 'unsafe for anything less than an army to venture into it'. It had been controlled by about 300 or 400 rebels, who were supported by an income of between 30,000 and 40,000 merks a year. 'The churches were quite deserted – no honest man, no minister in safety.'

Now, however, thanks to the methods he had adopted for quartering his troops and imposing discipline on the local people, matters had greatly improved. He doubted if 'the little people' could take the Test, because they would not be able to understand it (who could?), but he thought that something equivalent might work, 'for amongst all the prisoners he made, he found none that was ambitious of the honour of martyrdom.'

His 'discreet' measures had persuaded whole congregations to return to their churches. He had personally checked this, ordering ministers to take roll-calls every Sunday and turning up the day before in those parishes where numbers were low, with the warning that he would be in church himself on Sunday, ready to hand out punishment to all those whom he did not see there. The threat of Claverhouse himself, sitting in the back pew and taking a personal head-count in church, had, it appears, been quite dramatically effective.

In conclusion, said his report: 'The rebels are reduced without blood; and the country brought to obedience, and conformity to the church-government, without severity or extortion.' Giving allowance for understandable exaggeration on the part of its author, that was a fair record.

None of Claverhouse's work at this time would have been possible, of course, had not the Duke of York, with the King's approval, favoured conciliation. James had by now returned to Edinburgh, determined to continue a policy of extending tolerance. He had been in regular contact with Claverhouse, who cannot have failed to catch the drift.

James had proved himself a popular Commissioner, and very far from the cold tyrant so often pictured. Historians have tended to call him a persecutor, sometimes in extravagant terms, but the evidence that he was vindictive rests almost entirely on the claim that he liked to be present when men were being questioned under torture, an allegation for which there is no supporting evidence.

James's main interventions in the Council's judicial procedures at this time seem to have been to prevent executions by offering a reprieve to those Covenanters who were prepared simply to swear 'God bless the King'. On one occasion he offered the chance of enlistment in his regiment in Flanders to six young men who faced hanging – a chance which, however, they rejected – and on another he intervened in the course of questioning, to prevent four suspects condemning themselves by their own testimony.

Even the Covenanters conceded that James was not personally to blame for their persecution, and one completely objective, if not positively hostile, source, the Earl of Sunderland, wrote:

I will venture to say the King's affairs [in Scotland] are in a better condition than they have been these seven years. We apprehended he [the Duke] would have disordered them, but we find quite the contrary. Take this on my word for I do positively affirm it to you.

James's arrival in Scotland also saw the start of a new and civilized era in the capital. For the first time since 1603 there was a court at Holyrood. Royal patronage encouraged both a cultural renaissance and the foundation of some institutions that survive to this day. For three years, between 1679 and 1682, the court became the focus for a flowering of the arts, while James's sporting instincts found outlets on the golf course and on the hills.

The Privy Council sent a letter to the King which said:

No breach of the peace, no libel, no pasquil [lampoon], have ever been discovered during his short abode here; so that this too short time has been the most peaceable and serene part of our life, and the happiest days we ever saw.

His young wife, Mary of Modena, whom he had married on the recommendation of Louis XIV when she was fourteen, and who was still only twenty-one, captivated everybody. She was, as of her admirers said, 'tall and admirably shaped, her complexion was of the last fairness, her hair black as jet, so were her eyebrows and her eyes.' She was, of course, as much a Roman Catholic as her husband, but for the time being that was less important than her contribution to the gaiety of the city. Although her early days there were saddened by the death of the sick child she and James had left behind in London, she introduced a new and cultured climate which was greatly appreciated by the gentry in Edinburgh. Her step-daughter, Anne, the future Queen, also came to Scotland. Unlike the Duchess she was firmly Protestant: King Charles had insisted on it.

The royal couple introduced dancing, and encouraged travelling actors to put on performances at the Palace. There were balls, supper-parties and civic receptions, and Edinburgh began once again to acquire the trappings of a capital city. There was a golf course at Leith where James played, and where he doubtless discussed the merits of hazel-shafted clubs and the latest balls (lead-painted, stuffed with feathers, and made 'of thick and hard leather, not with pores or grains or that will let a pin easily pass through it', as Thomas Kincaid, a young chemist and a fanatical golfer of the time, described them). James missed, however, his favourite sport of stag-hunting, as he explained to William of Orange:

Where the stags are, there are such hills and bogs as 'tis impossible to follow any hounds, so that hare-hunting and shooting are the only sports one can have here. After June is once over there will be very good shooting at heath-pouts [grouse] of which and partridge there are great store here.

The grouse season began on 3 July, somewhat earlier than it does in the modern era.

James had also begun extending his patronage to areas which would have a significant effect on Scotland's cultural and professional life. With his encouragement, the Royal College of Physicians, the Advocates' Library, and, later, the Order of the Thistle, all came into being. He gave his support to the Physic Garden and the Royal Company of Archers. Through him the City of Edinburgh and the University received new charters. In mathematics, surgery, engineering and cartography, the advances which took place thanks to his enthusiasm transformed Edinburgh, and made it a city with a promising future.

It was one of James's ambitions that Edinburgh should expand. He commissioned Sir William Bruce to design the precursor of what was to be, seventy-five years on, the North Bridge. Later, after he became King, James asked Bruce to redesign what remained of the old abbey as a Roman Catholic chapel for the Knights of the Thistle. To accommodate the Protestant worshippers thus dispossessed, James presented them with a substitute in the shape of the Canongate Church, designed by James Smith.

He won no gratitude for this, and even less when he also established a printing press for the dissemination of Roman Catholic literature as well as a Roman Catholic school staffed by Jesuits. In all this the King showed a side of his character which was to lose him friends, supporters, and finally his throne: on the one hand admirably tolerant, an encourager of free worship and a supporter of open justice; on the other hand, so insensitive to public opinion that, to promote his own beliefs, he could trample roughshod over the sensitivities of a Protestant nation.

But, in those early years in Scotland, there were only a few dissenting voices, and the reputation he made for himself north of the border was one element in ensuring his acceptance as a successor to the throne, and in calming anti-Catholic hysteria in England. Midway through the Duke's term in Scotland, on 15 October 1681, Andrew Hay, a lawyer in Edinburgh, wrote about him:

Here all things are very quiet. Yesternight His Highness the Duke's birthday was celebrated with bonfires and ringing of bells and a ball at the Court. His Highness doth carry himself with so great temper and diligence, is so just in his payments, so merciful in all penal matters, so impartial in giving his judgment in court, so humble, so civil and obliging to all sorts of people that he hath gained the affection of all understanding and obligable persons, though there be a sort here of presbyterians (disowned by others of the same nickname) whom nothing can oblige.

And the Earl of Balcarres, writing a later assessment of James's period in Scotland, concluded:

All other things in the Government were as easy, and managed with as much justice, as ever was known in any age . . . nor was there ever in the Council and Session more justice and despatch of affairs shown, not soldiers better paid, nor with less trouble to the countries where they quartered.

If this picture of Scotland's settled state can be believed, then some of the credit must go to James's friend and confidant, John Graham of Claverhouse, for what he had achieved in settling the west. He had done so by sensing the mood of the people, and convincing his superiors that his way was the best way to handle them, thus demonstrating the skills of a politician as well as a soldier.

In this he was undoubtedly reflecting the instincts of the Duke of York and thus of the King. And perhaps it was a two-way process. With his own good sense and complete self-confidence, Claverhouse, in his correspondence with James, may well have played a significant part in influencing royal opinion.

CHAPTER EIGHT
Criminal Libel

'There was much transport, flame, and humour in this cause'

Sir John Lauder of Fountainhall

It is hardly surprising that, despite his 'discreet' approach to the establishment of the rule of law, Claverhouse should make enemies. He was by now identified throughout the west as in charge of state policy, and though his methods were fair, he was, for those still in rebellion, a marked man. There was an incident in June 1682 which he reported to Queensberry, and which the Marquis plainly believed was an assassination attempt.

He had stayed on in Edinburgh after delivering his report to the Privy Council, and had made plans to rejoin his troop in Galloway on 14 June. In the event he delayed his departure by a couple of days, a decision which probably saved his life. Riding without an escort through the bare hills of the upper Tweed, he met a traveller on the track near a place called the Bille who told him he had attended a funeral the previous day where all the talk was of a large party of rebels who had been in the area barely six hours earlier. There were more than a hundred of them, he said, and they had crossed over from Clydesdale to Teviotdale, where they had split up into small groups as if in search of someone.

Claverhouse questioned people in the area, including a local minister, in whose house some of the men had actually stayed, and heard conflicting stories. Some said the men had been 'seeking the enemies of God', and had been asking specifically about Claverhouse – where he was and when he was expected. Others said they were simply fleeing from the west. They had plainly scared the local people with their rough questioning, but in the end they had turned round and ridden back the way they had come. They did not sound like men in flight, thought Claverhouse, and he was inclined to believe that he had indeed been the target. When he reached the change-house at the Bille, where a dragoon was stationed, he sent an express back to Edinburgh with a report on the incident to the Lord Chancellor, 'for I thought it fit the quarters should be advertised not too secure, when these rogues had the impudence to go about so.'

Queensberry thought Claverhouse had been lucky to escape. As he told the Chancellor some days later: 'It was good he did not come a day sooner; for certainly their design was against him.' But Claverhouse had more dangerous, if less obvious, enemies closer to home. His commission as Sheriff-Principal of Wigton had brought him into direct conflict with the most powerful family in the area, the Dalrymples of Stair and Glenluce.

Charles II is once said to have remarked that, if there was ever trouble in Scotland, there was always a Campbell or a Dalrymple at the bottom of it. That was to give undue credit to the Dalrymples, whose notoriety stemmed from just two generations. Nevertheless, between them, Sir James Dalrymple, later Viscount Stair, and his son, Sir John, later the Master, then Earl, of Stair, succeeded in arousing more animosity than most clans. It was Sir James's family which inspired the dark legend that became Scott's *Bride of Lammermoor*. Sir John needed no fiction to become the brooding villain of the Massacre of Glencoe. Both were brilliant and civilized men, lawyers and Scottish patriots who had a vision of a more settled future for their country. Yet both concealed a streak of passion beneath a bland exterior, a passion that could, in the case of the son at least, erupt into destructiveness. Sir James, the great lawyer and Lord President of the Court of Session, bitterly resented a visit paid to him by Claverhouse in the early summer of 1682 at his house of Carscreoch in Galloway, a modern mansion set on bleak moorland, of which a contemporary remarked that 'it might have been more pleasant if it had been a more pleasant place.'

Claverhouse warned him with some asperity that he 'had need to walk warily' and choose his friends carefully if he was to stay in favour with the Government. Since Sir James was at the time trying to find a way of avoiding taking the Test, and had appealed unsuccessfully to the King and the Duke of York to help him out of his predicament, the warning touched a sore nerve. There was also something profoundly irritating about the way this thirty-four-year-old Captain had taken it upon himself to hand out advice to a distinguished sixty-three-year-old who was not only Lord President in Edinburgh but a powerful laird in Galloway. Sir James complained about Claverhouse's conduct to the Marquis of Queensberry, who was a relation of his, but got no satisfaction.

His son, Sir John, was a more formidable opponent. His estates round Castle Kennedy in the far south-west, towards the Rinns of Galloway, were the largest in the area, and, as Heritable Bailie of the Regality of Glenluce, he was himself charged with carrying out Government policy against religious dissidents. It was a policy for which he felt only distaste, and he did everything he could to mitigate the severity of the penal laws.

Sir John, also a lawyer, and every bit as clever as his father, was described as 'a perfectly calm and passionless man', but harsh in language and capable of a brand of invective that won him few close friends. His enemies were more outspoken. 'He was false and cruel, covetous and imperious, altogether destitute of the sacred ties of honour, loyalty, justice and gratitude', wrote Sir George Lockhart of Carnwath, who added for good measure: '... and lastly a man of very great parts else he could never have perpetrated so much wickedness.'

Sir John, like his father, was resentful of Claverhouse's jurisdiction and the right he had been given by the Privy Council to use his house and chapel as a garrison if necessary. Claverhouse for his part simply suspected that both the Dalrymples were, at heart, subversives. Their houses, he believed, were 'constant haunts of rebels', and he told Queensberry he was determined that 'this jest shall pass no longer here, for it is laughing and fooling the government'.

In August 1682, Claverhouse had a chance to challenge Sir John Dalrymple directly, when he seized the goods of a rebel laird who had abandoned his house within Dalrymple's judicial territory. Furious at this interference, Dalrymple 'severely expostulated' to the Privy Council at Claverhouse's 'meddling'. But Claverhouse was perfectly confident of his own rights as sheriff, and ordered that a message should be read from the pulpit at Glenluce church, summoning local people to attend a court hearing of the affair. Dalrymple responded by forbidding any of his tenants to attend, so that, when Claverhouse turned up at the courtroom door, he found just two people there – one was Sir John Dalrymple, the other his father, Sir James. What exactly transpired between them was to become a matter of dispute, but it appears that the Dalrymples offered Claverhouse a substantial bribe if he would desist from interfering in their affairs. It was brusquely rejected.

Sir John Dalrymple was now determined to test Claverhouse's jurisdiction head on, and, on 15 August, he summoned his own court at Glenluce and appointed as its officials two men whom Claverhouse had already identified and fined as rebel sympathizers. With Dalrymple presiding, they began trying cases which Claverhouse believed were well outside their competence and imposing fines which he considered derisory. Claverhouse's response was rapid and provocative. He arrested a number of the Dalrymples' tenants, including Sir James's factor, and charged them with attending conventicles and being absent from church. The fines imposed on them came to a total of nearly £1,000 sterling, an enormous amount, later described by Lauder of Fountainhall as 'exorbitant'.

Sir James had by now realized that his chances of escaping the Test were negligible, and had slipped out of the country with his family, to join William of Orange in Holland. He blamed Claverhouse for forcing his departure, and gave vent to his feelings in an angry letter to Queensberry:

> I was so rudely treated by Claverhouse; having fined my factor and tenants near a thousand pounds sterling; and there was said to be a citation against myself! ... It is like, great noise will be made of my consciousness to some great guilt; but I thank God I am conscious of none, but have most loyally and affectionately served the King....

His son, however, was determined to fight Claverhouse all the way. He presented the Privy Council with a Bill of Suspension, made out in his name and that of his father, which argued that the fines imposed by Claverhouse were illegal, since he had already dealt with the cases and handed down his own (much lighter) fines. The Council considered the petition and reserved judgment until November, ordering the tenants to be set at liberty for the time being, and the fines sequestrated. The Council sounded an ominous note for Dalrymple, however, when it observed that:

> heritable Bailies or Sheriffs, who are negligent themselves in putting the laws to execution, should not offer to compete with the Sheriffs, commissioned and put in by the Privy Council, who executed vigorously the King's laws.

The bitterness of the argument was beginning to cause a considerable stir in Edinburgh, at the Council and in the corridors of the Court of Session, with eminent lawyers taking sides in the affair. The King's Advocate, Sir George Mackenzie, wrote to the Chancellor, Haddo, now elevated to be Lord Aberdeen, on behalf of his friend

Claverhouse, and was backed up by Mackenzie of Tarbat, the Lord Clerk Register, who seemed to question Dalrymple's judgment: '. . . the business 'twixt Claverhouse and Sir John Dalrymple seems to grow. I wonder of Sir John's prudence', he wrote.

Others took up the Dalrymple cause, and Claverhouse grew concerned that the balance might tilt against him. He asked the Council for leave to go to London to present his case at court, but permission was refused by the Duke of York, who said that he would look after his interests himself. The decision worried Claverhouse: 'I know how much one's presence prevails with the good nature of the King and Duke', he wrote to Queensberry.

Instead he had to resume his duties in Galloway. Matters had not improved in his absence, and he found it necessary to remind another adversary, Viscount Kenmure, that he needed his castle as a garrison. He wrote to him in October 1682, saying that he should clear his possessions out because the soldiers were going to move in on 1 November.

The quartering of troops was the cause of a growing number of complaints, all of which had to be investigated. The rules for quartering were clearly laid down, but the soldiers had a great deal of latitude in their application, and there were several cases of violence or wanton damage, with crops being destroyed or animals stolen, allegedly in the course of a search for suspects. Anyone who was harmed had the right to lodge petitions with the army, and cases of hardship or abuse were supposed to be examined by an officer. But these were not always followed up.

Faced with a number of complaints against his soldiers, Claverhouse decided to deal with them at one sitting by summoning any outstanding plaintiffs to a special court at Strathaven. It was not a wise move. Several petitioners got together to mount a case against Claverhouse's brother, David Graham, quartermaster to the troop, and produced a series of instances of gross hardship clearly designed to inflame the local people, who had turned out in force. Claverhouse, who later suspected that Dalrymple's hand was behind it, had to order his men to hold back the crowd, which was threatening to get out of hand.

He was still trying to control his court when Dalrymple walked through the door and sat down on the bench. With Claverhouse momentarily reduced to a stunned silence, Dalrymple took over the proceedings and began turning the case against the Sheriff himself. In front of a delighted crowd, he accused Claverhouse of contravening the Acts of Parliament, abusing his position, exceeding his jurisdiction, and, by imposing fines, directly flouting the Privy Council's instructions.

Claverhouse was outraged. Shaking with anger, he shouted at Dalrymple to keep silent in court, and, when he refused to do so, he threatened him with arrest and ordered his soldiers to drag him forcibly out of the court. Dalrymple himself later described what happened:

> Claverhouse became so rude and enraged that though there were an hundred present who were not members, yet Claverhouse did cause his soldiers and officers take [me] by the shoulders from the table, which was an indignity that his Majesty's justice, and princely generosity, does not allow to be offered to a gentleman.

For the watching crowd, it was an extraordinary confrontation. As one commentator put it later: 'Nothing half so entertaining has occurred in the head-courts of Galloway or Dumfries from that hour to this.'

Plainly, however, matters were now out of hand, and Claverhouse decided that he in turn would have to take legal action. He began preparing a case of criminal libel. Taking advice from Sir George Mackenzie, he presented the Privy Council with a Bill of Complaint which set out specific charges against Dalrymple, and stated his intention of appearing personally to prove every item on the charge sheet. He was encouraged by hearing that the Duke of York had written to Queensberry on his behalf. His letter, dated 2 December 1682, said: 'I am absolutely of your mind as to Claverhouse: and I think his presence more necessary in Galloway than anywhere else; for he need not fear anything [Dalrymple] can say of him, his Majesty being so well satisfied with him.'

On 14 December, Claverhouse formally indicted Dalrymple before the Privy Council, and the case opened before a committee of the Council's members. Neither participant was able to conceal his dislike of the other, and Claverhouse's temper very nearly got the better of him. At one stage, as they were discussing legal procedure, he threatened to box Dalrymple's ears, which was, as Dalrymple's counsel, Sir John Lauder of Fountainhall, drily recorded in his account of the case, 'an intolerable affront to his Majesty's Government, and indignity to the liege so injured.' 'There was', Fountainhall recalled, 'much transport, flame and humour in this cause', and nothing like it had been seen in the courts since the Argyll case. The composition of the jury chosen (or volunteering) to hear it reflected the intense interest it had aroused. The jury drew its membership from the mightiest in the land, including the Lord Chancellor, the Primate of all Scotland, the Lord High Treasurer, and the Lord Privy Seal.

In the event, however, it was a somewhat one-sided affair. Almost from the start it became clear which way the case was going when, after Dalrymple's answer to the charges had been read, he was immediately taken to task by the Chancellor for the aspersions he had cast on Claverhouse's conduct. His counsel asked for permission to produce witnesses, but this was refused. After some legal debate, Dalrymple was told to restrict himself to specific cases involving himself and his tenants. The plaintiff, Claverhouse, on the other hand, was allowed a relatively free rein. Evidence was produced about Sir James Dalrymple and the behaviour of his family, despite Fountainhall's protestations that this was irrelevant. And much time was taken up with discussing the real state of affairs in Galloway.

Claverhouse was clearly on good form. When Dalrymple argued that the local people were 'turned orderly and regular', he replied that 'there were as many elephants and crocodiles in Galloway as loyal or regular persons.' This was held to be an excellent joke, for it was not long since the first elephants ever to be seen in Scotland had been exhibited in Edinburgh, creating great excitement in the capital. Nobody pointed out that in making the joke, Claverhouse was contradicting his own claims, made to the Council a few months earlier, about the settled state of law and order in Galloway.

The case was heard in three sittings, and finally, on 12 February 1683, the Council gave judgment. It was a triumph for Claverhouse; a disaster for Dalrymple. Claverhouse was acquitted of any wrongdoing, and Dalrymple's charges were found to be

> ... not proven to infer any crime, fault or misdemeanour against the said John Graham of Claverhouse; but, upon the contrary, that the said John Graham of Claverhouse has done his duty, and acted in the prosecution of the commission given to him for the discovery and punishment of disorders in Galloway, faithfully and diligently, conform to the trust reposed in him, to the great advantage of His Majesty's service.

Fountainhall, gloomily recording the judgment, noted that the Chancellor also commented on the way Claverhouse had handled the case, and 'complimented him so far, that they wondered that he, not being a lawyer, had walked so warily in so irregular a country.'

Dalrymple was found guilty on every charge. He was stripped of his judicial office in Glenluce; fined £500 (some members of the Council wanted it to be £1,000); ordered to pay for all Claverhouse's witnesses' expenses; and ordered to be committed as a prisoner in Edinburgh Castle until he paid, 'and further during the Council's pleasure.' But he did not stay behind bars for long. On 20 February, he was freed, but not yet permitted to return to Galloway. He was given liberty only within the bounds of Edinburgh, 'craving the Secret Council pardon' and 'acknowledging his rashness'.

Despite that acknowledgement, Dalrymple was to remain a thorn in Claverhouse's flesh, and a cause for continued complaint. A year later, he was arrested again, this time at the house at Newliston near Edinburgh which he had been given as part of the dowry of his wife, Elizabeth Dundas. Again he was sent to prison, only this time the fine was £5,000, which Dalrymple found hard to raise. He was phlegmatic about his fate, however, telling friends that he was paying for the 'original sin of my Presbyterian father'.

For Claverhouse, the rewards for his service in Galloway did not need to wait for the verdict of the courts. On Christmas Day 1682, a commission, drawn up in Whitehall, gazetted 'our right trusty and well beloved John Graham of Claverhouse' to be Colonel of a newly formed regiment, 'His Majesty's Regiment of Horse'.

It was to be composed of his own and the two other independent troops which had been originally raised in 1678, together with a fourth troop 'to be added thereunto', though not at any further expense. The soldiers were to come from the foot guards and the Earl of Mar's regiment, supplemented by nine horsemen from the independent troops, a slight case of robbing Peter to pay Paul. Still, not only did the new regiment fulfil the ambition Claverhouse had originally had of gaining a command of his own, but it gave him something for which he had long argued – a proper force for the maintenance of order in the still-volatile west of Scotland.

Less than three months later, the newly-promoted Colonel Graham was on his way south to join the Duke of York for some leisurely hunting and cock-fighting at Newmarket and for the rather more demanding task of advancing his own material interests.

CHAPTER NINE
Court Manœuvres

'I am as sorry to see a man die, even a whig, as any of themselves. But when one dies justly, for his own faults, and may save a hundred to fall in the like, I have no scruple.'

John Graham of Claverhouse

In the early years of Charles II's reign, there had been much talk in Scotland of the 'fundamental laws' that governed the country. In the absence of a powerful parliament, and with bitter dissent over the allegiance of the Church, the debate concerned not only matters of natural justice, but questions about the real authority of the King, whether the Privy Council was a legitimate body, and how the bishops could rightfully exert control over unwilling congregations.

The political opposition to Lauderdale had spoken of the need to reassert 'the fundamental laws of the nation'. The Covenanters argued that they were in tune with the 'fundamental laws of the land'. The King's prerogative, on the other hand, said his supporters, was upheld by 'fundamental laws of the kingdom', and the activities of religious dissidents in the west were held to be against 'the fundamental laws and liberties' of private citizens. Quite what those 'fundamental laws' were and who was or was not in breach of them was a matter for fierce argument, both in and out of the courts.

Such arguments reflected the uncertainty of the times. Charles's swift moves to reassert the crown's control of the Church through the appointment of bishops had been dictated as much by the need to impose the King's authority as by any basic concern about religious protocol. And though his crown servants in Scotland accepted the right of the King to issue proclamations and impose sanctions to back them up, there was considerable doubt as to how far he could go. No less an authority than Sir George Mackenzie, the King's Advocate, argued that it was unlawful for a king, with or without Parliament, to act against the fundamental laws of the land. And the Covenanters, when they claimed that Charles had 'inverted all the ends of the government', were saying much the same thing.

In the 1680s, the test of whether someone was in rebellion frequently came down to a series of simple questions, such as whether the suspect was prepared to condemn the murder of Archbishop Sharp, whether he had been at Bothwell Brig, whether he had taken the Test, whether he acknowledged the King's authority, and so on. Time after time, interrogators like Mackenzie were faced with defiant Covenanters, whose initial 'crime' had not perhaps been a major one, but who condemned themselves quite deliberately by giving answers such as that of Henry Erskine, an 'outed' minister from near Berwick, who rejected the authority of the King by telling Mackenzie: 'My Lord, I have my commission from Christ, and though I were within an hour of death I durst not lay it down at any mortal man's feet.'

Mackenzie was concerned enough about his own role as prosecutor to write a 'Vindication', which was published after his death, and which described the meticulous process he claims to have used to establish his own 'scruples' about prosecuting. Only if they were satisfied, and if 'the ablest advocates' concurred, would the case proceed. He was claiming, in short, to have acted as a surrogate defence counsel, thus reflecting the personal doubts of a man who appeared to the outside world as a convinced and convincing advocate of the King's cause, and to the Covenanters a persecutor.

'Scruples' was not a word that ranked high in the lexicon of John Graham of Claverhouse. His views on religion and politics were clear. He believed firmly in the right of the King to determine the law, and accepted episcopacy, not only as the family religion, but as an expression of royal authority. Conventionally religious himself, he held family worship at home, and went regularly to church, to the satisfaction of at least one strict Presbyterian lady in Edinburgh who 'could not believe a good thing of any person of his persuasion, till his conduct rectified her mistake'. But he was suspicious of Presbyterianism, particularly in its extreme forms. By rejecting the bishops, it was implicitly, in his view, rejecting the control exercised by the King and placing control instead in the hands of rebellious preachers. He saw it, increasingly, as a threat to good order. His role, as a soldier and a member of the justiciary, was to minimize the threat.

That simple goal was about to become more complex, however, for he was on the point of joining the ranks of the legislators by becoming a member of the Privy Council. It was, perhaps, the natural outcome of two months spent in the spring of 1683 in the inner circles of the royal court in London, Newmarket, and Windsor.

Claverhouse had travelled south in early March full of the scheme he had used to such effect in Galloway to settle the area. During his early weeks in England, plans were drawn up to extend the approach he had adopted into something like a full judicial system. A letter sent to the Privy Council from London in April announced the setting up of a Justiciary Circuit, which would sit in Stirling, Glasgow, Ayr, Dumfries, and Jedburgh in June and July. Its brief was to hear criminal cases, impose the Test Act, with its oath of loyalty to the King as head of the Church, and put 'the law vigorously in execution against all persons who, since our late Indemnity, have been or shall be hereafter found guilty of any fanatical disorders or irregularities, especially those who continue obstinate in them.' The Claverhouse touch was there in an offer of royal clemency: a complete indemnity was to be offered to anyone taking the Test on his knees before 1 August that year, and there was a promise that no more trials would be held, except for new offences, from 1 January 1684 for three years. It was a case of carrot and stick.

Although the proclamation was long and detailed, this was not the only business on which Claverhouse found himself engaged. Once again his skills as a courtier were deployed, not just on his own behalf, but on that of his superiors, including the Marquis of Queensberry, who, as Treasurer, was now virtually running Scotland in conjunction with the Chancellor Lord Haddo, now Earl of Aberdeen.

Claverhouse had brought letters from Queensberry, and a request from him to act as a go-between with the Duke of York. Despite his position, Queensberry was a naturally suspicious man, convinced that his enemies were seeking to undermine him, constantly in need of reassurance. Claverhouse pandered to his concerns, and passed his messages on, with gratifying results:

> I spoke to the Duke concerning what your Lordship gave me in commission; and he desired me to assure you, that he had all the esteem imagineable for you, and that nobody had offered to do ill offices with him; and if they had, they would not have succeeded, and expressed himself very kindly and frankly of you.

The letter was written from Newmarket, where the royal party was enjoying some racing and hunting. Life there, it appears, was congenial, for in the same letter, Claverhouse added: 'It is hard to get any business done here. I walked but nine miles this morning with the King, beside cock-fighting and courses. I have not spoken as yet concerning the muster-master, but I shall...'.

Claverhouse was treating Queensberry with some care ever since an unfortunate altercation in which Queensberry had accused him of exceeding his instructions in the west. He had confronted him in his Edinburgh lodgings and soundly berated him. Claverhouse almost certainly responded in kind, but complained later that he 'was not used like a gentleman'. He was convinced by the exchange that Queensberry wanted him out of public service altogether, but he relied on his friendship with the Duke of York to ensure his survival: 'I flatter myself with the thought that his Royal Highness has more goodness for me than to sacrifice me to the humour of anybody', he wrote to Aberdeen.

That was certainly true and, once he was down at Newmarket, Claverhouse basked in royal approval. He and the Duke of York saw eye to eye, particularly on military matters, and Claverhouse was able to convince him that far from building an empire in the west, he had simply been trying to run an efficient operation. He managed to persuade the Duke that efficiency would be further improved if his soldiers were re-equipped, and in May that year the Privy Council agreed that he could send up from England '150 ells of red cloth, 40 ells of white cloth, and 550 dozen of buttons', so that his regiment should be as smart and glittering as those he had seen in the south. His troopers would certainly outshine General Dalyell's dragoons who had just imported 2,536 ells of 'stone-grey cloth' to be made up into uniforms at the factory at New Mills near Haddington. Dull though the General's chosen colour might be, it gave to the regiment the name by which it would be known – the Scots Greys.

Claverhouse was also engaged on a matter which had as much to do with his own advancement as with Queensberry's. There was, that spring, a mounting scandal at court concerning the late Duke of Lauderdale's successor, his brother, Charles Maitland, Lord Hatton, who was Master of the Royal Mint. Hatton, it emerged, had, over the years, corruptly extracted no less than £72,000 from the public purse by means of reducing the copper content of the coins and minting coinage weighing some 17,000 stone more than was officially accounted for. Soon after the news came out, the Warden of the Mint was found dead at his home, having committed suicide. Hatton himself spent much time in London trying to defend his position.

The matter was debated at length in the Lords, and an investigating committee, set up to examine the affair, proposed that Hatton should be fined the same amount as he had stolen. The King reduced the sum to £20,000 but that still meant virtual ruin, the loss of the Lauderdale fortune and property. The scandal was the talk of the court, and it was one from which three men, Aberdeen, Queensberry, and Claverhouse, believed they might benefit.

Aberdeen had his eye on the fine, which could well come his way, and Queensberry was in pursuit of a dukedom. Claverhouse was determined to have the Hatton property, for it included the Castle of Dudhope, a place he knew well, since it stood high above the town of Dundee, not far from the Claverhouse estates.

Dudhope was a solid, round-towered construction of medieval origin and considerably fortified in the 1600s. It was well sited, and a place of considerable strength – a citadel rather than a home. It had been the property of the Scrymgeour family, for whom Charles II had created the Earldom of Dundee, but had been passed by the crown, with its estates, to Hatton, when the first Earl of Dundee died without issue in 1668. Claverhouse's enthusiasm for Dudhope may have been sharpened by the fact that his family boasted descent from the Scrymgeours.

Claverhouse tried to argue his case at Newmarket, but found it difficult to make headway: 'It is very hard to do anything either with King or Duke; for the Duke hunts, besides going wherever the King goes.' The next thing he heard was that Aberdeen himself had his eye on Dudhope, and he wrote, on 20 March, in some consternation to Queensberry, saying that he was quite prepared to buy the land if he could not get it for nothing:

> I must beg your Lordship's assistance in that business of the lands of Dudhope. My Lord Chancellor designs nothing but to sell it and buy lands in the north. . . . I have no house, and it lies within half-a-mile of my land; and all that business would be extremely convenient for me, and signify not much to my Lord Chancellor, especially seeing I am willing to buy the land. I would take this for the greatest favour in the world, for I cannot have the patience to build and plant.

It was not strictly true to say that he had no house of his own, because there was always Glenogilvie, but that was not, in his view, a house that accorded with his new status, and status was particularly important to him at that point: he had just received confirmation that, on Queensberry's recommendation, he was to become a Privy Councillor. He did not hesitate to thank his patron, and offer him his continued service: 'My Lord, I am sensible, as I ought to be, of so much goodness, and lose no occasions here to do you any little service you allowed me.'

There was indeed a 'little service' that Queensberry was particularly interested in his doing, and that was in regard to the dukedom. Claverhouse was well aware of his ambitions in this direction, though it was a necessary fiction that Queensberry should pretend diffidence, and beg Claverhouse 'not to meddle with it'. To a practised courtier, that was as good a signal to press ahead as any, and, since Aberdeen had given Claverhouse 'christian liberty' to pursue the matter, he took the opportunity of sounding out the Duke of York, being careful to say that he was, of course, acting quite independently of Queensberry himself. The response was favourable enough for him to raise the matter, after dinner in London, with the Earl of Middleton, joint Secretary of State for Scotland, whom he persuaded to accompany him on a visit to the Duke of York. An appointment was made at St James's Palace, and towards the end of March the two men were ushered into the Duke's private room, where a long and intimate discussion took place.

This was power-broking at the highest level. It is interesting to record that Colonel Graham, who, despite his impending elevation to the Privy Council, was still no more than a middle-ranking officer and a local sheriff, was, on that spring afternoon, discussing the affairs of Scotland with the King's brother and the Secretary of State.

The conversation began, inevitably, with the scandal of the Mint, then Claverhouse raised the question of the Queensberry dukedom. James was hesitant. There were, he thought, difficulties. But Claverhouse pursued the matter: 'We discussed all,' he wrote later, 'and convinced him, and made him acknowledge it, after having given many arguments from different heads; and then we tossed the business from hand to hand so that we brought him quite about.' Other names cropped up – that of George Gordon, Marquis of Huntly, for instance. Surely he too should be a Duke? And Mackenzie of Tarbat, the Lord Clerk Register. James was obviously in generous mood as Claverhouse reported:

'Is it an Earl?' he asked, and would have agreed to that.

'No, but a Viscount', said Middleton.

It was all extremely friendly. 'We had the frankest conference that I believe ever was', reported Claverhouse, and the fact that they were handing out patronage like medieval despots did not escape them.

'[James] told us, laughing, that we would all be as great tyrants as my Lord Lauderdale was.' There was, of course, just one difficulty. James was not himself entitled to hand out titles. He had to make representations to the King, and the King was far from enthusiastic. When Claverhouse next called on James, he said that he 'had used all the arguments he could to persuade the King, but he could not move him to it'.

Claverhouse suspected that some jealous English tongues had been at work, but James told him that Charles had been turning down all requests for honours because there had been so many. As Claverhouse reported to Queensberry on 10 April:

> [The Duke] told me the King had been so vexed with the nobilitating people here (for when the door was once opened all would be in), that he could not willingly hear anything upon that subject ... the Duke in the end told me it was impossible.

Instead, James suggested they should wait until the climate was more favourable. Claverhouse told Queensberry not to be downhearted:

> I think I need not tell your Lordship how concerned I was. If it had been for my life I could do no more. But, my Lord, I hope you will bear patiently a little delay.... For the greatest men in England are glad to get it after many pulls. Therefore continue cheerfully your endeavours in the King's service, and it cannot fail.

Though Queensberry's interests were blocked, Claverhouses's had been significantly advanced. On 26 April he was able to tell the Marquis:

> As to the Mint, there is a letter ordered for your Lordship, telling that the King's pleasure is, that my Lord Lauderdale dispose to the Chancellor the lands about Dundee, and to me the house and jurisdiction; for which I render your Lordship hearty thanks.

He would, in fact, have to pay for Dudhope rather than getting it for nothing as he had hoped. But he had been helped by receiving a proportion of the Hatton fine. It was, of course, his own lobbying rather than any intervention by Queensberry which had won the day, and Queensberry, it appears, was far from pleased with the outcome. In his suspicious mind were now sown the seeds of a quarrel which would almost equal the Dalrymple affair.

For the time being, however, he kept his counsel. The transfer of Dudhope was, in any event, delayed. For though judgment was given, dividing the fine of £20,000 between Aberdeen and Claverhouse, with

Aberdeen receiving £16,000 and Claverhouse £4,000, the property at Dudhope was made dependent on Hatton's transferring it to Aberdeen in return for the whole of the fine. Only then would Claverhouse be allowed to buy the castle and lands. It was a situation fraught with legal difficulties. Not for another year would Claverhouse be able to claim his new seat, and then only at a very disadvantageous price. If he had not been so determined to get it, he might well have simply taken his £4,000 and left it at that.

His time at court in London was now nearing an end. He should have gone north early in May, for James wrote to Queensberry then that he was sending him to Scotland with messages. But there was first some business to attend to at Windsor.

Old General Dalyell had travelled south in a furious temper, demanding to see the King. He had always been resentful of Claverhouse's commission in the west, and was suspicious now of his close connections at court. But what had really annoyed him was to learn that Claverhouse's promotion to colonel had brought him considerable benefits at his, Dalyell's, expense. He was to receive the same pay as Dalyell collected in his capacity as a colonel of the dragoons – £1 and 6*d*. a day. But that was not all. It emerged that, to give Claverhouse the extra money, two of Dalyell's staff officers would have to be 'discharged'.

An indignant Dalyell arrived at Windsor and was duly given his audience with the King, who calmed him down and told him that of course he could have his officers back. 'I believe now he sees he needed not to have made so long a journey', wrote James to Queensberry,

> but that a letter from him would have done as well. But I am apt to think that his having spoke to the King himself will have helped to have satisfied him; for he proposed some things that were not very reasonable, yet he readily acquiesced to his Majesty's pleasure.

In the presence of royalty Dalyell was always amenable.

Claverhouse stayed on at Windsor, and he was there when, on 11 May 1683, the King signed a letter, announcing officially that 'our right trusty and well-beloved Colonel John Graham of Claverhouse' was now to be elevated to the Privy Council. Next day, his brother David was commissioned as joint Sheriff of Wigton. Two days later, Claverhouse was on his way back to Scotland, and on 22 May he was sworn in as a Privy Councillor, taking the Test and swearing the oath himself for the first time in front of his peers.

His first task was to accompany the circuit court that he had helped to create as it set about its business. It opened on 5 June 1683 at Stirling. Although General Dalyell was meant to be in charge while the court was at Stirling, Claverhouse made it his business to be there on the first day, supervising the troops who stood guard outside the building. The coaches which rattled into town beneath the Castle, carried an impressive band of lawyers. Headed by the Earl of Perth, who was Lord Justice-General, they included Lauderdale's son, Lord Richard Maitland, who was Lord Justice-Clerk, and Sir George Mackenzie, who, as Lord Advocate, was to act as prosecutor.

The significance of the occasion was not lost on the citizens of Stirling or on the surrounding shires of Clackmannan, Kinross, Perth, and Fife, whence large numbers of people, nobles as well as commoners, flocked in to take the Test. There had been some intimidation, and considerable pressure exerted beforehand, by rebel sympathizers, in an attempt to reduce the numbers, but the judges pronounced themselves well satisfied as the doors opened and the first of the crowd pushed in.

A new method had been devised for the taking of the Test, to avoid any cheating or – as had happened before – the giving of false names. Each person swearing the oath had to have two witnesses to testify to his identity, chosen from amongst those present in court. Each swearer went down on his knees in front of the bench, read out the words of the oath, and swore it. The clerk of the court then drew up a certificate, which was signed by him and the two witnesses, with the time and place of the swearing. This was sent to the Privy Council. Each swearer was given a document to prove that he had taken the oath.

There does not seem to have been much prevaricating about the almost impossible terms of the Test. As Claverhouse had remarked before, few of those swearing it had read the whole of it and fewer still understood it. Those, however, who said they needed time to study its terms were allowed to do so, in return for a surety and an undertaking that they would come back within a fixed period of time.

The size of the crowd seems to have acted as a stimulus to doubters, and by the end of the first four days, the court declared itself pleased with the results it had achieved. 'This Justice Air has succeeded marvellously', wrote Claverhouse to Queensberry:

> Many gentlemen of good quality ... [and] above a hundred and fifty rebels, commoners, have here taken the Test, and I believe almost all will, so that the number of fugitives will be few. The Judges go on very unanimously, and my Lord Advocate does wonders.

One man, accused of murder, but acquitted, was so overwhelmed by the sight of so many people on their knees that he promptly fell to his and asked to be allowed to take the Test too, 'to show his affection for the King's service'. The court assented.

Only one man gave trouble, and he was to be the first one they sentenced to death. William Bogue came forward with what Claverhouse described as 'a false sham certificate', with the space for a Christian name blank (the word 'sham' was a relatively novel one in those days). He was asked whether he had genuinely taken the oath, but refused to say. The judges then pressed him on the old test cases of Bothwell Brig and the murder of Sharp, but he declined to give the right answers. The public in the well of the court began demanding that his case be sent for trial, which was done immediately, in the same courthouse. With Mackenzie prosecuting, Bogue was found guilty of high treason and sentenced to death.

Bogue was ordered to be taken to Glasgow to be hanged there on the following Wednesday, despite a last minute confession, and an offer to take the Test. There were reasons for both the delay and the place of execution, as the Lords Justice explained in their report to the Privy Council:

> This being the first case of this nature, and that there is matter of prudence as well as law in it, we did therefore delay the execution till Wednesday next in Glasgow, betwixt and which time we may hear your Lordships' advice who are there. And it was thought the execution would be more terrible at Glasgow than here.

The 'matter of prudence' involved the question of whether the hanging of a man who had offered to take the Test would act as a deterrent to others. Claverhouse was in no doubt as to what should be done, as he explained to the Lord Chancellor on 9 June:

> [It cannot] be thought any surety for the Government, the taking of the Test by men after they are condemned; seeing all casuists agree that an oath imposed where the alternative is hanging cannot any ways be binding.

He thought that to show mercy would be to expose the court to ridicule, and he did not hold with the argument that execution might put others off:

> It may be said that his case may be mistaken, and it may deter all from coming in. Experience of this day answers that. Above twenty have taken the Test since he was condemned.

And he added, revealingly: 'I am as sorry to see a man die, even a whig, as any of themselves. But when one dies justly, for his own faults, and may save a hundred to fall in the like, I have no scruple.' It was a fair summing up of the Claverhouse philosophy, but in the letters he sent that day there was, perhaps, just a little too much eagerness for reprisal to be entirely consistent with a concern for justice.

Word had come from the Duke of Hamilton that a party of troopers from the Horse Guards, escorting a prisoner to Glasgow, had been ambushed at a place called Inchbelly. A party of seven men had caught them in a narrow pass and shot two of the Guards, leaving one dead and one badly wounded. The prisoner had escaped. Next day, two of the assailants – 'the insolentest rogues that ever I spoke to', according to Hamilton – were captured and sent under escort to Glasgow, to face almost certain execution.

Claverhouse's reaction was interesting: 'This new murder they have committed gives us all new vigour', he said. And, writing to the Chancellor: 'I am impatient to be in Glasgow, where we will have new matter.' It would be an exaggeration to say that he was acquiring a taste for harsh measures, but certainly his attitude was hardening.

Sir George Mackenzie, on the other hand, was merely contemplating how much this judicial exercise was costing him. 'I shall not see one dollar in all this circuit', he wrote gloomily.

On 12 June, the Lords Justice made an almost royal progression into Glasgow, with the condemned man, Bogue, riding behind them. They were accompanied along the way by many of those who had been at court with them in Stirling, and, by the time they reached the City, the crowd had swelled to thousands.

A scaffold had been erected in the marketplace, and Bogue, having decided to withdraw his confession, died as a martyr, albeit a somewhat flawed one. Next day, the two who had been captured after the ambush were also executed, having suffered bravely the cutting off of their right hands. Their bodies were hung up in chains.

The gallows were left standing 'for the better instruction of the great number of rebels who are cited to appear before this Court', according to the Lords Justice, and the hearings went on. Once again the numbers taking the Test were gratifyingly high, with gentlemen and commoners swearing the oath 'most cheerfully'.

From Glasgow, they proceeded to Dumfries, where they sat from 26 June to 2 July, putting the town to the expense of £1 10s. 'for a pound of candle ilk night to Claverhouse's troop, when they kept guard the time the Judges were here', and £2 10s. 'for deals and nails for raising a seat to my Lord Justice-Clerk'. The next stop was Jedburgh, where, according to the Lords Justice, 'our entry was as noble and splendid as any place elsewhere we have been.' But, as the court was making its stately progress through the Borders, word came from London of a serious plot against the King and his brother, with a Scottish cabal closely involved in it.

The idea had been to seize or assassinate the King and the Duke of York as they were returning from Newmarket, at a large mansion near Ware called the Rye House. In the event, the plan, set for March 1683, had miscarried, for a serious fire at Newmarket caused the King and his party to return early to London, and the attack never took place.

The conspiracy was found to stretch beyond Whig opponents of the King, men like the Earl of Shaftesbury and the Duke of Monmouth, as far as the western shires of Scotland. The Reverend William Carstares, acting for the Earl of Argyll, was in touch with the conspirators, and Carstares was closely in contact with some powerful Scottish Whigs – Sir John Cochrane of Ochiltree, Campbell of Cessnock, and Baillie of Jerviswood – who had been frequent visitors to London.

When news broke about the plot, word was sent north to be on the lookout for some of those the Earl of Moray, joint Secretary of State, called 'the hellish plotting crew'. Not all the names had yet come to hand, but a proclamation, offering £500 a head for their capture, was drafted by the Privy Council, and a copy was dispatched to Claverhouse. On 5 July, he was in the saddle with his troop, ready to patrol the borders near the Buccleuch estates which Monmouth owned through his wife, as he reported to Queensberry:

> I have commanded forty dragoons to the Langholm, which is the heart of the Duke of Monmouth's interest; and twenty there at Annan. My troop lies at Moffat, and a part of Captain Strachan's troop at Dumfries, to catch what may escape the two advanced posts. They have orders conform to the proclamation.

Campbell of Cessnock and Baillie of Jerviswood were arrested and sent north to Edinburgh for interrogation and trial. And another supposed conspirator, Sir Alexander Gordon of Earlstoun, was picked up in Newcastle, to be questioned by Sir George Mackenzie, who heard from him the name of Sir John Cochrane. He, according to Earlstoun, had kissed the King's hand one day and gone to a meeting of the conspirators on the next. But Cochrane had disappeared, and it was probable that he was by now across the water in Holland.

Earlstoun, a big man, built like a bull, was threatened with torture, but bellowed so loudly that he frightened his torturers. They thought that he had gone mad. Although he had papers on him from a wanted preacher, James Renwick, he was, in the end, neither tortured nor executed. Others were not so lucky. Carstares was captured, and brought to Edinburgh, to be interrogated by Mackenzie. There, he was horribly tortured, and, since Claverhouse was on the investigating committee of the Council, it was probable that he witnessed it. Carstares held out bravely, but in the end succumbed and gave his torturers some limited information about the plot. Baillie of Jerviswood, who was not centrally involved, was held in prison for so long that his health broke. He was, nevertheless, still executed, his sentence evoking loud protests from the people of Edinburgh.

An excommunicated minister, William Spence, who had been secretary to the Earl of Argyll, was subjected, not only to 'the boot', which involved the leg being placed inside a metal boot into which wedges were hammered, but to sleep deprivation and 'the use of a new invention and engine called the thumbikins which will be very effectual', according to Council minutes. The thumbscrew had in fact been used intermittently in Scotland since the fifteenth century, but this may have been a new variety. Since General Dalyell supervised the interrogation of Spence, this may explain the myth that he imported the thumbscrew from Russia.

Claverhouse never wrote down his views of torture, but Mackenzie did. He believed it be a justifiable part of the legal process, though he disliked it intensely, and considered it an unsatisfactory way of eliciting information, since evidence so gathered was always suspect. There was a strange dichotomy in the Scottish attitude to such barbarity. On the one hand, it was often practised, but, on the other, if a prisoner died under torture, those who had ordered it could stand trial for murder.

With the ending of the first court circuit, which completed its tour at Ayr without having had to order any further executions, Claverhouse was released to take up his duties in the west again. His presence in Galloway was not as regular as before, since he was an assiduous participant at Privy Council meetings. He attended thirty-three of them in seven months, and he was constantly on the road to and from Edinburgh.

Conditions in the west he found unsatisfactory. The garrisoning, to which he attached so much importance, was inadequate, and he found himself increasingly at odds with his superiors on the subject. They in turn sought to undermine his position. Perhaps they were irritated by his arrogance, perhaps they were jealous of his links with the court. More likely, their reaction was caused by his inability to conceal the contempt he had for those who performed less well than he in the service of the King.

The Duke of Hamilton was one of the main complainers, pouring poison about Claverhouse into Queensberry's ear, accusing him of talking about the Marquis behind his back, of being 'an informer', and warning him that he had 'reason to distrust his kindness'. Queensberry, to whom such talk was fuel for his natural suspicions, wrote in alarm to the Duke of York, who sought, unsuccessfully, to pacify him.

Claverhouse's own manner did not help. Nor was his news welcome. He had already warned the Council that matters had deteriorated in the 'Shire of Wigton, of which I have the honour to be Sheriff', and that, although neighbouring shires were well garrisoned, his own territory was still short of troops, with the result that rebels were filtering in from the north. But he had little hope that anything would be done. 'Nothing that comes from me now is relished here because of my Lord Treasurer [Queensberry]', he told Aberdeen. And he was enraged to discover that Hamilton and others had been discussing plans behind his back for another 'Highland Host', bringing the clans down again to take over from Claverhouse and the dragoons. Although the idea came to nothing, it was evidence of a lack of confidence in Claverhouse's ability. General Dalyell, as usual, was having as little to do with him as possible.

To prove that he was still in control of events, Claverhouse drew up a new plan for garrisoning the west, and persuaded the Chancellor that it should be presented to the Council for approval. Aberdeen said that it seemed a satisfactory idea to him, but, when it came before the Council early in September 1683, the matter was referred back to Dalyell. Again, Claverhouse was not at his diplomatic best: 'I took the liberty to tell my Lord Chancellor, that if the Duke [of York] had been at that Board, as he was when I was first sent to Galloway, I would have been believed in matters of that country.' That cannot have endeared him to the Council. But on this occasion, a letter from Queensberry, offering to provide accommodation for Dalyell's troops, and thus some form of garrisoning, came to his assistance, and 'all was done in Council with great *eloges*', as Claverhouse wrote later, adding: 'The General said nothing.'

The whole affair suggested to him that his command was at risk, and he went so far as to ask the Chancellor how the Council wanted to dispose of his troop. The response was not reassuring: 'The Chancellor shunned to make answer; but, being pressed, all he answered was, that they took nothing from me.' Aberdeen was of a view that the troops should stay in the west. General Dalyell said bluntly that they should go to Fife, and, when Claverhouse protested that they would be 'useless to the King's service' there, the matter was referred once again by Aberdeen back to Dalyell. It was a stalemate which left Claverhouse depressed: 'I know not how it will be', he told Queensberry, 'but I am sure I am very indifferent.'

The truth was that in the absence of his patron, the Duke of York, he had no natural political support. He sensed it himself, but was determined to rise above it: 'I see not that the Court grows much here', he wrote to Queensberry from Edinburgh in October. 'I find myself worse there every day; but I take no notice of it.' Furthermore, as soon as he was officially gazetted a full member of the Privy Council, he had to surrender the Sheriffdom of Wigtown, and this removed his local base of power.

He was still, however, a colonel, and was punctilious about anything concerning his troops. The cloth he had imported from England had not proved entirely satisfactory, and he told Queensberry that he intended to send some of it back because it was not exactly the right colour. The cost, he assured his master, was 'mightily reasonable'.

It was, however, rather more expensive than General Dalyell's plain grey cloth which was nine shillings an ell for officers, and six shillings an ell for the men. Furthermore, the factory at New Mills which made up the uniforms had still not been paid for their 'ride cloath' in November 1688, five years later.

The political climate was now beginning to change in Scotland. Since the death of Lauderdale, Aberdeen and Queensberry had, between them, masterminded affairs from the capital, while the joint Secretaries of State, the Earls of Moray and Melfort, had been the King's advisers at court. But Aberdeen's hold on power was beginning to slip, and there was much talk about appointing a 'Juncto' of senior ministers – a term recently coined to describe the rump of the English Parliament – to govern Scotland.

Claverhouse was eager to promote the idea, and wrote about it in some detail to the Duke of York. Most of his information he picked up in Edinburgh from a close friend, Lady Erroll. She was a Drummond, sister to the Earls of Perth and Melfort, and a fund of good gossip. Since Perth was being talked of as a future Chancellor in succession to Aberdeen, she was deeply interested in the outcome of the Juncto discussions. Lady Erroll's brother was married to the Duke of Hamilton's sister, so her connections were impeccable. She had an apartment at Holyrood, and boasted that she 'ran Scotland'.

In early November 1683, Claverhouse was again with Lady Erroll, who had seen Aberdeen and was able to tell him that the Chancellor believed he was still holding on to power, though most people thought that his position was weakening. Aberdeen, it appears, was 'mad' against Claverhouse over the Dudhope affair, though, as Claverhouse pointed out, 'I have more reason to be so against him.' Aberdeen was also furious that some of his confidences, imparted to Queensberry, were now the talk of Edinburgh. Since he had also made them to Lady Erroll, that should not have surprised him.

On 13 December, the Juncto was formally set up, and became, in effect, a new Cabinet for Scotland, referred to as 'the Secret Committee'. Aberdeen retained his post as Chancellor, but power was now to be split between him and seven others. Queensberry, as High Treasurer, was the key figure. Lady Erroll now had both of her brothers in positions of power – Perth as Justice-General, Melfort as Treasurer-Depute.

One side-effect of the new committee was to reduce the influence of the lesser members of the Privy Council, including Claverhouse. There was not now as much in Edinburgh to detain him as there had been before, so in January 1684, he was back on duty with his regiment in the west. It was a command that brought him increasingly into conflict with General Dalyell. When, on 22 April, the Council recommended that Claverhouse be given command of all the troops in Ayrshire, including Lord Ross's troop, five companies of Lieutenant-Colonel Buchan's foot regiment, and half of the troop of Horse Guards, Claverhouse felt compelled to clarify the chain of command with Dalyell.

The General, it emerged, was so put out by the extent of Claverhouse's new duties that he refused to see him. Claverhouse called on him at his lodgings in Edinburgh, only to be told that he had gone out to dinner. Shortly afterwards, a copy of the Council's order was sent round to Claverhouse by Dalyell with the message that the General had nothing to add to it.

Claverhouse was taken aback. The Act of Council referring to his new duties stated specifically that, before Claverhouse and Buchan could take up their new commands in Ayrshire, the General had to give his written assent. So he sent Dalyell's servant back, to say that he would call on the General after dinner that evening. When he arrived, however, he was told that the old man was lying down, and had not been well for some time. 'I offered to stay till he was awake', said Claverhouse, 'but his man told me, I needed not, for he would give me no other orders.'

The result was stalemate, for, as Claverhouse said, 'I can do nothing without his orders.' He decided that, rather than wait, he would simply go down to Ayrshire, join Ross there, and wait for the General to issue his instructions. He posted his companies and visited the garrisons in Galloway, Dumfries, and Clydesdale. But still he heard nothing. Finally, he wrote to the General, asking him to send his orders to Glasgow, and pointing out that 'if the King's service was retarded, the blame should not be on [him].' Finally, on 19 May 1684, the orders arrived bearing the General's signature.

Claverhouse's tour of the west had proved mildly encouraging, he reported to Queensberry: 'The country is much disposed to peace and order, and I will answer for both in all those countries as long as the forces continue thus posted, and England keeps quiet.'

His account, on that day, was less detailed than usual. This was because another matter now preoccupied him. Claverhouse was contemplating marriage again. He had met and fallen in love with an Ayrshire girl, and was pursuing her with his customary application to detail. There was only one drawback – he could hardly have decided on a less suitable match.

CHAPTER TEN

A Marriage Disturbed

There's ancient men at weddings been
For sixty years or more;
But sic a curious wedding-day
They never saw before.

Anon.

The marriage was unsuitable because the lady's family was Whig. It was unsuitable because her grandfather had been in trouble for harbouring rebels. It was unsuitable because her father had died, in the year of Bothwell Brig, with a minister by his side praying for a Covenanting victory. And in 1684 it was particularly unsuitable because she was the niece of Sir John Cochrane, who was at that moment wanted for questioning in connection with the Rye House plot.

Jean Cochrane, who was barely twenty to Claverhouse's thirty-six, was the daughter of William, Lord Cochrane, and granddaughter of the Earl of Dundonald. The family were substantial landowners in Ayrshire and Renfrew, and Jean, the youngest of six children, grew up at the family seat, the Place of Paisley, which stood next to the magnificent ruins of the old abbey.

The death of her father in 1679, when she was fifteen, meant that her grandfather, the Earl, played an important part in her upbringing. He had represented Ayr as a member of parliament in 1647, and had been raised to the peerage as Lord Cochrane of Dundonald by Charles I. Then, after the Restoration, he became a member of the Privy Council, and was created an Earl by Charles II. He had, however, made himself unpopular with the Government by harbouring fugitives, and had only narrowly avoided prosecution.

Dundonald's Presbyterian tendencies were probably only mild ones, but his son William had married into a family of stern Covenanters. Lady Catherine Kennedy, daughter of the sixth Earl of Cassilis, Jean's mother, was a fierce supporter of the rebel cause, and it may well have been she who gave house room at Paisley to some wanted men and persuaded her husband in 1678 to refuse the Government's bond. He also challenged its right to make masters responsible for their servants' appearance at church, which earned him a stiff reproof ('without laughing') from the Earl of Perth. Certainly, it was she who, when her husband was dying, called in an 'outed' minister to pray over him. It was later recorded by Sir John Lauder of Fountainhall that the minister had 'prayed God to bless the rebels in the west with success', which, in the year of Bothwell Brig, was provocative talk.

Claverhouse may have met Jean Cochrane first in Edinburgh, where she stayed for some time in her grandfather's house in the Canongate while he attended the Council. But it was when he resumed his duties in Ayrshire that they got to know each other better. The intermediary may well have been the young Lord Ross, whose father had defended Glasgow at the time of Drumclog, and whose troop was now under Claverhouse's command, since Ross was a cousin of the Cochranes. But in any event Claverhouse was a regular visitor at Paisley, where some of his troops were quartered.

Jean's portrait shows that she had the long straight nose and the determined chin of the Cochranes. She was slight and pale, but with a cheerful mouth and eyes, clearly of strong character, which she must have been to brave the grim disapproval which her mother immediately voiced of the marriage. Claverhouse proposed in the autumn of 1683, and Lady Catherine pronounced herself adamantly against the match. Nothing would induce her to assent to the betrothal of her daughter to a man she viewed as a persecutor. Dundonald, however, gave his approval, which was critical, and Jean's brother, the heir, supported him.

Dundonald even used the match to inquire whether it would help free him of the risk of prosecution for his family's activities, which elicited a ribald response from Moray, the joint Secretary of State, who wrote to Queensberry in September that:

> The Advocate's brother told me one of the pleasantest stories imagineable this day, that the Chancellor had sent to the Earl of Dundonald to tell him that the match he intended with Claverhouse was no ways able to secure him, but if he would let Gordonstoun [a sixty-year-old twice-married old rogue] have his grandchild, he would secure him, at which

mother and daughter were so alarmed, they immediately ran out of town.

The impending marriage caused no little talk in Edinburgh, and one can imagine that Lady Erroll was not short of comment. But Claverhouse was in love. Nothing else would have induced him to contemplate such a disastrous liaison, one which went against all his political and religious instincts, and which would seriously threaten his career. In love, as in all things, Claverhouse pursued his interests singlemindedly. Nothing – the hostility of his prospective mother-in-law, the dark mutterings of his enemies in Edinburgh, Hamilton's gossip and Queensberry's suspicions – was permitted to come between him and the object of his affections.

Not that he was unaware of the problems. Writing in May 1684, to Queensberry, he argued his case on strategic as well as romantic grounds, by pointing out the advantages of a relationship with a Whig family: 'I must say my new allies that I am like to make, is not unuseful to me in the shires of Ayr and Renfrew', he wrote. 'They have the guiding of those shires, and they do strengthen my hands in the King's service.'

However, the gossip plainly unsettled him. On 19 May he wrote an anxious letter to Queensberry, defending his own position, and the reputation of the Cochranes:

> I looked upon myself as a cleanser that may cure others by my coming amongst them. Besides, that I saw nothing singular in my Lord Dundonald's case, save that he has but one rebel on his land for ten that the rest of the lords and lairds of the south and west have on theirs.

He said it was unfair to blame Dundonald for Sir John Cochrane of Ochiltree's crimes – 'He is a madman, and let him perish' – and he pointed out that no one had bothered particularly about the Cochranes until they heard that Claverhouse was going to marry one of the daughters. If they really wanted to pick on him, then there were other, worse cases that should be taken up as well: 'One man may cast in the mire, as we say, what ten will not take out.' In the end he asked the world to judge him by his loyalty alone: 'Whatever come of this, let not my enemies misrepresent me ... I will, in despite of them, let the world see that it is not in the power of love nor any other folly, to alter my loyalty.'

He was put out, however, to learn that the Duke of Hamilton, who was in much the same position – his daughter Susanna wanted to marry

Jean Cochrane's brother John –, had taken the precaution of writing to ask the King's permission before giving his approval. It was something Claverhouse had omitted to do, but which he now swiftly put right. Permission was granted.

He had by now achieved the ownership of Dudhope. It had taken a year since the committee investigating the Hatton affair had given its verdict, and much pressure had been exerted at court on Claverhouse's behalf before a satisfactory solution was reached. He had to pay £6,000 Scots for it, which was more than he had contemplated, but, finally, on 23 April 1684, the deeds were assigned to their new owner.

With the Crown Charter of Dudhope Castle went the lands of Castlehill, the office of Constable of Dundee, and the absolute right to be first magistrate and officer under the King in the town of Dundee and all its territories 'in all times coming'. This last elicited a formal protest from the provost of Dundee. There was a long tradition of self-government in the royal burghs, and the town resented the fact that the Constable held judicial powers which they regarded as their own. The matter was not to be finally concluded – in Claverhouse's favour – until May.

The following month, Colonel John Graham of Claverhouse and the Honourable Jean Cochrane were married. The wedding took place at Paisley on Tuesday 10 June 1684, with a guard of honour formed by his own troopers, dressed in the brand-new red tunics he had ordered for them. The kettle-drummers and trumpeters wore grey. The bride's mother could not bring herself to be there. The register was signed by Jean, the bride, whose signature leant forward; by Jean's grandfather, in the quavering writing of an old man; by her grandmother, Euphame Scott, Countess of Dundonald in a splendid flourish of curlicues; and by her brother, Lord Cochrane. Amongst the witnesses was Claverhouse's friend and brother-officer, Lord Ross, writing in a fine manly hand. Claverhouse signed firmly as 'J. Grahame', with the initial J characteristically looped through the G. Claverhouse settled on his wife an annuity of 5,000 merks and the liferent of Glenogilvie. Her dowry for him was 40,000 merks.

The wedding day did not end quite as expected. The guests were in mid-celebration, when a messenger arrived for Claverhouse carrying news from General Dalyell that there had been trouble at a conventicle at the Black Loch in Lanarkshire, and that a party of armed fugitives was heading into Renfrewshire.

It was not an auspicious start to married life, but the news left Claverhouse with no choice. He saddled-up immediately, said goodbye to his bride of a few hours and their guests, and set off with Ross to gather their troops and begin the hunt. This was a pattern often repeated in the years to come, but all Claverhouse would say about the call in his subsequent report to the Lord President was: 'They might have let Tuesday pass.'

General Dalyell had learned of the conventicle while he was in Glasgow and had sent a party of troopers and dragoons to investigate. They reported that about a hundred men and women had gathered on Saturday night for an outdoor service at the Black Loch near Motherwell, and that the men were armed. The dragoons pursued them southwest towards Hamilton, but lost them south of the Clyde, and returned 'very much fatigued' to Glasgow to report to the General. The officer in charge estimated that there were about eighty armed men and twenty women.

Claverhouse sent orders to his colleague, Colonel Buchan, who had most of the troops down at Dalmellington, south-east of Ayr, and told him to meet him at Newmilns. He then took half of the Horse Guards – twenty-one men, he noted, instead of fifty – and sent Ross with his troop and some dragoons to scour the moors towards Muirkirk, while he branched north-east to Lesmahagow. All next day was spent traversing 'many moors and mosses', as Ross described them, between Clydesdale and Ayr, ending up at Strathaven. Nothing was seen. Colonel Buchan was told to head back south, keeping an eye out as he went. On 12 June, Claverhouse returned to Paisley and his postponed wedding night.

He was not there for long. On the morning of Friday 13 June, he had word from Buchan that some of his men had run into an ambush. Shots had been exchanged with a small band of rebels and one soldier was wounded. Buchan was now heading towards Cumnock to cut the insurgents off from Galloway. Claverhouse immediately set off to join him. He was with him by nightfall, and heard that the band was now down to fifty-nine, and had been seen crossing Airds Moss, 'running in great haste, barefooted many of them, and taking horses in some places to help them forward.'

But, though he, with Ross, Buchan, and Captain John Strachan, ordered up from the south end of Galloway, scoured the country, they could not find them. 'We were at the head of Douglas', wrote Claverhouse later.

> We were round and over Cairntable. We were at Greenock-head, Cummer-head and all through the moors and mosses, hills, glens,

woods; and spread out in small parties, and ranged as if we had been at hunting, and down to Blackwood, but could learn nothing of these rogues.

They picked up scraps of information, about a rebel commander who was 'a lusty black man with one eye' and about a man with a velvet hat and a man with a grey cap, but, though they offered money, and examined witnesses under oath and 'threatened terribly', they could not pin down their quarry. The ground was reasonably dry because it had been an exceptionally hot summer, but much of it was wild uncharted country, and the troops 'complained mightily of the march'. Finally, at Kilbride on 15 June, Claverhouse stood the troops down and sent a full report to Dalyell in Glasgow before returning to Paisley, this time for a slightly longer stay.

The General meanwhile was cross. He had heard nothing in the interval from Claverhouse, despite sending him two expresses, and had not been able to communicate any orders. The whole procedure appeared to him disorganized. He sent a testy letter to the Council, complaining that Claverhouse's tactics were wrong, and that it had always been his view that the army should stay in its garrisons in the summer and not risk small parties of troops running round the country exposing themselves to rebel bands – rather as a certain Captain Graham had done at Drumclog not that many years ago.

On 16 June he did receive reports from both Claverhouse and Ross, but they did nothing to improve his temper. He dispatched another letter forthwith to Edinburgh:

> I received the enclosed late yesternight ... They will speak for themselves. But if each man acts after his own fancy, without any order, his Majesty's affairs may suffer; and I doubt not but they will, if some one have not the direction of the war. For this two days bygone I could not determine whether to draw together the whole forces, or march with a part of this garrison. For it looked very like a general insurrection....

That view was reinforced a month later when the escort of a party of sixteen prisoners being taken back to Edinburgh was ambushed on the drove road which ran along a narrow pass at Enterkin between Thornhill and Sanquhar. Again the attack was successful, and one soldier was killed, others wounded, while all but two of the prisoners escaped.

To the Secret Committee in Edinburgh, it seemed as if Dalyell's reading of the fresh trouble in the west might be right. The Earl of Aberdeen had finally been replaced as Chancellor by Lord Perth, to the delight of Perth's sister, Lady Erroll, and Queensberry now felt himself able to come up to the capital to assert control and deal with the new rebellion which seemed to be beginning.

On 14 July he appointed Claverhouse to a committee set up to inquire into the Enterkin incident, with instructions to draw up a report and make recommendations. One result was a proclamation, published on 22 July, announcing a 'hue and cry' against those who had taken up arms again or who had failed to come forward to the Court of Justiciary the previous year. They were now to be prosecuted. A list had already been published containing more than 1,800 names, and the proclamation spread the net even wider: anyone harbouring one or more of the 1,800, or withholding information about them, could be subject to the demands of the law. On 1 August 1684, another proclamation, perhaps the harshest that had yet been issued, ordered an immediate examination of all prisoners held 'for being in the late rebellion', and instructed magistrates to proceed to execute them within six hours if they were found guilty.

On the same date, Colonels Claverhouse and Buchan were confirmed in a joint command in Ayrshire, with powers to examine suspects under oath, while other troops were stationed in Glasgow, Edinburgh, Fife, Teviotdale, Galloway, Nithsdale, and Dumfries. Dalyell was in overall command and movements were subject to his orders. That still left Claverhouse with a great deal of autonomy, however, and he used it to organize searches from Ayr in the west as far as Moffat to the east. Once again he was shocked at the lack of good intelligence on his own side and the almost uncanny amount on the other. 'They have such intelligence that there is no surprising them', he wrote in early August.

> When we came here [Strathaven], they told they heard of my coming; and last night I was asking if there were any troops at Newmilns, as I came from Mauchline, and though it was under night, and nobody but my own servants, they told me my Lord Ross's troop was there, and that I was expected. I fear we do nothing; for so soon as I come, I find they acquaint all the country, expecting a search.

On 9 August, however, his troops had a stroke of luck when they stumbled on six men sleeping in the open near Closeburn in Dumfriesshire. Shots were fired, and all were taken prisoner, three of them being badly wounded. They were escorted to the Tolbooth in Edinburgh, where they were accused of having been at the Enterkin ambush. Though they denied it, they were found guilty and executed on 15 August, just four days after their capture.

This was, according to at least one Covenanting historian, the beginning of the notorious period known down the centuries as the 'killing time'. It certainly marked the start of a period of growing harshness. But for Claverhouse, whose name is primarily associated with the persecution, the summer of 1684 was an unaccustomed period of leisure. In mid August, he was able to take some leave and travel north to spend time with his bride at the new family seat of Dudhope, where, in the sunshine, its light-grey stone built on two sides of a square, with gardens and orchards behind and parkland stretching down to the edge of the firth, justified its description as 'an extraordinary pleasant and sweet place.'

He was not entirely idle, for he took a personal interest in the affairs of Dundee, of which he was now Constable. It is worth recording that his first intervention was to limit the severity of the law to an extent that was remarkable for the times. He had been down to the town's Tolbooth and found some men imprisoned there for petty theft. Their punishment was, traditionally, execution, but Claverhouse objected strongly and sent a petition to the Privy Council that the sentence be replaced with something more lenient. There is no record of what the Privy Council members privately thought of this request, but they assented to it, and on 10 September announced:

> ... full powers and commission to the said Colonel Graham of Claverhouse, Constable of Dundee, to restrict the punishment appointed by law, against such persons within his jurisdiction already made prisoners, or that shall hereafter be made prisoners, upon account of the foresaid petty and small theft, or picking, to an arbitrary punishment, such as whipping, or banishment, as he shall find cause.

Considering that this was seventeenth-century Scotland, and that torture and execution were often sentences for capital crimes, considering also that in England hanging was continued as a punishment for petty theft for more than another century, Claverhouse's intervention shows a view of the law quite notably liberal for his time. His view did, however, reflect the essential pragmatism with which he was always to view questions of crime and punishment, however severe the latter might be.

He thought, for instance, that it was unjust for people to be held responsible for crimes committed by others. Thus, when it was proposed that a new bond should be circulated in the south-west requiring landowners to be held responsible for their tenants, he objected, arguing his case to Queensberry in a very straightforward manner:

I think it should be altered; for it is unjust to desire of others what we would not do ourselves; for I declare I think it a thing not to be desired, that I should be forfeited and hanged, if my tenant's wife, twenty miles from me, in the midst of hills and woods, give meat or shelter to a fugitive.

This view was good justice, but poor politics. This was precisely the argument that had been put up by his grandfather-in-law, Dundonald, and rejected. For Claverhouse, who was still, in the eyes of people like Queensberry, an object of suspicion because of his marriage, proposing leniency towards Whigs was not a sensible course to pursue.

The relative leisure of Dudhope days did not suit him for very long. He had not been there for much more than a fortnight when he wrote to Queensberry that he was ready to take up new duties whenever he was commanded, and that, even if Queensberry did not have anything immediate to suggest, he would come and see him in Edinburgh on the off-chance. 'Though I stay a few days here,' he wrote, 'I hope nobody will reproach me of eating the bread of idleness; seeing nobody has, and nobody will go more cheerfully about anything that concerns the King's or your Lordship's service ...' The order came finally in early September, when Claverhouse was told to accompany another itinerant court, set up under the auspices of the Privy Council but not quite as grand as the previous one. It was, however, headed by the 'Prime Minister' of Scotland, Queensberry himself.

There were just three judges: Queensberry, Claverhouse, and Queensberry's son, James, Lord Drumlanrig, who by now, thanks to his father's patronage, had command of a troop of horse. The way justice was administered under this curious trio bore more resemblance to a court-martial than to a circuit court, and, though fining and imprisonment were the only sanctions applied, the questioning that went on in the courthouses of Dumfries, Kirkcudbright, and Wigton dispensed with legal niceties and went straight to the issue of obedience. The 'judges' were empowered 'to call and convene all persons guilty of conventicles, withdrawing from public ordinances, disorderly baptisms and marriages, and such like disorders and irregularities.'

Wives whose husbands failed to appear before the court were ordered not to cohabit, and vice versa; children were not to live with parents who were found guilty; neighbours were instructed to testify against neighbours; and always there was the knowledge that soldiers, armed with lists of names, would be following up the orders of the court. Inevitably, as it progressed, it left behind an aura of fear and suspicion. There were to be no hangings this time, but there had been a number of executions since the first circuit court went on its leisurely tour of the south-west: three for treason in February, and five for the same crime at the Glasgow market cross in March.

The prisons, from Dumfries in the south to Dunnottar Castle in the north, were now beginning to bulge. Dunnottar, near Stonehaven, which was every bit as terrible as, and in many ways worse than, the Black Hole of Calcutta, had not yet been used for inflicting punishment, but conditions in its dungeons were barbarous nevertheless.

Those prisoners who were judged 'penitent' were ordered to be transported to the American plantations, or the 'canebrakes' of the West Indies. This was often judged a worse fate than being sent to the freezing dungeons of Dunnottar or the windy cells on the Bass Rock. Life on the plantations was brutal, and often short, with many perishing from disease or ill-treatment. Others were lost on the way there, the worst case being that of the prisoners who had been held at Greyfriars after Bothwell, who were shipwrecked off Deerness in Orkney. The Captain, William Paterson, battened down the hatches so they could not escape, and beat back those who tried to scramble ashore on to the rocks. More than 200 were drowned, and a monument now commemorates them on the high Orkney cliffs.

It was not, perhaps, surprising that events in Scotland had begun to take a more violent turn. The Cameronians, who represented only a small minority of the western Presbyterians, were nevertheless implacable in their opposition to the Government, and were believed by the authorities to represent a massive movement. Their statements and beliefs, which represented a distorted view of the National Covenant itself, placed them firmly on the wrong side of the line between accepting and rejecting the King's authority over the Church, and therefore, the nation. As the reprisals grew harsher, so did their response, until blood was demanded for blood. With their strong roots in the Old Testament, they found little difficulty in sanctioning vengeance in the name of the Lord. Resistance built up, as so often before, round a handful of preachers, of whom one in particular stood out.

As a young student, James Renwick had been present when the Lanark Declaration was posted and the market cross defaced in January 1682. He was already a rebel, having helped cut down the bodies of some Covenanters who had been executed in Edinburgh. Later he was sent to Holland to study for clerical orders. Amongst the outlawed Cameronians, achieving ordination was a difficult but crucial step, and Holland was one of the few places where they could be certain that the

John Graham of Claverhouse, Viscount Dundee by Sir Godfrey Kneller

The Manner of the Barbarous Murther of
JAMES,
Late Lord Arch-Biſhop of St. Andrews,
Primate and Metropolitan of all Scotland,
And one of his Majeſties moſt Honourable Privy-Council of that Kingdom; *May* 3. 1679.

The murder of Archbishop Sharp on Magus Moor, 11 April 1679

John Graham of Claverhouse, painted while serving abroad as a mercenary soldier

The Duke of Lauderdale, for many years Charles II's principal adviser on Scottish affairs

Charles II in later life

James, Duke of York and Albany, who later became King James II of England and VII of Scotland

General Thomas Dalyell of the Binns

The battle of Bothwell Bridge, 22 June
1679

Left: Convenanting flag captured at Bothwell Bridge by the Hon. Archibald Rollo

Below: Standard of Lord Rollo's troop of Horse bearing the Rollo family motto

Bottom: Dudhope Castle, which Claverhouse acquired in 1683

Lady Jean Cochrane, who married
John Graham of Claverhouse on 10 June 1684

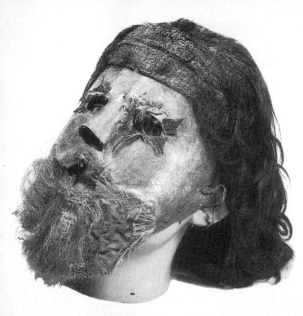

The mask of the Revd Alexander Peden

Lieutenant-General Hugh Mackay of Scourie, who commanded the Government forces at the battle of Killiecrankie

training was properly supervised. In the summer following his ordination, Renwick was back again to preach in Scotland, prepared if necessary for martyrdom. He had a natural ability to inspire his congregations, and he offered a full-blooded challenge to the Government, rather as Cargill and Cameron had done. Indeed, his first full sermon in Scotland took Cargill's last text, from Isaiah, as its theme: 'Comfort ye, comfort ye my people.'

Over the next year, Renwick traversed the country, high on the wanted list. A series of dramatic escapes from Government troops brought him a justified reputation for skill and daring in the course of his fugitive mission. He urged courage on his followers: 'Let us be lions in God's cause, and lambs in our own' was one of his favourite sayings.

The mystique that surrounded him was echoed by another legendary preacher, the mysterious Alexander Peden, who flitted amongst the hills, disguised on occasions by a mask. Peden's mask, an extraordinary and elaborate object, with a false beard and moustache, was also used by his disciples to suggest that sometimes its owner was in two places at once. When worn by a follower at night and seen only through a window by candlelight, it could deceive people into reporting his presence in one part of the country while he was preaching in another. Renwick never hid his face, but relied instead on a fleet horse, which stood near him as he preached, and became a familiar hallmark.

On 8 November 1684, in response to the growing sense of persecution felt by the Covenanters, Renwick issued a Declaration which was to have far-reaching results. It disowned the authority of the King and his government and attacked their system of justice. It claimed that sentence of death was being passed on citizens of the country, not on the basis of crimes against the state, but simply because they subscribed to a different faith: 'We utterly detest and abhor that hellish principle of killing all who differ in judgment or persuasion from us, it having no bottom upon the word of God, or right reason', ran part of it. It went on to threaten the forces ranged against them with 'punishment according to our power and the degree of their offence.' That appeared to be a licence to take life, if necessary, as a way of responding to persecution. The reaction in Edinburgh was one of near-panic. The Secret Committee described the document as one 'declaring war with the Government and threatening to kill us all'.

Ten days later, Renwick's Declaration was translated into action. Two Life Guards, Thomas Kennoway and Duncan Stewart, who had a reputation for severity, were followed to an inn at Swineabbey, west of

Blackburn, where the Guards were garrisoned. They spent the evening drinking, and then, as they emerged, they were shot down by a waiting party of rebels.

The cold-blooded murder of soldiers – as opposed to the killing of them in military confrontation – was something new, and it horrified the Council in Edinburgh, and the Duke of York when he heard of it. Tarbat, the Lord Clerk Register, wrote to Queensberry, still on tour with his court, in some alarm:

> For God's sake take care of yourself; for now that these villains are at the utmost despair, they will act as devils, to whom they belong ... I think all other matters are to be left till those wild cats be catched.

The Council met on 22 November and passed a resolution which was, in effect, a licence for summary execution. The Renwick Declaration was to become a new touchstone, and anyone refusing to disown it under oath, 'whether they have arms or not, should be immediately killed before two witnesses.' On 25 November, the words of the oath were agreed. Claverhouse was not present in the Council when the order was approved, but he was there to sign it, and there is no record of his objecting to its terms.

The killing of the two soldiers was followed by another murder, this time of an indulged minister, Peter Peirson, of Carsphairn in Kirkcudbrightshire, who was shot at the door of his manse by a gang of five men, led by one James Macmichael, and including a nephew of James Mitchell, who had attempted to assassinate Archbishop Sharp. Peirson had been an isolated man in the neighbourhood, known as 'a favourer of popery', and was outspokenly hostile to Whigs. He was said to have been an informer, and he may well have been, but his death shocked many Presbyterians.

Renwick immediately condemned the killing and said it was 'contrary to our Declaration'. He added, however, that it was 'not materially murder'. It was clear, therefore, that both sides had issued broad licences to carry out executions on their behalf, though the interpretation was to be a matter for their agents, whether officers of the Government or wandering bands of rebels. One of the former was, of course, Claverhouse, and he was accused of carrying out just such an execution in early December, when, it was alleged, one William Graham, a tailor from the village of Crossmichael in Kirkcudbright, was killed.

The allegation was, specifically, that Claverhouse had pursued him as he was attempting to escape, had questioned him, and had then shot him dead. But the details were not written down until six years later, and there is no reference to a William Graham in the Council records for that month. Considering that this would have been the first such execution on the spot, and that Claverhouse himself would have submitted a meticulous report on the incident, that version seems unlikely. William Graham's gravestone in Crossmichael gives the date of his death as 1682, which cannot be right, and claims he was 'instantly shot dead by a party of Claverhouse's troops'. The facts undoubtedly relate to James Graham of Crossmichael, whose fate at this time was documented. He was picked up, questioned about the Declaration, and sent on to Wigtown, to Dumfries, and then finally to Edinburgh for trial. He refused to disown the Declaration, and was executed at the Gallowlee on 9 December 1684.

A week later Claverhouse was directly involved in action. On Tuesday 16 December, a party of about a hundred rebels invaded the town of Kirkcudbright, which was not at the time garrisoned, killed the sentinel at the Tolbooth, released all the prisoners, took the town drum and any arms they could find, and vanished into the countryside. Claverhouse, who was searching the country a few miles north of Kirkcudbright at Bridge of Dee, came across a small band of rebels, gave pursuit, and caught them on Auchencloy Moor. A brief skirmish followed, which ended with five of the rebels dead and three prisoners taken. Amongst the dead was James Macmichael, who had led the attack on the minister of Carsphairn, though Claverhouse did not realize that at the time. The prisoners, Robert Smith of Glencairn and Robert Hunter, were taken for trial at Kirkcudbright, where Claverhouse sat in judgment along with Captain Bruce of Earlshall and Captain Lord William Douglas, his junior officers. Sentence of death was passed, and the two were immediately executed.

Meanwhile word had reached Claverhouse that one of those left dead on the field at Auchencloy was Macmichael, the Carsphairn murderer. He therefore sent orders that his body be disinterred from the graveyard at Dalry church, where it had been taken for burial, and hanged on the local gibbet. This has been condemned as an act of spite, but it was, interestingly, a procedure consistent with the law of *læsa majestas* laid down by Sir George Mackenzie, the King's Advocate, and intended as a demonstration that justice had been done, even after death.

Justified or not, it was the first case in which Claverhouse had acted as judge, jury and executioner, and his enemies were not slow to associate him with what they saw as the brutalities of the time. The graveyards of the Covenanting 'martyrs', which are still today so much a feature of the churchyards of the west, were beginning to spread, and with them the legends. Of the executions carried out at Kirkcudbright, the epitaph later ran:

> This monument shall show posterity,
> Two headless martyrs under it do lie,
> By bloody Graham were taken and surprised,
> Brought to this town, and afterwards were siz'd;
> By unjust law were sentenced to die,
> Then first they hang'd, then headed cruelly.

The days when Claverhouse could boast that Galloway was 'as peaceable and as regular as any part of the country this side of the Tay' were over. In their place had come a time of fear, suspicion, oppression, and hatred. Death, for the Covenanters, whose hiding places were growing fewer and further between, was a thing to be lived with daily, and often to be prayed for.

Peden, the preacher, always credited with gifts of prophecy, said: 'The day is coming in these lands that a bloody scaffold shall be thought a good shelter.' And Renwick echoed him: 'Death to me', he said, 'is as a bed to the weary.'

CHAPTER ELEVEN
The Killing Time

*'To men I can be answerable, and as for God, I'll take him
into mine own hand'*
John Graham of Claverhouse (attrib.)

So far, relations between Claverhouse and Queensberry, while uneasy, had remained just this side of civility. But towards the end of 1684 they became, suddenly, overtly hostile, and threatened Claverhouse's career with disaster.

Queensberry had never acknowledged the help Claverhouse had given him at court towards his ennoblement. Indeed, looking at it from his lonely outpost in the west of Scotland, it had seemed to him that rather more work had gone into the advancement of Claverhouse's own career than of his. He had complained about him to the Duke of York, claiming that he was playing a devious game, but James had defended him by testifying to his reliability: 'He is not a man to say things that are not', he wrote. But, given Queensberry's nature, and the number of friends more than willing to feed his doubts, his suspicions of Claverhouse were at least understandable. When therefore, on 3 November 1684, he finally achieved his ambition, and became His Grace the Duke of Queensberry, he did not immediately rush to bestow favours on the man who had done so much to help him towards his new eminence. Rather the reverse. He had now got everything he needed out of him, and from now on he would do everything in his power to prevent the advancement of a possible rival.

Claverhouse, for his part, had long resented the way that Queensberry disposed of vacant military commissions, handing them out to friends and dependants rather than to properly qualified military officers, and in July 1684 he had genuine cause for complaint when

Lord Drumlanrig, Queensberry's son, was promoted to the Lieuten-ant-Colonelcy of Claverhouse's own regiment. In August, Queens-berry's brother, James Douglas, whose original training had been as an advocate, was made Colonel of Linlithgow's regiment of foot, and in November, another son, Lord William Douglas, was given a troop under Claverhouse's command. Throughout all this time, Claver-house's own brother, David, had not advanced beyond the rank of cornet.

He appears to have expressed himself with typical force on the subject, for Queensberry again wrote complaining to the Duke of York, and the Duke expressed views on the subject to Moray, who reported back:

> I find [the Duke] displeased, as he has good reason, at his [Claver-house's] carriage, and as freely as the short time would allow me, I told the ill consequences of the fiery temper of young men, who ought to understand themselves better than to fail so grossly in their duty to such as the King chiefly trusts.

But Claverhouse would not allow the matter to rest, and his resent-ment finally boiled over at a meeting of the Privy Council on 11 December. A petition had been presented from some of Colonel Douglas's soldiers, complaining that they had been turned out of his regiment, and the arrears of pay they were owed had been used to buy uniforms and boots for some of the other soldiers. Douglas, it appeared, was something of a martinet, insisting that his soldiers be of the same height, to improve the appearance of the regiment, and giving out strict orders about the length of beards, the kind of cravats his men wore, and the ribbons they used to keep their hair out of their eyes.

To Claverhouse this was nonsense, and he took up the soldiers' petition in front of the Council, saying that such things did nothing for morale and would simply discourage people from joining the army. Queensberry immediately took affront, and Lauder of Fountainhall, who was recording the exchange at Council, noted simply: 'Thus grew the difference between Claverhouse and the Treasurer.' Clearly, Claverhouse had failed to keep his famous temper in check, for the ensuing fracas was immediately reported by the Chancellor, Lord Perth, and his brother, Melfort (now joint Secretary of State), to the Duke of York, in London, whose confidence in Claverhouse was badly shaken: 'When I come down to you', he told Queensberry, 'Claverhouse shall know I am not satisfied with his behaviour to you.'

Hints were now dropped that Claverhouse had other faults. He had not, the word went round, been tough enough on the Ayrshire Whigs, because of the Cochrane connection. Queensberry used that as an excuse to withdraw him, at least temporarily, from his duties in the west. Four of his six troops had already been placed at the disposal of Lord George Drummond, who had been given justiciary powers in the western shires, and in January 1685 Claverhouse was ordered to hold his own court elsewhere, on the other side of the country, in Fife. Finally, on 15 January, Colonel Douglas with his troops moved into Claverhouse's beloved Galloway, simply, as Fountainhall noted, 'to put a rub on Claverhouse'. Douglas does not seem to have performed too well, however. A skirmish took place in January in which one of his officers was killed, the first lost in action in six years. Douglas himself was very nearly shot, and would have been if a rebel carbine had not misfired.

The vendetta against Claverhouse was by no means finished. Someone had suggested to Queensberry that he might inquire into the fines collected by Claverhouse in Galloway in the course of his term there. Claverhouse had always argued that they were used to pay for his soldiers' expenses. The money was, he said 'both for expense and reward; and this I may safely say was spent.' But they were substantial sums of money, often running into five figures at a time, and no accounting had been done. Queensberry raised the matter with Melfort towards the end of the year, and at the same time he questioned whether Claverhouse should now be asked to pay for the 'gift' of the estate of Freuch in Galloway, which he had acquired in 1681.

It was a measure of how far the Duke had by now been influenced against Claverhouse that when Melfort raised the matter with him, he was disposed to take action. On 24 January, Melfort reported back to Queensberry:

> I waited for a fit opportunity to move the Duke in Claverhouse's affair, and am now commanded to tell your Grace that though the Duke desires nothing in the two years' rent of the forfeited estates [of Freuch] to be done till he comes to Scotland, yet he orders the fines uplifted by Claverhouse to be counted for, and paid in, or any other bond to be sued for, that he or any other may upon that account be owing to the King; so without a grudge, you may call for them.

For Claverhouse the matter was one of the gravest concern, partly because of the money, partly because he had not been able to argue his case. He was desperate to go to London to see the Duke, but the opportunity was denied him.

On 6 February 1685, Charles II died, and the Duke of York ascended the throne as James VII. The proclamation of his accession in Scotland was signed on 10 February by the entire membership of the Privy Council, and Claverhouse's signature was there with the others. But he must have wondered what it counted for.

Only one day after the accession, Melfort was again writing to Queensberry from London, describing Claverhouse's conduct as 'impudent' and 'malicious'.

It is hardly surprising that, in those hectic days after the death of the King, James should have found little time for such petty wrangling. He told Claverhouse not to come to London, but he seems to have had 'uneasy consequences' about the affair.

Melfort continued to make mischief: 'I am really sorry at Claverhouse's carriage', he said, 'though you know my opinion of him before this fell out ... But if he will play the fool he must drink as he brews.'

In March 1685, Claverhouse was summoned to the Council in Edinburgh to be confronted by Queensberry and was ordered to account for the fines collected in Galloway. He said that his brother David, now Sheriff-Depute of Wigton, was calculating the figures, and he asked for time. He was told that he could have five or six days. He retorted that five or six days was the same as none at all, given the distance to be travelled. 'Then you shall have none', snapped Queensberry.

On 2 March, Queensberry confirmed that his brother was to take over officially in Galloway in place of Claverhouse, although, as Fountainhall noted, 'Claverhouse's name was more formidable there'. The next day, Claverhouse was formally stripped of his place on the Privy Council. The 'pretence', said Fountainhall, was that Claverhouse, 'having married a daughter of a fanatic family, viz. Dundonald, he was not fit to be trusted with the King's secrets.' And on 27 March, Douglas was given the vacant commission of Sheriff of Wigton, with Claverhouse's signature notably absent from those confirming the order. There remained only his military command. But that, at least, he retained. His commission as Colonel Graham was renewed on 30 March.

In the space of three months, a man who had held full civil and military powers in the west of Scotland, answering only to the highest in the land, was back to being a plain soldier. It had, however, taken two Secretaries of State and a Lord High Treasurer to do it.

Queensberry himself went to London in late March, and returned with more powers, as Lord High Commissioner to the Scottish Parliament. No opportunity was lost to blacken Claverhouse's name, but the King, it seems, was now a reluctant critic, and suggested to Lord Moray that Claverhouse might be restored 'to place and favour' if he wrote to Queensberry acknowledging his faults. Moray, the politician, hastened to steer the King away from such a notion. He pointed out that Claverhouse, who was 'of a high, proud, and peremptory humour', might think that his fall from grace had been against the King's wishes, 'which would certainly blow up his humour to a greater insolence than ever; besides which he would certainly talk of it with insufferable conceit and vanity.' James was not immediately per-suaded, but agreed to drop the matter for the time being. And Moray wrote to Claverhouse on 18 April like a headmaster ticking off a schoolboy:

> Now, I shall say from myself, as your friend and well-wisher, that I am sorry you have not before this time, addressed yourself to [Queens-berry] who, I dare confidently say, would very generously receive it, and recommend you respectfully to his Majesty. It is from kind inclina-tions towards you that I take this freedom. And do me the justice to believe I am your hearty well-wisher, and, Sir, your faithful servant.

With 'well-wishers' like this, Claverhouse might well have thought he needed no enemies. In any event, he does not appear to have heeded the advice, for, on 28 April, Moray wrote to Queensberry from London expressing the fear that Claverhouse, Pimpernel-like, might have slipped into London:

> Some said confidently, they had seen his servant on the Exchange. Others, that they saw himself in a coach. But I cannot find any good ground for it; besides that, Lord Melfort told me this morning that he had a letter from him by post yesterday, and that there is no such thing as his coming from Scotland at all.

Moray's anxiety stemmed from the grave doubts he was beginning to have about the King's attitude, for he was aware that James, at heart, was still Claverhouse's friend and intended to restore him to power at the earliest opportunity. All that was needed was a formal apology to Queensberry, which Claverhouse seems finally to have given. Moray passed the matter on to the King, saying that, in his view, the apology was not enough, but James 'walked up and down a great while silent, and then said he would consider of it.'

Which he did. And, having done so, he decided in Claverhouse's favour. Despite all the lobbying conducted against him, Claverhouse was now, by royal command, to be restored to the Privy Council.

Moray, grinding his teeth, framed the letter and sent it off to Queensberry:

> Whereas, in consideration both of the loyalty and abilities of our right trusty and well beloved John Graham of Claverhouse, Colonel of our regiment of horse in that our ancient kingdom, we have thought fit to add him to our Privy Council there...'

By the time Claverhouse resumed his seat in July 1685, events had moved on in the west, with dramatic and bloody consequences.

An indemnity had been offered to those who were fugitives, if they took the oath within twenty days, but it was a cramped and mean indemnity: property holders were not entitled to it, nor were vagrant preachers, nor persons under sentence for fining, nor those implicated in the various recent murders and attacks. And the tone of the Government in Edinburgh did not suggest much leniency. On 23 April, the Chancellor, Lord Perth, told the reconvened Committee of Estates:

> We have a new sect sprung up among us from the dunghill, the very dregs of the people, who kill by pretended inspiration, and instead of the temple of the Lord, had nothing in their mouths but the word, wresting that blessed conveyance of His holy will to us to justify a practice, suggested to them by him who was a murderer from the beginning....

This was a clear reference to James Renwick, and the courts were given powers of 'fire and sword' to question and convict him and his followers. Renwick had few friends amongst the more moderate Presbyterians. They condemned his Declaration, and called him 'the great cause and occasion of all the trouble in this country'. But his adherents remained obdurate.

The indemnity was no help to those who were already imprisoned. On 18 May, 274 prisoners were dispatched from Edinburgh to the dungeons of Dunnottar Castle. They were already in a poor state, and many of them were too old, sick or infirm to travel. But, on 24 May, more than 150 of them, men and women, including three ministers, arrived at the prison roped together, and were packed into a vault measuring fifty by fifteen feet, where starvation and disease took their toll.

No one knows how many died in that terrible place, but on 24 July the Privy Council found that of 283 prisoners, 177 had been banished from the kingdom, forty-nine had been 'cut in the ear' – had had their ears sheared, a common punishment for offending Covenanters –

fifteen had been detained further, two had been remitted, and four had been dismissed. The figures do not add up. There are 36 missing.

When, on 21 April, a fresh commission was given out to Lieutenant-General Drummond for 'pursuing, suppressing, and utterly destroying all such fugitive rebels as resist and disturb the peace and quiet of his Majesty's government', the 'killing time' could indeed be said to have begun. The severity with which the law was applied depended very much on the nature of those in charge, and varied dramatically from place to place. Some, like Sir Robert Grierson of Lag, once Claverhouse's neighbouring sheriff, and the prototype for Walter Scott's Sir Robert Redgauntlet, acquired a lasting reputation for cruelty. Lag hanged two men on an oak tree at Irongray church after they had refused to take the oath, and is said to have rounded up a churchful of people, ringed them with soldiers, and forced them to take the oath, dismissing them with the words: 'Now you are a fold of clean beasts, ye may go home.' He shot the stepson of Viscount Kenmure, who was suspected of being a staunch Whig, and tradition has it that later, at Kirkcudbright, when Kenmure met Lag, the two came to blows, and that Claverhouse had to separate them.

Another 'persecutor', in Covenanting eyes, was Captain Peter Inglis of the dragoons, formerly under Claverhouse's command, who ordered an old man of seventy, Thomas Ritchart of Muirkirk, to be shot at the gallows for harbouring his son, who was on the fugitive roll. But Ritchart was at least given a trial before his death. (Inglis was demoted shortly afterwards when he was judged to have been lax in guarding prisoners in Newmilns Tower. A gang of sixty men broke open the Tower with sledgehammers and rescued the prisoners there, losing only one man, John Law, who was shot as they made their escape.)

The 'killing time' was certainly a period of sustained brutality. But it is important to examine those episodes which, over the years, have become its icons, particularly since the man whose name was and is most closely identified with them, was John Graham of Claverhouse.

By May 1685, Claverhouse was back in the saddle, and in charge of his troops again in Ayrshire. Within days of his return he was involved in one of the most controversial incidents of his military career, and the one which, more than any other, gained him his reputation as 'bluidy Clavers'. The case of John Brown, 'the Christian carrier', has become a much-elaborated legend, but, as with so many of its type, the details which appear most damning are those which were only recounted later as the story was embellished.

On 1 May, Claverhouse and a troop of dragoons rode into the village of Priesthill in Muirkirk parish and questioned a man called John Brown, described by the church historian Robert Wodrow as a man 'of shining piety' who spent much time instructing the youth of the village in religious matters, and was 'no way obnoxious to the government'. He was, however, in Government terms, a nonconformist. He was said to have been visited the previous night by his friend, the preacher Alexander Peden, who called Brown 'a clear shining light, the greatest Christian that ever I conversed with'. Peden left him next day, on that 'fearful morning, a dark misty morning', after predicting that something dreadful would happen.

Claverhouse, according to the story, did not ask Brown to take the oath, but told him instead to say his prayers, which he did 'in a peculiar judicious style, he having great measures of the gift', according to Wodrow. Claverhouse then instructed his soldiers to shoot him. When they refused to do so, he 'was forced to turn executioner himself, and in a fret shot him with his own hand before his own door, his wife with a young infant standing by'. Brown's final prayer was said to have made such an impression on Claverhouse that he could never thereafter forget it.

As Brown lay dead on the ground, Claverhouse is said to have turned to his widow and asked her:

'What thinkest thou of thy husband now, woman?'

'As much now as ever', she replied.

'It were but justice to lay thee beside him.'

'If ye were permitted, I doubt not that your cruelty would go that length; but how will ye make answer for this morning's work?'

To which, according to the story, Claverhouse answered:

'To men I can be answerable, and as for God, I'll take him into mine own hand.'

Later versions had Claverhouse interrupting Brown's prayers, and his widow scooping up the dead man's brains, covering him with his plaid, and weeping over him as the soldiers rode away. The latter details are repeated in at least two other Covenanter stories.

These accounts, dramatic as they are, were compiled at least thirty years after the event. The only convincing version is a contemporary one, and it comes from a first-hand witness, Claverhouse himself. He was, of course, a biased source, but, as with all his reports, the one that he sent to Queensberry on 3 May 1685, two days after the event, was a model of spare and precise detail. He had no reason to defend his actions, and there can be little doubt that it is accurate so far as it goes:

On Friday last [1 May], amongst the hills betwixt Douglas and the Plellands, we pursued two fellows a great way through the mosses, and in end seized them. They had no arms about them and denied they had any, but being asked if they would take the abjuration, the eldest of the two, called John Brown, refused it, nor would he swear not to rise in arms against the King, but said he knew no King; upon which, and there being found bullet and match in his house and treasonable papers, I caused shoot him dead, which he suffered very unconcernedly.

The other man, John Brown's nephew, whom Claverhouse called 'John Brownen', offered to take the oath but refused to swear that he had not taken part in the release of the prisoners at Newmilns. 'So I did not know what to do with him', continued Claverhouse:

> I was convinced he was guilty, but saw not how to proceed against him; wherefore after he had said his prayers and carbines presented to shoot him, I offered to him that if he would make an ingenious confession and make a discovery that might be of any importance for the King's service, I should delay putting him to death, and plead for him; upon which he confessed that he was at that attack of Newmilns, and that he had come straight to this house of his uncle's on Sunday morning.

Meanwhile, Claverhouse's soldiers had found an underground shelter with swords and pistols in it, which Brownen said belonged to his uncle, who had been in hiding since Bothwell Brig. He gave convincing detail about the Newmilns incident, and about two recent conventicles, and then offered Claverhouse the names of his uncle's confederates. He confessed that he had a halbert in his possession but said it had been given to him by a man who had already been taken prisoner. Having heard his story, Claverhouse spared his life. He concluded his report:

> He has been but a month or two with his halbert; and if your Grace thinks he deserves no mercy, justice will pass on him, for I, having no commission of justiciary myself, have delivered him up to the Lieutenant-General [Drummond] to be disposed of as he pleases.

As so often with Claverhouse's letters, there is a simplicity about the narrative that makes it hard to doubt. He is uncomplicated about the shooting, which he might have been expected to excuse. And he is honest about his change of heart in offering a man his life. He might, after all, with doubts still hanging around his Whig marriage, have wanted to prove his credentials by carrying out a summary execution.

As to his decision to execute Brown but spare his nephew, the procedure seems to have been straightforward. If Brown did refuse the oath (and even the inscription on his gravestone at Priesthill says he was murdered because he 'durst not own the authority of the then Tyrant [the King]'), Claverhouse had the power under the resolution of the Privy Council dated 22 November 1684 legally to execute him, provided two witnesses were present. On the other hand, since the nephew had agreed to testify, Claverhouse no longer had jurisdiction to decide his eventual fate. In both cases he obeyed the rules.

Furthermore, Brown, far from being innocent, turned out to be amongst the wanted men listed in the royal proclamation of May 1684, and, two months before his death, he was named as one of those excluded from the indemnity ('John Brown, an old man, in the fugitive roll, refuses the allegiance, and so ought not to have the benefit of the indemnity').

Nevertheless, this was the first man that Claverhouse had executed without trial, and, though he obeyed the rules to the letter at a time of singular repression, it is perhaps not surprising that that action should have been used thereafter to blacken his reputation. Furthermore, although he had offered the nephew Brownen a reprieve, in return for information, he seems to have done nothing, thereafter, to see that he was spared.

Five days later, Brownen (who was sometimes referred to as 'Browning' or 'Binning') was brought before Drummond's commission at Mauchline, and convicted along with four others. They were all sentenced to hang at the town-end and to be buried in a common grave – there was no mention of the deal that Claverhouse had made.

These executions, too, became a famous tale of brutality. Daniel Defoe, whose history of these times is a tangle of wild exaggerations, has Claverhouse carrying out the executions. Another version, by the Covenanter Alexander Shields, says that Claverhouse, James Douglas, and the Earl of Dumbarton disposed of the five men 'without legal trial or sentence', giving rise to the famous epitaph at Mauchline:

> Bloody Dumbarton, Douglas and Dundee,
> Moved by the Devil and the Laird of Lee,
> Dragg'd these five men to Death with gun and sword,
> Not suffering them to Pray, nor Read God's Word;
> Owning the Work of God was all their Crime.
> The Eighty-Five was a Saint Killing Time.

But Claverhouse had nothing to do with their execution. Two at least of the victims were put on trial by Drummond, and there is no reason to believe the others were not as well – the 'Lee' referred to was Cromwell Lockhart of Lee, one of Douglas's Sheriff-Deputes who would have sat on the case. But neither Dumbarton nor Claverhouse was there – Dumbarton because he was in London at the time, Claverhouse because he no longer had any jurisdiction. His only connection was that he handed over John Brownen for trial.

The harshness of the Government's measures reflected another fear. Rumours abounded that the exiled Earl of Argyll was planning an invasion along with the Duke of Monmouth. In anticipation of Argyll's arrival, Highland troops were rallied by the Council, and new dispositions made in the military hierarchy.

Old General Dalyell, who would have been in command, was finally nearing the end of his life. He was to die aged seventy, in August that year, while taking his supper, wine-glass in hand, and admiring the painted ceiling of his mansion in Black Jack's Close in Edinburgh. 'He never was merrier than just when the fit seized him', wrote Lord Perth to Queensberry. He was buried with full military honours.

For the time being, the Earl of Dumbarton was made Commander-in-Chief of the armed forces, to co-ordinate defences against Argyll's invasion. He was a soldier of immense experience, having been, as Lord George Douglas, a page of honour to Louis XIV, and then having risen to Major-General in the French army. A Roman Catholic, he was denied command until James VII came to the throne. (His regiment, later the Royal Scots, still marches to the tune of Dumbarton's Drums.) James decided that both Claverhouse and Douglas should be promoted to the rank of brigadier, but he told Moray that he wanted Queensberry to withold their commissions, 'to be made use of in case of any rebellion, but not otherwise'.

Claverhouse's regiment now consisted of six troops, captained by the Earl of Drumlanrig; Lord Ross, whose father had been in Glasgow at the time of Drumclog; Lord William Douglas, Drumlanrig's younger brother; the now ageing Earl of Airlie; and Colin Lindsay, third Earl of Balcarres, probably Claverhouse's closest friend. He was well-loved for his genial manner and generous nature, and married, as his second wife, Claverhouse's first cousin, Lady Jean Carnegie. Claverhouse himself still captained his own troop, and had Bruce of Earlshall as his captain-lieutenant, while his brother David remained a cornet.

Claverhouse's duties were to patrol the Ayrshire countryside which by now he knew so well, and report any signs of trouble. It was here that he encountered, probably for the first time in Scotland, Highland soldiers, for they had been drafted into his area as traditional opponents of Argyll, to help resist the invasion.

On 10 May he found himself in dispute with a Highland officer over yet another execution. Andrew Hislop was a young man from Gillesby in Annandale who lived with his widowed mother. They had, for some time, been sheltering a wounded rebel, and, when he died, they buried him in a field at night for fear they would be accused of 'resetting', that is, harbouring a fugitive. Secrets of that kind were hard to keep in Annandale, and word of the night-time burial reached the local steward-depute, Sir James Johnstone of Westerhall. He ordered the corpse to be exhumed, and, as a punishment, destroyed the widow's house. Andrew, her son, was found wandering in the fields by Claverhouse and his troops, and was brought before Johnstone. Whether Johnstone had the right to try him was doubtful. Nevertheless he ordered Hislop's execution.

Claverhouse was clearly unhappy with the decision, and asked the commander of a Highland infantry company, which was in the same place at the time, to carry out the order, which he refused to do, and 'swore he would fight Claverhouse and his dragoons before he did it.' Claverhouse then ordered his troops to shoot Hislop, after telling Johnstone that the responsibility was his. Hislop died with a bible in his hand, refusing to pull his bonnet over his eyes.

Claverhouse's conduct here was neither honourable nor militarily sound. The nature of Hislop's crime was doubtful. If he had simply failed to swear the oath, Claverhouse was likely to have dealt with the case as summarily, as he had that of John Brown. But if he was accused of harbouring a fugitive, then execution was not the automatic sentence. Claverhouse's uneasiness suggests either that he was not convinced of Johnstone's jurisdiction, or that he was doubtful about the sentence. In fact, under a Commission granted to Colonel Douglas on 27 March, Johnstone had been given justiciary powers, but if Claverhouse did have any doubts, his clear duty was to refer Hislop to Lieutenant-General Drummond, who held the overall commission in the west. By carrying out Johnstone's request, while attempting to shift responsibility, Claverhouse fell below his own high standards.

There was another execution at this time. A tombstone in the churchyard of Colmonell in Carrick, reads:

> I Matthew McIlwraith in this parish of Colmonell
> By bloody Claverhouse I fell
> Who did command that I should die
> For owning Covenanted presbytery.
> My Blood a Witness still doth stand
> 'Gainst all defections in this land.

There are no records of the circumstances of Matthew Meiklewraith's death beyond the fact that it took place. However, his name is listed as that of a fugitive on the vast roll of wanted men published in May 1684, and the inscription on his tombstone suggests that he may have testified before Claverhouse and been found wanting. In that case, and if he refused to swear the Oath of Abjuration, he was probably executed in the same way as John Brown. Without further evidence, however, the case is unproven.

On the same day that Claverhouse was dealing with Andrew Hislop in Eskdalemuir, the most notorious of all the Covenanter executions took place. Even the most zealous of Presbyterian historians does not implicate Claverhouse in the case of the Wigtown martyrs, but perhaps because he was so closely associated with the persecutions of the time, or because his brother David's name was involved, the crime has sometimes been laid at his door.

Margaret M'Lauchlan and Margaret Wilson, aged sixty-three and eighteen respectively, were arrested and imprisoned in Wigtown early in 1685, allegedly for failing to drink the King's health, perhaps for resetting, or attending conventicles. They were tried on 13 April by Sir Robert Grierson of Lag, sitting with Captain-Lieutenant Thomas Windram, Captain John Strachan, and Mr David Graham, Sheriff of Galloway. It has always been assumed that this David Graham was Claverhouse's brother, the cornet. This is an error. All the other names are listed by their correct military and civilian ranks in the Commission of 27 March 1685, by which Colonel James Douglas was given justiciary powers in the area. On the roll of those serving under him, there is a 'Mr David Graham'. No other soldier is listed other than with his correct rank. Clearly this is a different David Graham. Furthermore, though Cornet Graham had, during his brother's period of office, acted as a Sheriff, that office lapsed at the time of Charles II's death and was not renewed. So the Graham connection with the Wigtown deaths is severed.

The two women were found guilty and condemned to death by drowning. This fate, an ancient Scottish punishment for treason, was prescribed under a clause agreed by the Privy Council (with Claverhouse present) on 13 January 1685, which instructed the commissioners that 'at this time you are not to examine any women but such as has been active in these courses in a signal manner, and these are to be drowned.'

The verdict in Wigtown was reported to the Privy Council, which bade the joint Secretaries of State ask for a royal pardon, and commanded the magistrates of Edinburgh not to proceed with the execution until word came back from the King. There are, however, no records of a response from London, and no explanation of why the magistrates in Edinburgh rather than Wigtown should have been involved.

Whether it was an error in documentation, or a lack of urgency is not known. But no word of the Privy Council's stay of execution reached Wigtown, and, on 11 May, the two women were tied to stakes in the Solway Firth as the tide came in. The older woman, Margaret M'Lauchlan, was said to have been tied nearest to the incoming sea, and to have been 'held down within the water by one of the town officers by his halbert at her throat', in order to persuade the younger one, Margaret Wilson, at least, to take the oath and save herself. Neither, however, would give in, and both drowned, testifying to their faith. Margaret Wilson sang part of the 25th psalm, with the words 'My sins and faults of youth do thou O Lord, forget', and one of the officers ran forward into the water to implore her to take the oath. 'I am one of Christ's children, let me go' she said, as the waters closed over her.

The circumstances of the Wigtown drownings have been examined and re-examined over the years, but we remain tantalizingly short of hard evidence. Much of the finer detail was published long after the event, and some historians have suggested that the executions were never actually carried out. But the original accounts were written in the lifetime of many who must have known the facts, and there is no reason to doubt that the executions took place.

Women suffered greatly during the repression, whether through being thrown out of their houses because their husbands were fugitives, or because they refused to attend the services of indulged ministers. There were few executions – the hanging of Isobel Alison and Marion Harvey in January 1681, after having been cross-examined by Mackenzie and threatened with torture by Dalyell, was an exception –, but there were many cases of gross ill-treatment. Oddly enough, however, though soldiers were frequently quartered on unwilling households, there are few documented cases of abuse or rape. Military discipline – especially in Claverhouse's regiment – was extremely strict.

On 20 May 1685, the Earl of Argyll finally landed, at Campbeltown on the Argyll coast, vowing to overthrow 'James, Duke of York, a notorious apostate and bigot Papist'. With him were Sir John Cochrane, Claverhouse's uncle by marriage, and Balfour of Kinloch, one of Sharp's murderers. Monmouth however, contrary to rumour, was not with him.

The invasion prompted Queensberry finally to confirm James's commissions to Claverhouse and Douglas, and they were promoted to the rank of brigadier on 23 May, the document being signed, ironically, by Claverhouse's 'affectionate friends' Queensberry, Perth, Dumbarton, and Tarbat, men who, between them, had almost brought about his ruin.

Claverhouse's promotion had not been granted without some heart-searching. Melfort, it emerged, had been ordered to make out a commission for Claverhouse as Brigadier of Horse, and Douglas as Brigadier of Foot. Moray, when he discovered, was appalled. He immediately pointed out to Queensberry that this would make Claverhouse senior to Douglas. James was not particularly concerned, but the two Secretaries, like characters out of Gilbert and Sullivan, waxed 'very hot on the matter', with Melfort, who was growing tired of Queensberry's supremacy, saying there was no reason why Douglas should be senior except that he was Queensberry's brother, and Moray arguing that there was every reason why Douglas should be senior *because* he was Queensberry's brother. After an angry discussion, Moray 'flung from him and went straight to the King and represented the case'. Melfort followed, and the King was forced to listen to his two senior Scottish advisers quarrelling in front of him. Sensibly, he took the diplomatic course and pre-dated Douglas's commission by two days, which gave him the seniority but without his having to confront the issue. 'Now, I beseech your Grace, say nothing of this', wrote Moray to Queensberry.

Argyll never attracted enough followers to his banner, though there can rarely have been a more widely advertised invasion. Distrust of the man himself was too widespread among potential supporters, and the Presbyterian movement in the west was deeply divided. His little force of 800 men dwindled as he crossed the Clyde, and he himself was captured near Paisley by a weaver named Semple who gave him 'a great skelp on the head' with a rusty sword. 'Ah, unfortunate Argyll', said the Earl as he sank to the ground.

Taken into Edinburgh at night, he was sent to the scaffold on 30 June, and beheaded at the Cross by 'The Maiden', the Scots guillotine, the sight of which is said to have so unmanned him that he had to be blindfolded. He managed, however, to say as he knelt that 'It was the sweetest Maiden ever he kissed, it being a mean to finish his sin and misery, and his inlet to glory, for which he longed.'

Amongst those of Argyll's confederates who were also captured was

Sir John Cochrane, with his son William. Both were taken, bound and bareheaded, by the hangman into the Tolbooth on 3 July. But the influence of Dundonald, and a well-placed bribe, saved them from execution. In England, Monmouth's invasion was no more successful. His troops were defeated at Sedgemoor on 6 July, and Judge Jeffreys, with his 'Bloody Assizes', completed the cleansing work.

Claverhouse missed all of the action because his task was to patrol the Borders, with his headquarters at Selkirk. He continued to question suspects – and, on occasion, send them for trial – once threatening a man with death for carrying a powder-horn, once ordering his men to fire their carbines in order to elicit answers from frightened villagers. Interrogation, as always in hostile country, was harsh, sometimes brutal.

In June he went first to Nithsdale, and then to Sanquhar, crossing Queensberry's own territory at Drumlanrig, still one of the most disaffected parts of the country. 'I may safely say', he wrote to Queensberry, 'that as I shall answer to God, if they had been living on my ground, I could not have forebore drawing my sword and knocking them down.'

The implied criticism cannot have improved the temper of Queensberry, who had been complaining yet again about Claverhouse's arrogance, this time to Dumbarton. One can occasionally understand Queensberry's irritation. Claverhouse could be a prig, and his conviction that he knew best in military matters was never less than total. On 16 June, he was ticking-off the Earl of Annandale for suggesting that he should hold back his troops from a proposed march to Annan. 'I am unwilling to shock anybody that serves the King in such a time', wrote Claverhouse, 'though I think it not just that my Lord, or any other, should think to exclude the rest of the forces from doing their duty.'

A month later, on 16 July, he resumed his seat on the Privy Council, then travelled north to Dudhope, missing by a week the admittance to the Council of Hugh Mackay of Scourie, who had returned from Holland with the Anglo-Scots Brigade to help repel Monmouth's invasion. Both men, who would later oppose each other in battle, were, for the time being, united in helping to stem the first crisis in James's reign.

With the west now under firm control, Claverhouse was finally allowed to travel south to London, to be greeted warmly by James. Queensberry was now the man out of favour, and he was ordered to repay to Claverhouse the £596 sterling he had extracted from him for the Galloway fines. 'What grates his soul the most', wrote Perth, 'is that Claverhouse has got back the money he caused him pay when in the height of his pique.'

Then, on 21 December 1685, came the most signal honour yet of Claverhouse's military career. His regiment was henceforth to be called 'His Majesty's Own Regiment of Horse', and was to have the rank and precedence that accorded with that title. The trumpeters of the troops, and the kettle drums of the regiment were to have their own livery, and Claverhouse clothed his troopers in red, laced and faced with yellow, the colours of the royal Stuarts. His rehabilitation was complete, and his reputation once again established.

As to his reputation as a brutal persecutor, that has been harder to shake off. The facts, however, do not justify it. There are only two cases in which he ordered summary executions – those of John Brown and Matthew Meiklewraith (the latter a doubtful one). In both of these, there was strict observance of Government instructions: the sentence was carried out by his own troops after he had correctly questioned the subjects and established their refusal to take the oath of abjuration. There was one case, that of Andrew Hislop, where he carried out an execution at the request of a civilian authority, though he appears to have questioned the authority. Here he certainly behaved less than honourably.

There remains the less-provable charge of vindictiveness in the execution of his orders. Claverhouse did, of course, have a quick temper, and he probably extracted information roughly, in the manner of impatient soldiers in the field who need it fast. He was, however, strict in observing the rules, and he would never have allowed undisciplined brutality in his regiment. No evidence of torture attaches to his name – which was not the case with Dalyell, for instance – but there is, perhaps, a hint that, in pursuit of what he called 'the plague of Presbytery', he acquired something of the zeal of those he was harrying. The eagerness with which he wrote of the witch hunts of the circuit court, his lack of concern at executions, and the occasional violence of his language in describing the rebel cause are suggestive of a man whose perception of duty could on occasion blinker him to the wider considerations of morality.

That he could, however, be humane is demonstrated by the concern he showed for sick prisoners in his charge, and he could apply himself to obtaining justice for those he considered wrongly punished (as with the malefactors of Dundee whom he rescued from hanging).

As to whether he was entitled to persecute men for their religious beliefs, it is worth quoting Sir George Mackenzie, who said that religion was no excuse for anyone 'to rise in arms, or to murder.' Mackenzie saw the role of the military as suppressing a rebellion, not a religion: 'The bulk of all the processes in King Charles II's and King James VII's reign', wrote the Lord Advocate, 'were against such as rose in actual rebellion.'

The context of the times must also be considered. There is no question but that the suppression of Presbyterian dissent in the western shires of Scotland inflicted enormous suffering on the population. But the statistics should be noted. In terms of human life, the final toll exacted through summary executions, or for attempting to resist arrest or escape capture, documented in written records in Scotland during the period of James's reign was seventy-eight. To that figure should be added the number of those executed after full judicial proceedings, which brings the total almost exactly to a hundred. Mackenzie estimated that the final figure, when those who were killed outside the judicial process were added, came to 200, 'and above 150 of these might have saved their lives by saying "God Bless the King"'. These figures do not, of course, include those who died in prison, who were drowned while being transported, or who perished in the harsh conditions of the colonies. He said that this should be set against a total of some 20,000 who were guilty of public rebellion.

These statistics should perhaps be compared to those of Judge Jeffreys and his Bloody Assizes, which were contemporary in England, under which about 150 suffered death and 800 were transported to the West Indies. Scotland did not have a monopoly of violent persecution.

CHAPTER TWELVE
Exit the King

*'There is but a small distance between the prisons and the
graves of Kings'*

James VII

In an age of intolerance, King James VII was a firm believer in
toleration. To allow the free practice of religion was, for him, not just a
matter of political convenience, nor a cynical device for permitting a
return to Roman Catholicism. It was central to his view of kingship.

Long before he came to the throne, he gave his blessing to a
declaration on behalf of the emerging colony of New York. It said:

> No person or persons which profess faith in God by Jesus Christ shall,
> at any time, be in any ways molested, punished, disquieted, or called in
> question for any difference of opinion on matters of religious concern-
> ment, who do not actually disturb the civil peace of the Province.

That statement has been called by one historian the 'first legal existence
of the American spirit of religious liberty which is enshrined in the
Constitution of the United States', and it remained a cherished ideal for
James long after he had gone into sad and bewildered exile at St
Germain-en-Laye.

He wrote once: '. . . that it was always my principle that conscience
ought not to be forced; and that all men ought to have liberty of their
conscience.' This doctrine extended to all denominations – Quakers,
Jews, Ana-Baptists, Anti-Sabbatarians, Independents. But it also, of
course, extended to Roman Catholics.

James seems never fully to have comprehended the depth of feeling
still aroused by any prospect of a return to popery, nor the ingrained
suspicion that at heart it was all he cared about. Perhaps, more import-

antly, he never understood how much it was feared by strong and vested interests. As Lord Balcarres, Claverhouse's friend, later explained to James in the memoirs he addressed to the King:

> The terror of bringing back a party who had ever lain at catch for the bringing down of the Monarchy, and had cost your predecessors so much time, blood, and treasure to humble, made even your firmest and faithfullest servants comply with your demands, but with an unwilling mind.

Lord Fountainhall put it more bluntly: 'A Papist qua Papist, cannot be a faithful subject.'

Those powerful figures, both in England and in Scotland, who watched James's moves towards toleration with suspicion and hostility ignored its general application, and saw only the steady advances made by those of the Roman Catholic faith. It was the Roman Catholics, of course, who had most ground to make up.

James's early moves towards a relief of the penal sanctions which existed against Roman Catholics were modest, and won approval from the bishops. But when, in 1687, frustrated by the lack of progress made by those who shared his faith, he introduced his first Declaration of Indulgence, he was unprepared for the fury it aroused. It was not just the extreme Presbyterians who condemned it, as an 'anti-Christian, intoxicating Toleration' which was 'brewed in Hell'. That model of reason and good sense Sir George Mackenzie said that to ease restrictions on those who dissented with the state on religious grounds would end in anarchy. His opposition led to his resignation.

The Indulgence was, indeed, sweeping. It permitted worship for all faiths, in houses or in chapels, thus making field conventicles irrelevant; bishops and clergy were given the right to the titles of their own churches and property; no one was to be debarred from public office because of his religious beliefs.

Scotland's ruling hierarchy had, by that time, shifted significantly, in tune with the King's new policies. Queensberry had stepped down from the office of High Treasurer. He had returned disillusioned from his visit to London at the end of 1685, and in February 1686 received a letter of dismissal from James, who announced that he intended to put the Treasury into Commission and to give the Duke of Gordon, a Roman Catholic, command of the Castle of Edinburgh, 'to make that town have more regard for my commands, and civiler to the Catholics by seeing it in the hands of one of that persuasion.'

Mackenzie took his dismissal from the post of King's Advocate, and his replacement by the egregious Sir John Dalrymple, philosophically – he was observed by Fountainhall 'putting on a gown as an ordinary advocate and appearing at cases at the Bar with his hat off.' But some of the changes amongst judges caused considerable unease, particularly when Balcarres observed one of them at the head of an anti-Catholic mob in Edinburgh 'with a halbert in his hand, and as drunk as ale and brandy could make him.'

Others thrived. Moray was made Commissioner to the Parliament after pretending, up to the last minute, to back Queensberry for the post; and Melfort continued as Secretary of State. The Duke of Hamilton, whose qualities of statesmanship were not outstanding, became a Lord of Treasury, and the Earl of Perth, who 'made a sudden clutch at the scarlet skirt' and became a convert to Roman Catholicism, continued as Chancellor. Perth did not help the King's cause in Scotland by celebrating mass openly at his house in Edinburgh, an action which caused riots in the streets and led a Protestant baker's boy to dowse Lady Perth with water from the town's gutters as she returned one day from worship.

There were promotions within the King's forces too. James Douglas, Queensberry's brother, who may not have been quite as bad a soldier as Claverhouse thought, was made Lieutenant-General and Commander-in-Chief, and Claverhouse himself was promoted to the rank of Major-General, with a pension of £200 sterling a year 'during pleasure'.

With the return of relative peace in the west of Scotland, Claverhouse's military duties were fewer, and he was able to spend more time on his estates at Dudhope. There, as the records of the town of Dundee show, he and his relatives and retainers were sufficiently numerous to occupy the first three rows in the church, and there, as Constable and Chief Magistrate, he took his seat regularly on the bench, and supervised such mundane but occasionally rewarding activities as exacting local tolls and taxes on behalf of the town. His income from the army was supplemented by a proportion of these, and, since Dundee was a wealthy port, his income for this source was not inconsiderable. On 12 February 1687, he is recorded as receiving 2,000 merks Scots, from taxes on 'Ale, beer, French and Spanish Wines'. A law suit with his relative Fotheringham of Powrie details a dispute over tolls from local fishermen.

He paid one visit to court towards the end of 1687, in the company of his wife and Lord Balcarres. They spent several months in England, and paid a visit to Bath, where they took the waters, before going to

London. There Claverhouse had his portrait painted by 'the best that was in England', according to Jean's description of the picture by Sir Godfrey Kneller. They returned to Scotland early in the new year of 1688 in time to witness the trial of James Renwick, the last of the famous Covenanting preachers, and focus of the whole Cameronian movement.

Renwick had been captured finally in Edinburgh on 1 February 1688, surprised in a friend's house on Castle Hill, and held after a chase along the Cowgate. He was placed on trial, with Livingstone, Balcarres, Tarbat, and Claverhouse amongst the witnesses for the prosecution. Although the sentence of death was inevitable, he was allowed a full hearing in court, and his execution was postponed until 17 February to allow him time for a possible recantation. There was none, however, and Renwick was hanged, at the age of twenty-six, in the Grassmarket, with the drums rolling to drown his final speech.

Presbyterian propaganda still made the authorities nervous. Claverhouse, who became Provost of Dundee in March 1688, found himself dealing with various cases of preachers who sought to go beyond the terms of James's Indulgences, and hold services which, in the King's words, threatened 'to alienate the hearts of our people from us or our government.' They were minor cases, however, and Claverhouse seems to have dealt with them fairly.

The Indulgences were by now alienating opinion at almost every level. But to every expression of opposition, James responded with more measures, more pressure for change, more hostility to his critics. He was, as one historian observed, like 'a man that rode post over hedges and ditches, rocks and precipices, so that in a very little time he must either break his neck or come to his journey's end.'

The birth of a royal son and heir on 10 June 1688, an event the King recorded with great joy and pride, brought that end much nearer. There was now a recognized 'Revolution' party in England, whose immediate response to the birth of a Roman Catholic heir to the throne was to suggest that the child was a changeling – a false rumour, but one that acquired immediate currency. William of Orange, who had first sent congratulations from Holland, soon joined the ranks of the sceptics. For him the birth, if genuine, meant that his wife was no longer heir to the English throne.

William's claim to the throne had been reinforced in 1677, the year he married James's daughter, Mary. He had always maintained close links with leading Protestant families in England, and had encouraged influential exiles from Scotland, like Sir James Dalrymple, his son Sir

John Dalrymple, and Argyll, to maintain an opposition to James, while he ostensibly remained on good terms with him. Amongst his senior officers was Hugh Mackay of Scourie, once Claverhouse's comrade in arms but now a general who owed his commission to King James.

Mackay gave him crucial assistance when an invasion was being planned by persuading the six regiments of the Anglo-Scots Brigade to stay in Holland. Their return to England was demanded of William by his uncle, and as British subjects they were obliged by treaty to obey. Mackay, however, advanced compelling reasons why they should not. Consequently only 50 officers out of 240 sailed for home in a yacht sent for them by James. The rest remained in the Low Countries, a vital component of William's army when he launched his invasion in November.

James had been told of William's preparations, but was convinced that his son-in-law was anticipating war with France. It was actually King Louis who finally broke the news to him, in mid-September, that William's hostility was directed against himself.

The word that an invasion was planned came as an equal surprise in Scotland. The Secret Committee heard it from an emissary sent by James himself, and ordered the army on to immediate stand-by, summoning Claverhouse from Dudhope to help stem yet another attempt to claim James's throne. Beacons were prepared for lighting as soon as any ships were seen off the coast of Scotland.

But it was only at the eleventh hour that James set about building up his own forces. He calculated that he could raise an army, with support from Scotland and Ireland, of around 40,000 men. But he did not count on the defections. Some amongst the 'persons of quality' to whom he turned for troops raised the men requested by the King, and then offered their services to William instead. Others pretended allegiance to James, but secretly sent messages of support to Holland. In Scotland, the divisions amongst James's ministers quickly became apparent.

The King relied on his Secretary of State, Lord Melfort, to give him information on the best course of action to be taken in Scotland, and to dispose of his forces there. Rarely can a monarch have been worse advised. On 24 September a royal letter was dispatched, on Melfort's instructions, ordering the army to prepare 'for such further orders as we shall think fit to send'. This was followed by a second letter, signed by Melfort, 'on the back of a plate', according to Balcarres, ordering the entire force, except for the garrisons of Edinburgh, Stirling, and Dumbarton castles, to march to Carlisle and then to Chester, where they would come under the command of the King's General, Lord Feversham.

Balcarres was not alone in thinking the advice insane. Instead of holding the army at the border or in the north of England, to secure it, Scotland was being left virtually undefended at a time when the country was deeply split. He blamed Melfort entirely, as he told James:

> [Melfort] wrote down an Order, not subscribed by your Majesty, but only in your Majesty's name, ordering that the army should immediately march, and that if any of your servants were afraid to stay behind, they might go along with the army .... With a sorrowful heart, your Majesty's orders were obeyed, for the consequences were too evident.

The army, under the command of Lieutenant-General Douglas, was just under 3,000 strong – 1,995 of foot, 841 of cavalry. The infantry was made up of two regiments later to become famous: Douglas's foot guards, which became the Scots Guards; and Colonel Thomas Buchan's regiment, later the Royal Scots Fusiliers. The cavalry included Lord Livingstone's troop of Life Guards, Claverhouse's regiment, which was 357 strong, and the Earl of Dunmore's Dragoons, which had once been Dalyell's Scots Greys.

In foul weather, short of ammunition, and without sufficient pack-horses for all his baggage, Douglas set off in the first week of October, heading through Moffat in the direction of Preston. Claverhouse went on ahead, leaving Douglas to wait for a party of Highlanders who were due to join him. 'We drink your health every day', wrote Douglas disconsolately to Queensberry, 'either in wine or brandy, and eats now and then a bit of cold meat on the march.' But, by the end of October, cavalry and foot were together again, and the army, complete with ammunition and baggage, had reached London. The men were quartered around the capital, with Claverhouse's troops installed in barracks at Westminster and Tower Hamlets.

On 5 November 1688, helped by 'a fair Protestant wind', the Prince of Orange's fleet landed at Torbay, accompanied by General Hugh Mackay and the Anglo-Scots Brigade. William assembled his forces and marched them to Exeter, where he waited. It was an exotic army: it included '200 negroes wearing embroidered caps with white furs and plumes of feathers' as well as 200 Finlanders in bearskin and black armour, some Danes, and several regiments of French Huguenots, both horse and foot.

Despite the mounting opposition in England to the King, and despite William's encouraging soundings amongst his Whig supporters, there was no guarantee that he would prevail. His own hesitancy suggested uncertainty, and if James had launched an immediate counter-offensive, he could well have thrown William's army back into the sea. Instead, he ordered his forces under the Earl of Feversham to take up quarters in Salisbury, where they would be joined by the Scottish regiments, and waited.

Claverhouse was now once again at court, at the King's hour of crisis, and James took the opportunity to present him with an honour which reflected the regard he had always had for his loyalty and good service. On 12 November 1688, Claverhouse was raised to the Scottish peerage and given the title Viscount Dundee and Lord Graham of Claverhouse. The warrant stated that his elevation was in recognition of:

> ... the many good and eminent services rendered both to his Majesty and his dearest Royal brother King Charles the Second (of ever blessed memory) by his right trusty and wellbeloved Councillor Major General John Graham of Claverhouse in the several offices and stations of public trust as well civil and military in which he has been employed for many years past; together with his constant loyalty and firm adherence (on all occasions) to the true interests of the Crown.

Both the timing of the honour and the decision itself were a mark of James's affection and regard. The new Viscount Dundee was not at this point commander of the Scottish army, but James was strongly aware of the need for reliable supporters, and in this at least his judgment was sound. General Douglas was shortly to defect. Dundee was a reliable choice.

On 17 November, James left London to join his troops under Feversham at Salisbury. What he found there was a disintegrating army, and open intrigue amongst his officers. Defections to the enemy camp were now a daily occurrence, the most notable being John Churchill and the Duke of Grafton, a bastard son of Charles II. Churchill's departure shocked even General Schomberg, William's commander, who later described Churchill as 'the only Major-General ever to have deserted his own colours'. One observer, George Clark, saw the King at Andover:

> I can never forget the confusion the court was in; the Lord Churchill had gone over to the Prince of Orange from Salisbury and the Duke of Grafton this morning.... Everybody in this hurly-burly was thinking of himself and nobody minded the King who came up to Dr Radcliffe and asked him what was good for the bleeding of his nose.

William was sufficiently encouraged to march out from Exeter. His advance guard was at Wincanton when James, uncertain and confused, withdrew to Reading. Next day, the King, 'in perfect health', according to the *London Gazette*, was back in Whitehall.

In fact, James may not have been in perfect health. Throughout this extraordinary period, when his throne hung in the balance, he seems to have acted like a man in a trance – or in a state of depression. Accounts from those who saw much of him in those last days, like Lord Ailesbury, picture him as apathetic, unwilling to listen to any advice that urged action, and incapable of concentrating on anything other than leaving the scene of such chaos and betrayal. This was behaviour quite out of character for a man who had always been one for action, whose own courage was not in doubt, and who had never shrunk from hard decisions. The inspiration that he had once given to the officers and men whose respect he had earned all those years ago when he commanded the navy, and which had prompted Turenne to say that if he were to conquer the world he would choose the Duke of York to command his army, seemed to have deserted him.

Balcarres's daughter said later that the King had suffered a burst blood vessel in his head which 'was the consequence of these agitations and sorrows', but he may simply have been weighed down by the defections of his friends and family. James was in many ways an ingenuous man, who took a simplistic view of political problems – and of politicians. He believed implicitly in those who gave him loyalty, and was deeply hurt when they changed allegiances. When he heard that his daughter Princess Anne and her husband, the Prince of Denmark, had gone to join the invader, he burst into tears, weeping: 'God help me, my own children have forsaken me.' And there is no doubt that he had been stunned by William's decision to invade. His cousin, Princess Sophia, said later:

> His Majesty wrote to me that it was a long time before he could bring himself to believe that his son-in-law and nephew intended to invade his country, and that it was for that reason he thought of taking defensive action when it was too late.

His visit to Salisbury must have confirmed him in the view that all was lost. The betrayals and the defections along the way amongst his advisers and his officers may well have contributed to his gloom. He returned to London a man deprived of energy and incapable of any decision other than to leave the country. For those who stuck with him, like the new Viscount Dundee, it was hard to believe that this was the King they had so admired.

Claverhouse, who from now on will be referred to, as all his contemporaries did, as 'Dundee', was amongst those who sought to persuade James not to abandon his throne. He proposed three choices for the King: to give battle, to parley with William, or 'to make his way into Scotland, upon the coldness he observed in the English army and nations.' But James was not listening. On 8 December, Feversham withdrew from Reading to Twyford, and two days later James sent him the astounding order to disband the army since he, the King, could not expect his friends to expose themselves by resisting a foreign army and 'a poisoned nation'. Feversham obeyed next day. The Queen and the young prince had already been sent to France for safety, and that morning James crossed the Thames to Vauxhall on his way to the coast, throwing the great seal of England into the river as he went.

Dundee was so shocked on hearing the news of the army's disbandment that, according to some, he broke down in tears. With no orders to guide him, he took his cavalry north to Watford, away from the line of William's advance, and waited. It was while he was there that he received a letter from William, who had once been his commander-in-chief. No copy remains, but Captain John Creichton of the dragoons later reconstructed it from memory. As he recalled, it said:

> My Lord Dundee – I understand you are now at Watford, and that you keep your men together. I desire you may stay there till further orders, and upon my honour none in my army shall touch you.
> W.H. Prince of Orange

If that was an overture, it was rejected. Word had already reached Dundee that Scotland was in a sorry state, and on 11 December, the day of the King's flight, Balcarres arrived in London to confirm it. Edinburgh was in the hands of anti-Catholic mobs, who had seized Chancellor Perth, and thrown him into a common gaol. Such mobs had also been active in London, where Catholic buildings had been burned and the Spanish embassy destroyed.

Balcarres suggested a meeting of any remaining members of the Privy Council, and on 13 December he, Dundee, Lord Livingstone, General Douglas, and old Lord Airlie assembled at the Duke of Hamilton's London house. The loyalties of two at least of those present – Hamilton and Douglas – were suspect. Hamilton had been in contact with the other side, and Douglas had actually suggested to Dundee that he might defect. Dundee had rejected the suggestion angrily, but since Douglas had sworn him to silence he was unable to say anything about it.

At the meeting, Balcarres produced a letter drafted by the Secret Committee for the King, and Hamilton demanded to see it. Balcarres refused to let him have the original, and showed him a copy instead, which provoked a serious disagreement, with Hamilton shouting at the others, and Dundee attempting to pacify him. They were right not to trust him, however, for Hamilton was interested only in backing the winning side.

Three days later, there was a sensation: the King, it emerged, was back in town. The *London Gazette* recorded it with its usual economy: 'Whitehall, December 16. His Majesty returned hither in very good health.'

James's flight had been a débâcle. He had taken ship at Sheerness, but was obliged to wait for the tide. While there, some Kentish fishermen had boarded the vessel, and, after discovering who the passenger was, had cheerfully taken care of him. The provisional government in London had then provided a military escort to bring him back to town, where he was greeted by ecstatic crowds. As he drove through the City, James was amazed to see the streets thick with people. They roared applause from the balconies, lit bonfires, and pealed bells. For a time, as he entered Whitehall, the King was roused from his apathy. He sent the Prince of Orange a message proposing a conference at St James's Palace.

That same day, Dundee and Balcarres went to see him, and found him attended only by a few Gentlemen of the Bedchamber. It was a very different meeting from the one Dundee had had all those years ago when he and the Duke of York, as James then was, had carved up the Scottish peerage between them. Now James was uncertain and hesitant. As they talked, one of the generals of the disbanded army came in and begged the King for orders to reassemble the troops and defend the capital. He said he could muster 20,000 men before the end of the following day. The King shook his head. 'My Lord, I know you to be a friend, sincere and honourable', he said; 'the men who sent you are not so, and I expect nothing of them.'

The King then invited Balcarres and Dundee to join him for a walk. It was a fine day, and the three men, unaccompanied, strolled down the Mall. As they talked, the King stopped and asked them why, when all the world had forsaken him, they remained loyal. Balcarres said that his faith in James was unchanged and that his loyalty 'to so good a master would ever be the same'. Dundee said so too. His duty was to the King and nothing would ever change that. James told them that he had decided, nevertheless, to leave. 'You know,' he said, 'there is but a small distance between the prisons and the graves of Kings.' He would go to France, and from there he would authorize Balcarres to manage the civil affairs of Scotland, and Dundee would receive a commission as Lieutenant-General and Commander-in-Chief of the Scottish army.

Meanwhile, William, having considered the King's invitation to a conference, and rejected it, moved, from Windsor, to Syon House in Brentford. From there he sent his Dutch guards to Whitehall. The King ordered his own Coldstream Guards to give way, and for a night was guarded by William's soldiers. At one o'clock in the morning, he was roused from bed, to find a delegation of William's three advisers, the Marquess of Halifax, the Earl of Shrewsbury, and Lord Delamere, waiting to tell him that he should leave London 'that very morning'. He was to go by water so that he would not arouse the crowds.

James left from the Whitehall stairs, heading for Rochester, and Dundee was certainly amongst the 'loyal nobility and others and the foreign ministers' who, according to Lord Ailesbury, 'came to pay him their last respects'. This time there was no mistake, and, by the time Christmas Day 1688 was being celebrated in London, James was hearing mass at Ambleteuse. On the day that the King left England, William of Orange proceeded 'in great magnificence' to St James's Palace.

There was no precedent for a peaceful revolution in England, no precedent for replacing, against his will, a living monarch by constitutional means, no precedent for handing the crown to a claimant who had no natural rights of succession. It says something, therefore, for the resilience of the English establishment that, in the space of three months, it was able to invent a solution. An election was held and a body assembled which, in the absence of a royal summons, could not be called a parliament, but was called instead a convention.

It met on 1 February 1689, and by the end of the month had drawn up a Declaration of Rights, which proclaimed illegal most of what James VII had done, and established the principles of free elections, the subordination of the crown to parliament, the illegality of a standing army in peacetime, and the supremacy of the common law. It was not a notably revolutionary document, indeed it was profoundly Conservative in tone, and represented a Tory victory over the Whigs by removing power from James VII rather than overthrowing him. The question it left unanswered was how to fill the throne.

Something of the intense excitement and confusion of the times can be gleaned from an after-dinner discussion which took place on 15 January at the Archbishop of Canterbury's lodgings, and was recorded by the diarist John Evelyn. Amongst the guests were Lord Ailesbury, who had seen James off from Rochester, and Sir George Mackenzie, who was down from Edinburgh:

> After prayers and dinner, diverse serious matters were discoursed, concerning the present state of the Public, and I was sorry to find there was as yet no accord in the judgments of those of the Lords and the Commons who were to convene; some would have the Princess [Mary] made Queen without any more dispute, others were for a Regency; there was a Tory party (then so called), who were for inviting his Majesty again upon conditions; and there were Republicans who would make the Prince of Orange like a Stadtholder.

It was William himself who supplied the answer. After staying silent for three months, he announced that he would not be regent, he would be King; and if the convention felt unable to offer the crown to him and to Princess Mary to rule jointly, he would simply go back to Holland. There was really no choice. Mary came over to England to join her husband, and, on 23 February, they formally accepted the offer of the throne, on which they would rule jointly, and with it the Declaration of Rights.

The Scottish party in London had meanwhile been holding frenetic discussions at the Ship Tavern in St James's Street, trying to decide what their attitude to the new ruler would be. On 7 January, the leading figures met William at St James's Palace, and were asked to propose a solution for governing Scotland. On 14 January, they advised him that, in similar fashion to the proceedings in England, a Convention should be summoned at Edinburgh, on 14 March, and they asked him to take on the administration of the kingdom in the meantime.

Dundee, who was by now stationed with his troops at Abingdon, stayed aloof from the discussions. He and Balcarres were marked men and potentially in danger, but Balcarres, who knew William well enough to go and see him, had several interviews with him at St James's Palace, trying to win his support. Balcarres told him, however, that 'he could have no hand in turning out his King, who had been a kind master to him, although imprudent in many things.' William eventually told him 'to beware how he behaved himself, for, if he transgressed the law, he should be left to it.'

Dundee used an intermediary for his contacts with William – Gilbert

Burnet, the historian, whose wife was Lady Dundee's aunt. Dundee was not interested in any accommodation, he said, but, as Burnet later wrote, wanted to know whether he could take his troops back to Scotland:

> [Dundee] employed me to carry messages from him to the King, to know what security he might expect, if he should go and live in Scotland without owning his Government. The King said, if he would live peaceably, and at home, he would protect him. To this he answered, that unless he was forced to it, he would live quietly.

It was not exactly a pledge of acquiescence, and he had left himself an essential caveat, but William accepted his offer, and, in early February Dundee and Balcarres, escorted by Dundee's faithful troop, headed back to Scotland, and the temporary security of Dudhope Castle.

CHAPTER THIRTEEN
Scaling the Heights

To the Lords of Convention, 'twas Clavers who spoke,
Ere the King's crown go down, there are crowns to be
  broke,
So each cavalier who loves honour and me,
Let him follow the bonnet of bonnie Dundee.

Sir Walter Scott

Lady Dundee was expecting her first child, and her husband stayed with her through the bleak February days of her confinement at Dudhope. For the moment, he was content to steer clear of the great national events unfolding in Edinburgh, and to preside, for the last time, over the small but absorbing details of local life.

On 24 February 1689, he held his last council-meeting as Provost of Dundee, and on 11 March, he signed, at Dudhope, a document discharging the town for his duty on malt brewed in the burgh:

> I, John, Viscount of Dundie, Grants me to have receaved ane Thousand merkes, which Alexander Cathcart receaved upon the fourth day of october last by past from John Grahame, Colector of the towne's gift of two merkes upon each boll of malt broun and sold within the town of Dundie, – the qulk sowme is payable to me termlie out of the first end of the said gift, and discharges the said town of the terme of martimes, Jaj. vic. eightie-eight, as witnesse my hand, at Dudhope the 11 of March 1689. – DUNDIE.

Three days later he and the Earl of Balcarres were in Edinburgh to attend the official opening of the Convention of Estates, a more momentous event than commercial transactions in Dundee, and one which would determine the future course of the nation.

The capital, when he and Balcarres arrived there, was quiet, but there were rumours that bands of 'wild western Whigs', for whom Dundee was an obvious target, had been slipping into town and were concealed in the streets and wynds. These men were Cameronians, 'the worst kind of Presbyterians', in the words of a contemporary, 'who think it their duty to murder all who are out of the state of grace – that is, not of their communion.' With the prospect of a new era of Protestant rule, they sensed that their hour had come at last, and they intended to seize it. What was more, the City was virtually unprotected against serious trouble. The three regiments of the Scots Brigade, which were still quartered in Southwark, were not expected in Edinburgh for some time. They did not embark for Leith until 13 March, when they left under the command of General Hugh Mackay, who was 'very indisposed for such an expedition'. (Mackay had been struck by a serious illness shortly after he had landed at Torbay and had been making a slow recovery ever since.)

Some of those who attended the Convention had brought their own guards into town. These were supposed to be limited to ten, but both the Duke of Hamilton and Sir John Dalrymple, who was now Lord Justice-Clerk, were said to have smuggled in armed Whig supporters as well. Though the Convention, when it met beneath the vaulted ceilings of Parliament House, discussed the removal from the capital of 'such persons as are not concerned as members or their servants in the meeting', nothing was done.

Despite the danger in the streets, that other obvious target, Sir George Mackenzie, found occasion, on 1 March, for civilized ceremonial: the formal opening of his beloved Advocates' Library, in Parliament Square, its shelves weighed down with gold-embossed volumes containing the 'fundamental laws' of Scotland, which were once again the subject of such furious debate. (Sir George explained the splendour of their bindings with a little joke: 'We think it just to clothe them in gold through whom our gold is gained', he said. And then, in the only (oblique) reference he made that day to the stirring events outside, he urged his guests to remember that the learning in those books was more permanent than bronze, and that even Caesar, the warrior, had admitted that the triumphs of Cicero, the lawyer, were greater than his own.)

The Convention met on 14 March and was immediately divided over the crucial question of electing a president. The two candidates were a contrast in style and attitude, reflecting the mixed ambitions of many of those who crowded into the hall to hear the speeches and to argue in the corridors.

John, Marquis of Atholl, had travelled south from his estates in Perthshire, which had suffered a terrible winter. There had been great storms, and the rivers and burns had frozen over, making it impossible for the mills to grind corn, and so leaving his tenants desperately short of bread. There was considerable hardship amongst the poorest of them, and even the threat of starvation.

Atholl had been worried that 'the rabble' on his estates might seize the opportunity of his absence to riot and plunder. His own ambitions, according to his wife, were simply 'to get leave to live peaceably at home and to enjoy his religion', which was Presbyterian. But he had not been particularly peaceable himself. He had led a small army of Highland clansmen into Argyll after the Earl of Argyll's rebellion, to seize land and exact compensation. The Atholl raid was a fearsome affair, in which clans like the Macleans and Macdonalds exacted revenge on their age-old enemies the Campbells.

Both he and his son, the young Lord Murray, who was more eager than his father for political advancement, thought that William offered the best chance of guaranteeing a peaceful future. But both were uncertain men, their loyalties deeply divided. Atholl had been a member of James's Secret Committee, besides being a clan leader with long-standing Stuart connections, and he found it hard to abandon King James's cause.

The rival candidate was William, Duke of Hamilton, who was of a different calibre altogether: choleric, ambitious, and a political opportunist. He had been brought up as a Roman Catholic and it was as William Douglas Earl of Selkirk that he married the redoubtable Anne, Duchess of Hamilton – henceforward it was her strong Presbyterian beliefs which shaped his politics. It had not always been thus: in London he had assured James of his 'great zeal for the King's service', and, even after the débâcle at Salisbury, had assured Dundee and Balcarres of his loyalty. But his natural instincts were for William, and once the ground slipped from beneath James's feet he declared for the Prince of Orange, and set about ensuring the smooth transition of power.

There was no guarantee, however, that he would succeed to the Presidency of the Convention. Atholl was the favoured candidate, and when Hamilton was declared the winner, with a majority of fifteen votes, the result came as a surprise. It reflected, however, the mood of those present. James had won few friends amongst the nobility with his Indulgences, and the prospect of his returning filled most of them with dismay. Hamilton, as the man who was unequivocally for William and stability, commanded most support.

The first business of the day was the security of the City, and in particular the 'insults and tumults' which members of the Convention were being subjected to on the streets outside. A little further away there was a more formidable threat.

Edinburgh Castle was still held by its Governor, the Roman Catholic Duke of Gordon, who had been appointed by King James, and who owed him his dukedom. With the powerful cannon on the Castle battlements capable of clearing the streets, if not demolishing the Convention itself, the great fortress posed a formidable challenge to those meeting within easy range of its battlements.

Dundee and Balcarres considered it vital that Gordon hold firm. Both men were committed to the restoration of King James, and, though they hoped that they could win round the Convention by argument, the proximity of Gordon's cannons would be a useful reinforcement. They had paid him a visit on their way north from London, and had been horrified to find him moving out with his furniture. They had hurried in and spent some time encouraging him to stay loyal to King James. Gordon promised to wait at least until the Convention had reached some decisions about the future.

But the Convention, when it met, decided that Gordon must be made to surrender the Castle, and the Earls of Lothian and Tweeddale were sent to persuade him to do so. They carried terms which would exonerate him of any crime against the new regime, and Gordon agreed that he would cede the Castle if he could see the terms in writing. Balcarres and Dundee immediately dispatched a messenger to remind the Duke that he had given them his word that he would hold fast; but Gordon's reply was not encouraging. Unless he received undertakings 'that it was of absolute necessity for [King James's] affairs not to yield', he proposed to accept the Convention's terms. He had no intention of throwing in his hand with a lost cause.

In the early hours of 15 March, and under cloak of darkness, Dundee set out for the Castle – a dangerous mission in view of his enemies in the streets – and managed to gain entrance through a postern gate. Once again, he sat down with Gordon in an attempt to bolster his resolve. He told the Duke that the supporters of King James were determined to stay loyal, and that they had already discussed a proposal by which he and Balcarres set great store: they had permission from James to hold an alternative Convention at Stirling Castle, where the Earl of Mar was Governor and was well disposed. The Marquis of Atholl and others, he said, were with them.

What Dundee did not yet know, but what he expected to learn

shortly, was that James had landed, with French troops, in Ireland, ready to challenge William's throne from there. Dundee and Balcarres had sent him the draft of a letter which they hoped would be completed and signed by him, to be read out to the Convention. They had set out the kind of conciliatory ideas which they hoped would rally support, and had encouraged many of those attending to expect that 'full satisfaction would be given in matters of religion and liberty.'

Gordon was sufficiently convinced to agree that he would withdraw the offer to surrender, and despite a delegation of heralds, together with 'two poursuivants in all the pomp of their official panoply' preceded by 'two trumpeters sounding their trumpets', sent by the Convention, he could not be persuaded otherwise. He was promptly declared an outlaw and all communication with him was forbidden. Guards were posted at the roads up to the Castle and at the postern gates, to prevent messages or provisions being sent in or out.

On the morning of 16 March, as Dundee and Balcarres took their seats at the Convention, Dundee was handed disturbing information. A warning had been received that his life and that of Sir George Mackenzie were in danger. Two men had been heard to say that a plot to kill both men was being hatched. Mackenzie immediately proposed a motion 'for security of members', and a witness who claimed to have heard the threat was summoned to tell them about the two men he had heard saying that 'they resolved to use these dogs as they were used by them'. The Convention noted the point, and then moved on to other matters: it 'could not postpone public affairs to consider private matters'.

Information was now laid before the Convention that a letter had been received from King James. That was momentous news. But, in the best tradition of committee meetings, there was a prior motion to be considered. A report 'anent the election for the town of Perth' was duly considered, debated, and agreed on. The Convention then turned to consider the first communication it had received from the man to whom, technically, it still owed its allegiance.

However hostile some of its members were to King James, and however much they wished him to stay in Ireland, or preferably go back to France, he was still the rightful king. Many of those present were deeply concerned at the prospect of declaring the throne forfeit, and believed that William was still, as Lord Sinclair put it, 'a foreign authority'. The dilemma they faced in debating the future running of the country was similar to that which had so exercised their opposite numbers in England, with the added concern that James, in alliance with the French king, could call on far stronger historical ties with Scotland than could William and his Dutch confederates.

A motion was proposed that James's letter be read out, but Hamilton was immediately on his feet. He had received another letter, brought by the Earl of Leven from the Prince of Orange, and he suggested that it should be read out first. Much discussion took place as to which should be heard, with the vote going to William's, since it was feared that James's letter might contain an order to dissolve the meeting. Since he was still King, he had the power to do that, while William did not.

Dundee was not greatly concerned which was read first. He knew, or thought he knew, that James's letter, its terms suggested by him and Balcarres, would be friendly and conciliatory. Having heard it, he hoped, the Convention would be moved away from any idea of demanding the forfeiture of the crown.

When William's letter was read out, the listeners heard with approval a warm and tactful message that ended with his assurance that,

> having nothing so much before our eyes as the Glory of God, the establishing of the true Religion, and the peace and happiness of these nations, we are resolved to use our utmost endeavours in advancing everything which may conduce to the effectuating the same.

James's letter was then read, and Dundee listened in horror as he heard a travesty of what he and Balcarres had proposed. Instead of the diplomatic words they had composed, there was an arrogant and critical message, full of condemnation of the King's opponents, and ending with a threat 'to punish with the rigour of Our Law all such as shall stand out in rebellion aginst Us or Our authority.'

The Convention was in uproar as the reading finished, and those who were amongst the King's supporters realized that it had swung opinion fatally against them. Some of those present claimed to detect behind it the hand of James's principal adviser, the Earl of Melfort. Subsequently, the truth emerged: Dundee and Balcarres's letter had never reached James; it had been intercepted by Melfort, who had sent his own version instead.

Melfort's political and military advice was consistently inept. It was he who had suggested summoning the Scots army south to attack William, leaving the country defenceless; it was also he who, almost uniquely amongst James's advisers, had actually left England ahead of the fleeing King. But James seems never to have realized how badly he was being served.

For the King's supporters, Melfort's letter and its impact on the Convention left only one course of action open – to summon the rival Convention at Stirling, and leave Edinburgh to the mercy of Gordon's cannon.

Dundee and Balcarres had been promised the support of the Governor of Stirling Castle, the Earl of Mar, and they counted on Atholl, who had promised to accompany them. A rendezvous was set in Edinburgh for Monday 18 March, prior to marching for Stirling. Dundee spent that Sunday preparing his escort and sending messages to potential supporters. Then, at about ten o'clock on Monday morning, together with George Livingstone, Earl of Linlithgow, and some fifty of his own troopers, he rode to his rendezvous with Balcarres and Atholl.

But over the weekend, Atholl had weakened. He had begged for a day's delay, and had persuaded Balcarres that it would be better to attend the Convention for one more day to disguise their intentions. Balcarres had reluctantly agreed, and he was on the point of leaving for Parliament House when Dundee and his troopers clattered down the street towards him.

No one had told Dundee that the plans had been changed, and when he heard the news he was, in Balcarres's words, 'mightily surprised.' He was of course furious, and changed plans did not suit his military temperament. Balcarres tried desperately to persuade him to stay. 'It was very evident his going away would give the alarm, which made me extremely earnest that he might stay one day longer', he said later. But Dundee was adamant. He had made an appointment with allies outside town, he said, and he would not let them down. If Balcarres changed his mind and came, he would wait for him on the Stirling road. But Balcarres, for so long his friend and ally, stayed behind.

Wheeling his troopers round, Dundee set off on a route through the town that would avoid the Convention and the curious crowds. He rode through the Netherbow port, a gateway between the town and the Canongate, then turned left down the Leith Wynd and up the hill to the base of the Calton Hill. From there he rode east along the Lang Gate, or what is now Princes Street. This put the North Loch, the great scooped-out hollow where the gardens and the railway now lie, between him and Parliament House high on his left. Ahead of him lay the Castle and the road west towards Stirling.

The sight of Dundee's troopers, their scarlet tunics and the yellow facings standing out against the Castle rock as they rode towards it, was to become the stuff of legend.

Gordon spotted him from the Castle wall, where, armed with a telescope, he had been keeping an anxious lookout with his sister. As the horsemen approached, he gave them a signal, and they halted. Dundee dismounted near the West Kirk, immediately below the great escarpment that reaches up to the battlements on the north-west corner of the Castle rock. He was now hidden from the town. Unseen by all but idle onlookers, he began to scale the cliff face at the one point where the climb was feasible. For a fit soldier, even when booted and spurred on, it was a matter of barely ten minutes before he reached the postern above him. At the top, the Duke of Gordon was waiting. And there, 'over the Castle wall', according to a breathless account of the feat, a final discussion was held. Dundee may have urged Gordon to join him, or he may have asked him to hold the Castle at all costs. Either way he was eventually to be disappointed. According to legend, Gordon asked him where he was heading, and Dundee told him: 'Wherever the spirit of Montrose shall direct me.' Then, before the alarm could be raised, he scrambled down, mounted his horse and rode with his troopers westwards towards Linlithgow, and the beginning of his last campaign.

CHAPTER FOURTEEN
The Highland Way

*'Dundee, the heroic leader of the North, knew not how to
yield, however adverse might be his fate'*
James Philip of Almericlose

The news of the meeting of Dundee and Gordon was brought to the
Convention while the two men were still conferring over the Castle
wall, and it caused pandemonium. What shocked the members was
that Dundee had got access to a man who had only just been proclaimed an outlaw. It was 'a crime of the highest nature', and reports
that Dundee had assembled 'a great body of horse' suggested that a
well-orchestrated coup might be under way.

Hamilton was incandescent with rage, as Balcarres described it:

> The Duke of Hamilton had hitherto behaved himself with temper and
> equality; but, like smothered fire, his natural temper upon this occasion
> appeared in all its violence. He told the Convention that now it was high
> time to look to themselves, since Papists, and enemies to the settling of
> the Government, were so bold as to assemble in a hostile manner.

Hamilton ordered the doors locked and the keys put on the table.
No one was to be allowed out until their loyalties had been put to the
test. And to concentrate the minds of those present, he ordered in
'some foot from the Western shires, which he offered to employ in the
public cause.'

So the rumours were true: Hamilton, doubtless supported by Dalrymple, had brought over armed Whigs to help him. When the Earl of
Leven brought them into the chamber, Balcarres was appalled: 'never
was seen so contemptible a rabble', he wrote.

For some time, the Convention sat immobilized, locked up with the 'wild western Whigs', wondering whether Gordon's cannons might be brought into play. Then word came that Dundee had ridden off, and that he had no more than fifty men with him. He was on the road to Queensferry, said one report. Hamilton dispatched Leven to secure the roads to and from the Castle, and then ordered an elderly officer, Major Hugh Buntine, to go after Dundee with a summons ordering his return. Finally, he unlocked the doors of the Convention and dismissed those inside, to Balcarres's great relief, since he had been 'little expecting to come off so well.'

Major Buntine seems not to have relished the task of meeting Dundee and his fifty or so men. He spent some time assembling a suitable escort of eighty horse, and by the time he set off, Dundee had a good two days' start on him. Buntine failed to catch up with him, and instead carried his message on to Dudhope. Nine days passed between his receiving orders and reporting back, and when he finally did so, the Convention demanded an explanation for the delay.

Dundee had spent the night of Monday 18 March 1689 at Linlithgow, and had then ridden on towards Stirling. When he got there, he found that the Castle was no longer in friendly hands, for the Earl of Mar, who was ill, had withdrawn his support, and, in Balcarres's words, 'joined the other party.' So Dundee took his troop briskly through the town, crossed Stirling Bridge, and headed for Dunblane.

It was there that he met the first of his Highland supporters, Alexander Drummond of Balhaldie, son-in-law of the most influential of all the Highland chiefs, Sir Ewen Cameron of Lochiel. It was plainly a rendezvous which Dundee had arranged beforehand, probably the one he had told Balcarres about as they argued on the streets of Edinburgh, and it is clear that some plan had been conceived in advance.

This was, for Dundee, no romantic venture. As a careful strategist and an experienced officer, used to planning expeditions in detail, Dundee had already taken early soundings amongst the King's supporters in the north. How far he had worked out what he now intended to do is uncertain. He had, of course, given William his word that he would live peaceably unless circumstances forced him to do otherwise. This seemed now to have happened.

From Balhaldie, Dundee heard news of Lochiel and the likely response of what Lochiel had referred to as 'the confederacy of the clans', whose support in any future action was crucial. Then they separated, and next day, 20 March 1689, Dundee rode back to Dudhope, some seventy miles away, to wait for news from James, to consider his plans, and, of course, to be with his wife when she produced her first baby.

Meanwhile, with Major Buntine still on the road, the Convention was in a state of considerable confusion. Word had been sent to Stirling 'to seal the persons of the Lord Dundee' together with his soldiers, but the message arrived a day after Dundee had ridden through town. In Edinburgh, the tiny band still loyal to James had been momentarily cheered when the Duke of Queensberry arrived from London with the Earl of Dunmore, still leaning towards the King. But, as Balcarres noted sadly, his Grace had stayed away too long and had missed the crucial first day at the Convention which might have swung things the right way. So Queensberry went back home to Drumlanrig.

There was still the Duke of Gordon, holding the Castle, and communication was maintained with him thanks to the redoubtable Countess of Erroll, 'who found a way to keep a constant correspondence with [him] all the time of his being blocked up', according to Balcarres. But the Duke would now not do anything except defend the Castle unless he had word directly from King James. With the collapse of the plan to hold a Convention in Stirling, most of those who claimed to be Jacobites slipped quietly out of Edinburgh and went back to their estates.

On 24 March, Mackay and his soldiers of the Scots Brigade arrived at Leith, and were asked to consider an assault on the Castle. They studied the defences and wisely decided to play a waiting game instead by trying to cut it off from intelligence and provisions. On 28 March, Mackay was commissioned Commander-in-Chief of the forces under the Convention.

Rumours about Dundee's intentions were rife. Some thought he would try to go to Ireland to join James there, others believed he was heading north. One account was accurate. A pamphlet bearing the enticing headline 'Great news from the Convention in Scotland' stated on 28 March: 'We hear no more of the Viscount Dundee since his withdrawing, but that he lives peaceably at his own house; it being indeed but vain for that party to think of attempting anything against the whole nation.' And, indeed, Dundee was content for the time being to see how matters turned out. Buntine had finally delivered his message calling on him and Livingstone to surrender, a message reinforced by the full ceremonial of a trumpeter who summoned the household of Dudhope, and a herald who read out the Convention's citation. In fact by this time Dundee's companion, Livingstone, had returned home, and most of Dundee's small escort had dispersed.

On 27 March, Dundee sent a reply to Hamilton:

> May it please your Grace, The coming of a herald and trumpeter to
> summon a man to lay down arms, that is living in peace at home, seems
> to me a very extraordinary thing, and, I suppose, will do so to all that
> hears of it. While I attended the Convention in Edinburgh, I complained
> often of many people's being in arms without authority, which was
> notoriously known to be true, even the wild hill men; and no summons
> to lay down arms under pain of treason being given them, I thought it
> unsafe for me to remain longer among them. And because some few of
> my friends did me the favour to convey me out of the reach of these
> murderers, and that my Lord Livingstone and several other officers
> took occasion to come away at the same time, this must be called being
> in arms. We did not exceed the number allowed by the Meeting of
> Estates.

He begged leave to refuse the summons on the grounds that his safety
could not be guaranteed, and because his duty lay with his pregnant
wife: 'I hope the Meeting of States will think it unreasonable I should
leave my wife in the condition she is in.' He promised to give 'security
or parole not to disturb the peace', and asked Hamilton to read his
letter out to the Convention 'because it is all the defence I have made'.

Hamilton was not impressed. In his view, Dundee's actions, particularly (it clearly rankled) his communications with the outlawed Duke
of Gordon, constituted treason. When he read the letter out to the
Convention, its members agreed with him and a proclamation was
drawn up, full of pomp and circumstance:

> Forasmuch as John Viscount of Dundee being cited by warrant of the
> Estates to lay down his arms under the pain of treason and to appear
> before them to answer for his corresponding with the Duke of Gordon
> after he was intercommuned, and the herald who cited him and the
> witnesses to the execution having upon oath verified the execution of the
> charge given to the said Viscount, and he being thrice called in the house,
> and at the great door, and not appearing, the meeting of Estates do
> declare the said Viscount Dundee fugitive and rebel . . . .

Dundee cannot have been surprised to find himself an outlaw. In his
time he had pursued many a rebel for less. But the proclamation was
the deciding factor which turned him to outright revolt. Lady Erroll,
writing in coded language to a friend, expressed her sadness that force
had won over argument: 'The zeal which some has to ruin others, and
the ambition others has to raise themselves, far outrun common
measures of reason'. Her words referred to Hamilton, and not Dundee. But the implication was the same for both.

Towards the end of March, Lady Dundee gave birth to a son, who was called James, Montrose's christian name, but also the King's. On 9 April, James Graham was christened at the little church in Mains near Dundee, with the Viscount's brother, David, as one of the witnesses, and Major William Graham of Balquapple as the other.

Two days later, William and Mary were declared king and queen of Scotland. A Commission of three Scots, headed by Sir John Dalrymple, had gone south to offer them the Crown, and, on 11 April, the announcement was made in Edinburgh, by no less a herald than the Duke of Hamilton, who personally read out the Act of the Convention proclaiming the new king and queen, from the market cross, much to Balcarres's disgust. He described it as 'the meanest action that he even himself could do; for he officiated as clerk ...'.

Balcarres himself was now in real danger. He had retreated for safety to his house in Fife, but, a few days after Hamilton's proclamation, he was arrested by Lord Leven and brought to Edinburgh, where he was thrown into a common gaol. He was later transferred to Edinburgh Castle, where he remained a prisoner during the whole of Dundee's campaign. He was thus behind bars when, on 16 April, Dundee raised the royal standard on Dundee Law.

From the moment he rode out from Edinburgh, Dundee had, in effect, been a rebel. Now he was openly declaring it. There seems never to have been any doubt in his mind about what he was doing. His loyalty to James was fundamental, both as a subject, and as officer, and as a friend. He had been raised from obscurity by James and owed him his title and status. As an episcopalian, he knew no reason to doubt James's honesty on religion. And as a Major-General, the very concept of changing sides was unthinkable. Dundee's letters are studded with references to the royal service, the importance of obedience, discipline, and good order, and his abhorrence of lawlessness. For him, the King was the ultimate Commanding Officer. His views echoed those of Sir Edmund Verney in England, who, at the outbreak of the Civil War, was faced with a similar decision, and who concluded: 'I have eaten his [the King's] bread and served him near thirty years and I will not do so base a thing as to forsake him.' It was, therefore, by a natural, and to him quite unsurprising logic, that Dundee, the great disciplinarian, now found himself a rebel.

The raising of the standard for King James was witnessed by James Philip of Almericlose, son of the Bailie of Arbroath, a cousin and close neighbour of Dundee's. A classical scholar, and a romantic and passionate poet, he took part in the campaign and translated the stirring events that he saw into a lavish epic of flowing Latin hexameters inspired by the verses of the poet Lucan.

James Philip described the scene as Dundee stood before a tiny band of some fifty followers on Dundee Law, overlooking the town, and announced the beginning of his campaign:

> He himself, mounted on his charger, brilliant in scarlet, in the face of the town, drew out in long line his band of brave youths, and on the very top of the Law of Dundee he unfurled the Royal banner for the Northern war. Around him gather his chosen companions, and young men, in high spirits. All mounted and in bright armour, they follow the Graham as he rushes to the field. Then triumphantly, he led them over the lofty ridges of the Sidlaw hills.

Dundee rode to his old home at Glenogilvie, and Philip spared a thought for Lady Dundee as she watched him leave: 'Go where the honour of your King commands', he had her saying. 'Thus speaking, she sadly took ... farewell of her husband; and with her prayers she followed him as he went, ardent for the war, straining her bright eyes after him as long as he was in sight.'

It was not long before word reached Dundee of the response from Edinburgh. Major-General Mackay had spent his first few days in the capital attempting to build up his depleted forces. The three Scots regiments he had brought over from Holland had been reduced by the removal of all the Dutch soldiers from their ranks. They now amounted to a total of 1,100 men instead of 3,600. The Convention had decided to levy 6,000 foot, twelve troops of horse, and 300 dragoons, but the recruitment had not progressed very far, and Mackay had been critical of the quality of the soldiers.

Thus, when he began laying his plans to pursue Dundee, he could only call on limited resources. He did, however, have experience amongst his senior officers. The three regiments brought over from Holland were commanded by himself, by Brigadier-General Barthold Balfour, whose family had served in the Dutch army for generations, and by Colonel the Honourable George Ramsay, second son of the Earl of Dalhousie, 'a gentleman with a great deal of fire, and very brave', as General Mackay described him, who was later to become Commander-in-Chief of the Scottish army, but who was not to distinguish himself against Dundee. The foot were commanded by Lieutenant-Colonel Lauder, the horse by Lord Colchester, and the dragoons by Sir Thomas Livingstone.

Livingstone would play a significant part not just in the campaign against Dundee but in the brutal suppression of the Highland clans thereafter. He had been born in Holland and had served under William as a colonel of foot. But after arriving in England he had been promoted to Colonel of the Royal Regiment of Scots Dragoons in place of the Earl of Dunmore – Lord Charles Murray, Atholl's second son – who remained loyal to James.

It was Livingstone whom Mackay first dispatched to 'stop the forming of a party' by Dundee. Livingstone had been stationed at Stirling to help concentrate the uncertain mind of the Earl of Mar, and the plan had been to seize Dundee at Dudhope. But when Livingstone found that he was no longer there, he set out for Glenogilvie. The dragoons, according to Mackay, were 'very well and secretly led on', but they were 'disappointed by the retreat of the said Dundee'. By the time they reached Glenogilvie towards 20 April, it was deserted.

Dundee had ridden out, 'with loosened rein, through the vales towards the mountains', as James Philip recounted it, past Kirriemuir and over the North Water Bridge, heading for the Highlands. Livingstone reported back to Mackay his 'mislucked design and the Lord Dundee's motion north.'

Mackay now decided that he himself would have to take the field. He was aware of the appeal that Dundee might have amongst the Highland clans, and he felt he could not allow him to 'play his personage among the nobility and gentry of the north.' He knew enough of that northern part of the kingdom to assess the possible support Dundee might have there, and those clan chiefs he himself might count on. Like the seasoned soldier he was, he planned his campaign well.

He selected Perth, Dundee, and Stirling as his operational bases, and sent 120 men from Lord Colchester's regiment to join Livingstone's dragoons in Dundee, the 'rendezvous of his party'. Balfour was left in command at Edinburgh, while Mackay himself made his way north, via Dundee, to Brechin and Fettercairn, where he hoped to close with the enemy. He counted on certain prominent Highlanders to give him support. One such was Ludovic Grant of Grant, Sheriff of Inverness. His family had virtually ruled the lands of Moray since the thirteenth century, and owned Castle Grant, a key stronghold commanding the Spey. Grant was a keen supporter of William, but for the time being he was still in Edinburgh, and slow to return to his northern territory, a dereliction of duty which Mackay noted as being 'without any design of prejudice to the service, though highly punishable, had he been a man of service.'

The Master of Forbes, who owned Druminnor Castle, south of Huntly, was another influential figure, though still a young man, and 'as yet bashful before his enemy, never having seen any', in Mackay's words. The Earl of Mar's estates north of Blair were also important, though the Earl himself was a sick man. But it was Blair Castle, home of the Earls of Atholl, which was the crucial garrison. It dominated the route north from Dunkeld to Inverness, and its control was to be vital for both sides. Mackay counted on Atholl for his support, and thought he had it, in view of the 'many protestations of his affection to their Majesties'. Atholl had been asked to have 400 of his men in arms, ready to capture and hold Dundee if he reached Blair. Later, however, when Dundee had passed safely through Atholl's territory, Mackay concluded that 'he had falsified his parole and played double game.'

In any assessment of the merits of the rival leaders, Hugh Mackay of Scourie is usually presented as dull, prosaic, unadventurous in contrast to Dundee, the dashing cavalier. His image was not helped by the fact that while Dundee's exploits were chronicled in heroic verse, Mackay described the campaign in ponderous and unwieldy prose. In fact, the two men were remarkably similar in their military background. They had received the same training on the Continent and both imposed high standards of discipline on their soldiers. Both believed in political morality, and were themselves incorruptible. What is more, when it came to strategic decisions, Mackay was every bit as capable of a bold decision as his rival.

Unlike Dundee, Mackay was a Highlander. He might, therefore, have been expected to enjoy a greater understanding of the men and the country in which he was now operating. In fact, as it emerged, the reverse was true. Mackay's origins were in the north-west of Sutherland, an area of wild beauty, strange volcanic hills, and steep cliffs, which had as little to do with Speyside or Lochaber as did the town of Dundee. Furthermore, he had left Sutherland early in his life, and had never returned, preferring the flat plains of Holland and the sensible Dutch to the Gaelic 'savages' from whom he had escaped. He had adopted Holland as his own country, married a Dutch heiress, and now looked on his former countrymen with the eyes of a foreigner, finding them exasperating, untrustworthy and illogical. Whether he had any feelings for distant Scourie is not known; but the name at least he retained.

Mackay was a good commander, brave, if not always inspired. He admired the fighting skills of the Highlanders, but considered them irrelevant to modern warfare – they bore no relation to anything he had seen at Neimegen or St Omer. Dundee, on the other hand, felt at home with them. Unlike Mackay, he knew how to play the diplomat with clan chieftains, however exasperating he found them. His character, which was open and engaging, brought him many friends, and he knew instinctively how to cajole the clans and their volatile leaders.

Dundee had ridden out from Dundee Law on 16 April 1689 and had headed directly north, through Kincardine O'Neill, Huntly, and Keith, reaching Gordon Castle a few days later. From there, he sent dispatches to James, telling him that he was going on to Inverness and was 'encouraging all persons to stand out, letting them see by his example there was no danger in it.'

At Forres, he learned that the dragoons who were quartered in Dundee were inclined to back the King, and he considered turning south again to recruit them to the cause. They had been left under the command of Lieutenant-Colonel William Livingston (no relation to his commanding officer, Sir Thomas), who was a secret sympathizer. From Dudhope, Lady Dundee had been in touch with him to persuade him to break out and join her husband. But, as Dundee headed south, he intercepted a messenger with word from Mackay that he himself was heading for the town and intended to strike north.

Dundee therefore doubled back to Cairn O'Mount, some thirty miles north of the town, and waited as Mackay marched towards him. By 29 April, Mackay was at Brechin, within eight miles of him, at which point Dundee wheeled west, crossed the Dee to Aboyne, and then turned north, over the Don, past Forbes's castle at Druminnor, to Huntly Castle, where he was in the friendly country of the Gordons. And there he spent the night of 30 April.

Dundee, says Philip, was 'not unskilled in meeting the strategy of an enemy', and Mackay was consistently left guessing by his movements. He had fully expected his rival to be at Fettercairn, north-west of Montrose, and had sent a party of foot and horse under the command of his nephew, Major Mackay, to seize him there. But Dundee had gone. Then, later, Mackay was deceived by his move westwards into thinking he was heading for the lowlands. But that had only been a feint. Finally, he was left behind when Dundee headed rapidly north towards Inverness.

Dundee's movements, of course, were made easier by the tiny size of his band of supporters. So far he had made little progress in summoning allies. His early companion, Lord Livingstone, had lost heart, feigned sickness, and stayed at home. Others were bolder: Dundee's 'agent' in the north was the Duke of Gordon's brother-in-law, the Earl of Dunfermline, a trained soldier who had seen service in the Netherlands under William of Orange, but who was now a fervent Jacobite. Dundee had written to him saying that he was 'extremely pleased that I should have the happiness to concert with you these affairs, that concerns us all so much', and Dunfermline had shown that he was ready to join him. On 1 May, he did so, when Dundee arrived at dawn at Gordon Castle. Their combined strength amounted to just over a hundred men.

Cameron of Lochiel had promised Dundee that he would have the backing of 'the clan confederacy', and when he had Dunfermline arrived at Inverness on 1 May, one part of that confederacy was there to meet them. There was, however, a little local difficulty.

Coll MacDonald of Keppoch had been asked to provide an escort to take Dundee west to Lochaber, and he had come with 700 men. The Lochaber clans prided themselves on their great warrior tradition, and few could outdo Keppoch, whose personal bard Iain Lom had recorded, with suitable embellishment, the feats of his clan in the service of Montrose. But they were also inveterate cattle-stealers. Not for nothing was Keppoch known as 'Coll of the Cows', 'whom love of plunder would impel to any deed of daring or of crime', as Philip described him. When John Drummond of Balhaldie, Lochiel's grandson, compiled the great chief's memoirs, he described Keppoch as 'a gentleman of good understanding, of great cunning, and much attached to King James'. But he added that he was always 'indulging himself in too great liberties with respect to those with whom he was at variance'.

One of those was Mackintosh of Mackintosh, who held land to the south of Inverness. Keppoch and his clansmen took the opportunity offered by their journey, to swoop down on Mackintosh's fields and cottages, seize as many of his sheep and cattle as they could drive before them, and then head north to Inverness. They reached the town on 28 April and immediately demanded money which they said was owed to them. When this was not forthcoming, they seized the magistrates and demanded a ransom. Inverness, which was then more of a sprawling village than a town, was surrounded by a rough palisade, which was its only protection. For three days, Keppoch and his clansmen camped outside it, threatening the town and its inhabitants with burning and pillage. Dundee found him there when he rode up to Inverness late on 1 May. The Keppoch chief confronted him with all the arrogance of his clan, 'his shield studded with brazen knobs and all plaided and plumed in his tartan array', as Philip wrote.

This was the first time Dundee had met face to face one of the Highland chiefs on whom he would have to rely, and he was not impressed. The lack of discipline amongst the clansmen appalled him, and he 'expostulated the matter ... in very sharp terms'. He ordered the MacDonald men to stand to their arms, and demanded to know what Keppoch was doing by threatening the town: 'He told him that such courses were extremely injurious to the King's interest', according to Lochiel's memoirs, 'and that, instead of acquiring the character of a patriot, he would be looked on as a common robber and the enemy of mankind.'

It says much for Dundee's force of character that Keppoch backed down. He made excuses about the amount of money the town owed him, but agreed not to burn it down. Instead, Dundee negotiated a payment to him of £2,700 Scots, which was logged in the records of Inverness as 'Given by the magistrates to Coll MacDonald to prevent the burning of the town.' He promised the town dignitaries that when King James was restored they would have their money back.

But Dundee may have been too overbearing for Keppoch. With Keppoch's 700 men behind him, there had been every chance of a pre-emptive strike against Mackay's approaching forces. Indeed, on 2 May, Dundee sent word to the magistrates at Elgin that he would be returning to their town, this time with reinforcements, in the form of 700 Highlanders. But, instead, Keppoch and his clansmen went home to Lochaber, driving Mackintosh's cattle before them. It was not the first, or the last, time that he avoided a battle. This was Dundee's first setback, and he was plainly disappointed – 'grieved', as Philip recorded, 'to lose so great an opportunity of giving battle to the enemy.'

Instead he stayed on in Inverness for the next six days, as Mackay began to pick up his trail. On 1 May the General joined the Master of Forbes, who had forty 'gentlemen of his name' on horseback together with 500 country people. But Mackay found these latter 'so ill-armed and so little like the work' that he dismissed them. Although he had only 200 foot-soldiers to back up his dragoons, he pressed on towards the River Spey. As he marched north, a messenger reached him from Elgin carrying Dundee's letter, passed on by the magistrates, who thus made it quite clear which side they favoured. It requested provisions for Dundee's troops, and it indicated that Dundee intended to arrive in the town on the next day, 2 May.

The General was, by his own admission, nonplussed by this intelligence. It appeared that the two forces were now destined to meet at

Elgin, but he was not ready for battle. A victory at this stage for Dundee would be disastrous for the Government's cause, 'because', as Mackay wrote, 'the whole north, by fair or foul means, would declare for him, there being nothing ... to oppose them, if that small handful were routed'. Yet to retreat south would hand control of Elgin, Moray, Ross, and Caithness over to the enemy without a fight, causing 'affront and disadvantage' to the Government.

It was a difficult choice. Mackay believed he could rely on support from the Laird of Grant, who was now heading north, and there was some promise of men from Lord Reay's Mackays in Sutherland, and Ross of Balnagowan in Ross-shire. But to fight a battle now was a gamble. The General weighed the matter up, and decided to take the risk. He made straight for Elgin, aiming to get there before Dundee. Dispatching a messenger to Brechin with orders to send reinforcements, he advanced at the double, with his 200 foot running so hard that they kept the cavalry at the trot. They covered the seven miles between the Spey and Elgin before nightfall on 2 May, allowing Mackay to establish that the way was clear, and giving him ample time to post guards.

Of Dundee there was no sign. Whether the letter had been a deliberate bluff or not was unclear, but his absence allowed Mackay time to address the task of summoning allies and reinforcements to prepare for an advance on Inverness. Word went out in the name of King William, but the response was disappointing. The local lairds, according to Mackay, had 'no true sense of the deliverance which God had sent them', and preferred 'to embrace the party which they judged most likely to carry it'. But the reinforcements from Brechin did arrive, and Grant finally appeared, ready to raise his men. By 8 May, Mackay felt ready to advance, and he wrote telling Tarbat in Edinburgh that he might well encounter Dundee with his MacDonald allies, 'if they stay'. At Forres, however, he learned that Dundee had left Inverness heading south.

With the departure of Keppoch, Dundee was left with forces of no more than about 200 men. His plan was to head down the south side of Loch Ness towards Lochaber, where Lochiel was waiting and where he hoped to raise more recruits. He visited Invergarry Castle, and then turned back to Killcumin (now Fort Augustus), where he spent the night of 8 May. Next day he went south and east, crossing the Spey at Cluny Castle, and traversing Glen Truim to spend the night at Presmuckerach, a farm owned by Malcolm Macpherson of Breachachy, who was forester to the Duke of Gordon.

He was now in friendly territory. The Macphersons of Cluny were, he heard, 'very keen and hearty in their inclinations for that service', and his soundings suggested that the time had come to rally the clans formally to King James's banner. Accordingly, from Presmuckerach on 9 May 'he issued the Royal letter to all the faithful clans,' as Philip wrote, 'bidding them be ready with their men by the Kalends of May [18 May], to follow the orders and the camp of the Graham'.

The gossip in Edinburgh, at this point, was that Dundee was a spent force. He was said to have barely one or two servants with him, to be harried by unfriendly natives, and to have sent an offer of surrender to General Mackay. It would not be long before he was dragged back to the capital, said those who knew, his sorry venture at an end.

However, the ink was scarcely dry on the rumour-sheets, when their message proved out of date. On the morning of 10 May, Dundee rode out from Presmuckerach, heading, not west, but south. At some point he had hatched another plan, as daring as it was dramatic. Following the River Garry beneath the Great Forest of Atholl, through 'dense woods of hazels', as Philip described them, he rode straight to Blair Castle, 'with its lofty battlements'. There, instead of hostility, he encountered a warm welcome from Atholl's factor, Patrick Steuart of Ballechin, a staunch loyalist. Scarcely stopping at Blair, Dundee rode south, through the Pass of Killiecrankie, to the tiny cathedral town of Dunkeld, here he captured an amazed captain of horse, who had been collecting Government dues. Dundee relieved him of the money.

At nightfall on 10 May, he rode silently out of town, and headed for the City of Perth. This was a bold move, for Perth was Mackay's principal barrier to the south, one of the three strongholds he had designated to withstand any attempt by Dundee to drive south towards Edinburgh or Stirling. Halting two miles out of town, Dundee selected a party of about seventy volunteers, and then, guided by the Earl of Perth's chamberlain, Thomas Crichton, crept silently into the City, where the magistrates were sleeping off a municipal banquet that had taken place that evening. By two o'clock in the morning, Dundee's men were in control of the streets of the 'Fair City'.

The two officers in charge of the garrison, William Blair of Blair, and Lieutenant Robert Pollock, were pulled out of their beds and arrested, 'the commander himself, snoring in deep sleep, not having yet shaken off the effects of the night's debauch', as Philip told it. Dundee silenced their protests curtly: 'You take prisoners for the Prince of Orange, and we take prisoners for King James, and there's an end of it.'

There was no looting. Dundee took forty horses and a part of the public purse, but forbade the rifling of any private money. Then, by eleven o'clock in the morning on 11 May, he was in the saddle again, riding out with his prisoners and troopers behind him.

The deed was not just an act of daring, it was a superb piece of propaganda – a signal to be read in the Highlands as well as in Edinburgh. It struck horror into the hearts of the watching Convention, but in Lochaber the message had a deeper significance. Montrose had won his first great military victory against heavy odds at Tippermuir outside the City of Perth. As an echoing gesture to the waiting clans, Dundee's raid could hardly have been bettered.

That night he dined at Scone Palace, much to the embarrassment of Lord Stormont, who explained later to the Committee of Estates that Dundee had 'forced his dinner from him'. Then he rode on to the Earl of Perth's seat, Stobhall. The Earl himself was a prisoner in Stirling, but he would not have denied Dundee the hospitality of his charming little castle. At both places, local lairds paid him visits, while his troop rode about the countryside collecting King William's taxes for him. And at Stobhall he was joined by a man who would become one of his most loyal followers, David Halyburton of Pitcur, a neighbour and friend, who was related by marriage to Sir George Mackenzie. He brought about a dozen horsemen with him.

At nightfall on 12 May, Dundee rode through the darkness past Coupar and Meigle, arriving next morning at Glamis, a place he knew well, and where he had a godson. He had now gone almost full circle, leaving Mackay far to the north of him, and arriving back at Dundee in the hope of luring Livingstone's wavering dragoons over to his side. After resting briefly at Glamis, he headed south towards the City, and, at five o'clock on 13 May, he breasted the Sidlaw Hills. His arrival caused alarm in Dundee. From inside the City walls, the magistrates watched anxiously as he circled round the City and then rode to the top of Dundee Law, a formidable-looking figure, dressed in armour, with a reinforced breast-plate and back-piece, and a helmet lined, according to one witness, with black fur.

The City fathers were not keen on offering any support to their former Provost, whose civic powers had always been resented, and who now threatened their stability. There were probably many in that place whose memories went back to the terrible sacking of the City by General Monck. Scouts were sent out, but quickly retreated when they were fired on. A sally towards the City walls by four of Dundee's troopers met with a burst of fire which left one of them dead. Inside, Livingstone's dragoons, under strict orders from their commanding officer, stayed put. At nightfall, Dundee pulled back, his mission unaccomplished. As he retreated, a party of scouts rode out from the City at his tail and watched him go. He spent the night at Glenogilvie with his wife, then set out again for the Highlands.

Dundee's lightning strike into Perthshire and Angus had been a fine piece of strategy. In Edinburgh the Committee of Estates met and ordered more troops from the south, while Colonel Barthold Balfour was ordered to cross the Forth to Burntisland to prepare for action. Mackay, isolated in Inverness, was not pleased when he heard the news. He immediately judged that Livingstone, by failing to attack Dundee, had proved himself 'either a traitor or a coward; for notwithstanding he was at least as strong as Dundee, and his horse in better case, he did not budge out of the town.'

However, Mackay was now probably in better military shape than Dundee. He had spent the time he had been in Inverness reinforcing the palisades of the town, and had sent for reinforcements. On the advice of Lord Tarbat, who knew the Highlands well, he had written to several clan chiefs, and had approached the Duke of Gordon's former agent, Sir Aeneas Macpherson, offering him a senior commission in the army if he would persuade the Cluny Macphersons to join him. The response from Sir Aeneas and the others, however, was either silence or it was negative. Mackay therefore ordered Colonel Ramsay north from Edinburgh with 600 men of the Scots Brigade. They were to march through Atholl and Badenoch, where they would rendezvous with Mackay himself. Ramsay was delayed for several days by a sudden scare that the French fleet was approaching up the Forth, but the ships, on inspection, turned out to be Dutch fishing vessels, and so, on 22 May, Ramsay headed north from Perth.

The after-effect of Dundee's raid, however, was still being felt. Ramsay met with a hostile reception in Atholl, and the further he went north the less safe he felt. He had received no message from Mackay, and there seemed to be a great deal of movement among the clans. The rumours spoke of many hundreds in arms, ready to launch a fearsome attack. Ramsay pressed on gingerly, sending a dispatch north to Mackay saying that he intended to persevere and head for Ruthven barracks. But then, almost at once, he changed his mind. Mackay's message to him had been intercepted by Steuart of Ballechin, Atholl's factor at Blair, who substituted a verbal instruction that Ramsay was to retreat, choosing, if he wished, a less dangerous route back. Ramsay seized on the message thankfully, and withdrew to Perth, blowing up his ammunition before he went.

The Government's intelligence had now broken down. On 25 May,

Mackay received Ramsay's message, but with no hint that he had changed his mind. He set off south the next day, a Sunday, leaving Ross of Balnagowan to hold Inverness with 300 or 400 men. Mackay had a hundred troopers, 140 dragoons, 200 foot, and 200 Highlanders supplied by with some Balnagowan and some Mackay support, in all about 640 men. Confidently expecting that he would meet Ramsay at Ruthven, Mackay had taken only two days' rations. But half-way there, he was met by an express from the Commander of Ruthven barracks saying that Ramsay had turned back. What was more, the report said, Dundee was approaching Badenoch, in his direction.

Dundee had made his way back to the west to meet and raise those clansmen who had responded to his summons. The journey had been the roughest he had yet made, and his troops were visibly tiring. The route he had chosen was through Rannoch Moor, one of the most desolate parts of Scotland, and the weather was atrocious.

> Now many of the wearied horses sink into the marsh and are lost in its depth [wrote Philip]. Failing to raise them, the riders place the saddles on their own shoulders and pursue their way on foot. I myself, having lost my horse, have to tramp by rugged path and hill, by rock and river.

They passed Loch Treig and Glen Spean, skirting Keppoch. Finally, on 16 May, two days ahead of the appointed time for the rendezvous, they crossed Glenroy, and, as Philip described it, 'Abria jam germio Gramum accipit ardua laeto' – 'Gladly, Lochaber receives the Graham into her bosom.'

In fact, Lochaber was by no means united in its enthusiasm for this champion of the Stuart cause.

CHAPTER FIFTEEN
Hill-walking

*'[Lochiel] was firmly of the opinion, that with their own
Chiefs, and natural Captains on their heads, under the
conduct of such a General as my Lord Dundee, [the
Highlanders] were equal to as many of the best disciplined
veteran troops in the kingdom.'*

John Drummond of Balhaldie

Dundee's knowledge of the north and western Highlands of Scotland
can only have been limited. His family came from Angus and Perthshire, 'the brae country', which, though it fringes the Highlands, has
closer links with the south. Until now he had never concerned himself
with the highland clans, nor spent time in their company. Above all, he
had no experience of Highland warfare, which was very different from
that envisaged by his own precise and ordered training. His first
encounter, with Keppoch, had not been encouraging.

In bridging that gap, Sir Ewan Cameron of Lochiel was not only an
essential ally, but a tutor. He was well over sixty now, with long
experience as a clan chief. He was also a devious politician, well
qualified for the nickname of 'Gled Wylie' – the Cunning Kite. Lochiel
had never been diverted from a ruthless ambition to further the
interests of Clan Cameron, whether it meant backing Campbells or
MacDonalds.

He was endowed with dark good looks, tireless energy, and the
courage of a wild cat. His mother belonged to the most powerful
branch of the House of Argyll, the Campbells of Glenorchy, whose
lands stretched westwards through Perthshire as far as the Atlantic

coast. Their ancient motto, simple and to the point, provides a clue to their prosperity: 'Conquest or keip thingis conquest'. When Lochiel's father died young, his teenage son was fostered by the Marquis of Argyll – MacChailein Mor, chief of the Clan Campbell – who was a powerful influence on him. Though Argyll failed to make the boy a scholar, he showed him something perhaps more important; he showed him where power lay, and how to use it.

According to Lochiel's grandson, John Drummond of Balhaldie, who compiled Lochiel's memoirs, in 1643 Lochiel underwent an experience which ensured his future as a King's man. After Montrose's defeat at Philiphaugh, some of the Royalist prisoners were taken to St Andrews. Argyll was there with his household, and, without telling anyone, Lochiel paid a visit to the cells where the condemned men awaited execution. Among them was Sir Robert Spottiswood, the King's Secretary of State for Scotland. A long conversation between the two made a deep impression on the young Highlander and convinced him that the King's cause was the only one he could in future support.

While there may be some truth in this story, it must be set against the fact that, throughout Lochiel's long life, self-interest always came first, allowing him to deal conveniently with both sides, from the Civil War to the Restoration. Knighted under Charles II, he was once referred to at court as 'the King of Thieves.'

The fall of Argyll had allowed him to seize valuable Campbell territory in Sunart and Ardnamurchan, and, when James VII fled, what loomed largest in his mind was less the blow to the Stuart cause, than the prospect of the new Earl of Argyll reclaiming his property. As early as March 1689, he had consulted the Glengarry MacDonnells, the MacDonalds in Moidart and the Macleans in Mull about the implications of William's new supremacy. He counted on their backing because for them, too, taking up the King's cause was a matter of securing their future against the return of an Earl of Argyll.

And for some, it was a simple case of survival. In early 1689, many Highlanders faced the prospect of actual starvation. The previous autumn's harvest had been reasonable, but the long winter, which brought heavy snow and frost that lasted on through to the month of May, meant that hay had run out long before the new grass grew.

Their bleak prospects were not improved by William's accession. The new Earl of Argyll had been prompt in pledging his loyalty, and had been one of those who went south to London to offer William the Scottish crown. On his return, he began raising men to 'protect' the forthcoming Convention. It was only a matter of time before his new status reunited the Campbells as a military force that would once more threaten the Lochaber clans.

The return of King James, on the other hand, would open up the possibility of expansion, of further raids into Argyll country, of a new and favoured existence under a friendly regime. News from the Convention in March that support had swung to William concentrated Lochiel's efforts. It is clear that he had been in touch with Dundee for some time, and when he dispatched Balhaldie to make contact with him after his rapid departure from Edinburgh it was to report on progress in the Highlands. Support at that point, however, was not great in terms of numbers. None of the Lochaber clans could muster much more that 500 men each, and, in Edinburgh, Viscount Tarbat told Mackay that the most they would bring to the field was about 2,500.

Tarbat in fact underestimated their strength. There was no reluctance on the part of the clans to supply armed men, for the fighting tradition was very much part of their lives, and the old forms of land ownership mostly required military service of a tenant as part of the contract. The traditional feu duty farm tenure required the services of 'hosting and hunting', where 'hosting' was the duty of organizing men for military service and of mounting campaigns. To fulfil this duty, the fighting men of a clan would be transformed into a regiment, and the chief would become its colonel, often with his relatives acting as officers under him.

A greater problem was keeping the clan armies together in the course of a campaign. The first objective of any clan in warfare was the seizing of booty, and once seized, the next aim was to get it back home. This was not a matter of greed, it was a simple question of ensuring survival through the next season.

There had already been some action on behalf of James amongst the clansmen. A small landing of men from Ireland had been effected earlier in the month of Kintyre, and a force of some 200 men under Sir Alexander Maclean, who was the son of the Bishop of Argyll, had conducted a series of running skirmishes with Government troops on land and at sea. Maclean was still campaigning when Dundee summoned the clans on 18 May.

Lochiel greeted Dundee 'with all imagineable honour and respect', according to his memoirs, and found him a house a mile from his own castle at Strone in Glenroy. There was not much, however, in the way of provisions that he could offer him or his men, and James Philip records the hunger that they all felt as they waited for the day of the rendezvous.

Mackay had done as much as he could to lure Lochiel to his side, but without success. Lochiel showed Dundee letters he had received from the General offering him a large bribe, the governorship of Inverlochy Castle, and the command of a regiment if he would bring his clan over to the Government side, but, said the Cameron chief, he had barely opened them.

By now the summons to Dundee's royal standard had spread throughout Lochaber, Badenoch, Atholl and Mar. The traditional method of raising military support amongst the clans was to send out a fiery cross – a spear crossed by wooden javelins dipped in tar and set alight – and this was duly done. The place fixed as the rendezvous was called, in James Philip's poem, Dalcomera, but is now Mucomir, on the north bank of the Spean, close to where it enters Loch Lochy.

As 18 May approached, some of the chiefs began to appear. Alasdair Dubh MacDonnell of Glengarry is generally credited as being the first to arrive, bringing with him some 300 men. He was a young man, described by Balhaldie as 'a very zealous asserter of the royal cause' and 'a person of great penetration and good natural parts'. But equally, like Lochiel, he was a political animal. 'He loved to meddle with no affair but what bore some distant view of honour or profit.' He was followed by MacDonald of Morar, who came with 200 of the Clanranald MacDonalds. Then there were a hundred MacDonalds from Glencoe, led by their grand old chief, Alasdair MacIain, and, already there, 400 Camerons under Lochiel. Then there were also 200 Stewarts of Appin and 200 Keppoch MacDonalds.

Those who were not there but joined later included the sixteen-year-old Captain of Clanranald, the MacDonalds of Sleat, Sir John Maclean of Duart, with his 200 clansmen, Macleans of Morvern, Coll, and Torloisk, the MacNeils of Barra, the Macleods of Raasay and the MacGregors. But to begin with, at Dalcomera, Dundee had fewer than 2,000 men with which to form his army.

What the clansmen lacked in numbers, they seem to have made up with the fierceness of their demeanour and the variety of their dress and weaponry. Most of the clansmen wore the Feileadh Mor, the big plaid, a length of tartan some five feet wide and sixteen feet long, which they folded into rough pleats before belting it round their waists. The remainder was used, in rough weather, like a cloak to cover the upper half of the body. At other times, looped over the left shoulder, it served a partly ornamental function. In this all-purpose garment, the clan regiments marched, ate, and slept. Under it they wore shirts, dyed with saffron, which they would knot between their legs on those occasions when the plaid was discarded. The bare legs thus revealed earned for the Highlanders the name given them by derisive Lowlanders – 'the Redshanks'.

There were, as yet, no recognizable clan tartans, though attempts had been made by individual chiefs to enforce uniformity. Some identification was provided by clan badges – sprigs of bog-myrtle or other plants. They were armed with a variety of weapons, a dirk stuck in the belt on the right hip, and a sword, basket-hilted and sharpened to a razor's edge on the left. For defence they carried a round leather shield, often studded with metal, called a 'targe'. Those who were armed with muskets generally had flintlocks, though some carried old-fashioned matchlocks. Long practice on the hill meant that they put their weapons to good use however out of date they might be.

Each clan brought its piper, and some, like the Keppochs, had a bard to record their deeds, to celebrate their victories or bemoan their defeats. The chiefs were often men of some culture and education, and Philip described each one in his stirring verse: 'Never with greater note of preparation did men assemble in such force, nor scattered clans cover the hills with so great a company', he wrote. Glengarry was 'mounted on a foaming steed, and towering in glittering arms ... claymore in hand, his cloak shining with gold'. Alasdair MacIain of Glencoe was 'turning his shield in his hand, flourishing terribly his sword, fierce in aspect, rolling his wild eyes, the horn of his twisted beard curled backwards'. Philip says he was 'covered as to his breast with raw hide', though later, after some judicious plundering, he acquired a brass blunderbuss and a fine buff coat.

Keppoch was there, wearing a helmet and flourishing a two-handed sword (the old-fashioned claymore, which most clansmen had discarded as too unwieldy for battle). His men were armed in addition with axes, javelins, and clubs, according to Philip. Lochiel, 'stiff in brazen armour, rising high above his axe-bearing line', was particularly ferocious: 'His very look, so fierce, might fright the boldest foe.' Dundee himself 'as a bright sun, glows in their midst, or shines as the moon at the full amongst the lesser stars.'

Dundee's own troop, still barely more than eighty strong, included his brother David, various Graham cousins, Lord Dunfermline with some Gordon followers, David Halyburton of Pictur, and a bright young advocate called Gilbert Ramsay who had exchanged the wig for the sword. Finally there was, of course, the bard himself, James Philip of

Almericlose, who recounted simply: 'I myself was bearing in my arms the royal standard.'

Dundee delayed his departure for a week as the clans drifted in, and spent the time in drilling them as best he could. He spoke little or no Gaelic and he knew only the bare minimum about clan warfare. But it is clear that from the start he was able to instil some discipline amongst the Highlanders, and Lochiel, on whom he leant heavily for guidance, gave him one central lesson about the fighting men he was now to command, a lesson which he always followed. In essence, it was that the Highlanders had their own way of fighting, and it was best to draw on that strength rather than to attempt to teach them the alien tactics which Dundee had been used to on the Continent. Balhaldie later set it down as he recalled it from Lochiel's own testimony:

> 'That to pretend to alter anything in their old customs, whereof they are exceedingly tenacious, would entirely ruin them, and make them no better than new-raised troops; whereas he was firmly of the opinion, that with their own Chiefs, and natural Captains on their heads, under the conduct of such a General as my Lord Dundee, they were equal to as many of the best disciplined veteran troops in the kingdom.'

Their tactics, he said, were essentially the same as those of the ancient Gauls, who used sword and targe successfully against the Romans. Nothing much had changed over the years, except that the short yew bow had been exchanged for the musket. The secret lay in tight discipline up to the moment of a charge, and then ferocity as they broke through the enemy ranks: 'The attack is so furious that they commonly pierce their ranks, put them in disorder, and determine the fate of the day in a few moments', said Lochiel. Dundee seems immediately to have grasped the point, and to have accepted Lochiel's advice. 'As there is no argument like matter of fact', said Balhaldie, 'he thought himself obliged to take them on the word of one who had so long and so happy an experience.'

Despite the enthusiasm of his small army, Dundee was still dependent on help from James in Ireland. There was still no word from the messenger he had sent there in April, and, though he repeated his request for reinforcements, there was again no reply.

James had advanced with his army towards Londonderry in March and had begun laying siege to it. It was an action which was to last for three months, with fatal consequences for the campaign in Scotland. He had sent over a mass of letters and orders to Scotland with a messenger called Brady, promising 5,000 men, but Brady had been captured with the papers at Greenock in April, and Dundee's pleas for assistance arrived as the siege was getting under way. Melfort, whose malign influence was to be the greatest single handicap to Dundee's efforts, intercepted any messages that arrived, and delayed, fatally, in responding to them.

Dundee was able to promise the clan chiefs military commissions from King James and some guarantee that their expenses would be repaid, but, without definite word that troops would join him from Ireland, he could offer little in terms of a strategy. On 28 May, therefore, he marched out from Dalcomera, to the sounds of pipes and bugles, with Glengarry in the lead, and the other clans following in order of precedence. They crossed through Glen Roy, the mountains of Garvamore, and the fords of the Spey, heading east through Badenoch to Raitts Castle, the ancient stronghold of the Comyns.

The next day, 29 May, was one for celebration, it being the anniversary of Charles II's restoration, a day so often marked as infamous by the Covenanters. Dundee, however, chose the occasion to address his chiefs and to remind them 'to observe its due offices and honours'. A bonfire was lit, and, to the sound of applause from the watching clansmen and the rousing pipes, Dundee proposed the memory of King Charles, the health of King James, and the triumphant return by the royal forces to Scotland.

On the next day, Dundee marched towards Ruthven Castle, which lay across the Spey, and was now held by a company of Grants under young Captain Forbes, brother of the Laird of Culloden. Forbes was expecting to be joined by Mackay and when called upon to surrender refused. Dundee sent Keppoch forward to offer him a second opportunity, and, when that was also refused, Keppoch began filling the moat with piles of wood, declaring that he intended to set the castle alight. Seeing that his attackers were in earnest, Forbes announced that he was willing to surrender. He and his men were allowed to leave the castle unharmed to rejoin Mackay if they could find him. On Dundee's orders, Keppoch then set alight to Ruthven and burned it to the ground.

The alarm reached Mackay as he was heading south from Inverness, and he halted to consider his position. He had barely 700 men, so once again a battle was risky. To fall back on Inverness, however, meant ceding much of the country between Inverness and Perth, so he decided to try and cut Dundee off from Gordon territory by marching rapidly down Strathspey. Again, with only two days' provisions, it was a bold move, but the objective, as Mackay wrote, was clear. (In his memoirs, which chronicle the campaign, he always refers to himself in the third person):

> To gain betwixt Dundee and the south, to be master as well of the retreat in case of necessity... and to see if, by such a speedy and unexpected motion, he might happily meet with a favourable occasion to fall upon Dundee's party in disorder and straggling, to which that sort of people are very subject.

He force-marched his troops for twenty-four hours south-west, the latter part in darkness, until he came within a mile and a half of Dundee's camp. He found it secured by a wood and a marsh which acted like a double trench, so, judging that his exhausted soldiers were in no condition to mount a difficult attack, he took up position in a nearby pass and waited until dawn. But the enemy had retreated. On 30 May, therefore, he sent for reinforcements, and marched four miles down the glen to establish a holding position at Culnakyle on the Spey, ten miles north-east of Ruthven.

Dundee never knew how near Mackay had been to him, though an alarm had been raised during the march from Raitts. He had himself marched north-east, in the same direction as Mackay, but well behind him. On the way, there had been a slight diversion: on passing the Mackintosh castle of Dunachton, the Highlanders noticed it was in flames. Keppoch, the Ruthven incendiarist, had set it alight, and once again Dundee turned on him in fury. He rebuked Keppoch in front of the entire army, and told him that he would rather serve as a common soldier amongst disciplined troops than command men like him, 'who seemed to make it his business to draw the odium of the country upon him.' He ordered him to leave, taking his men with him.

Keppoch now, perhaps for the first time in his life, apologized publicly. He had, he said, attacked Mackintosh's castle only because he thought he was an enemy to the King. He promised to be obedient in the future. Reluctantly, Dundee accepted his excuses, and the army moved on towards Alvie, on the Spey. Riding ahead, Captain Alexander Bruce, formerly one of Livingstone's dragoons, but now with Dundee, found some of Mackay's troops still encamped there. He invited them to change sides, and was greeted by shots, which he returned with enthusiasm. Then, fearing that he might be cut off, he galloped back to rejoin the main force.

Delighted at the prospect of striking at the enemy, Dundee pressed forward. But Bruce had stumbled on only a rearguard detachment, which had hurriedly withdrawn to join Mackay's main force, at Culnakyle. Here they were in a well-protected position, where open ground would allow the General's cavalry 'to gallop through those Highland foot, who apprehend nothing so much as horse in the midst of this plain', as Mackay described it. He kept his men stood to, with horses saddled and bridled, and outposts in the woods reporting every two hours to alert him in case Dundee decided on an attack.

There Mackay was joined by Livingstone's dragoons, who had marched from the City of Dundee, and there he first learned of disaffection amongst his own troops. Two men claiming to be defectors from Dundee's side came to the camp and asked to speak to him privately. The General was suspicious, but agreed to hear one of them in the presence of Livingstone. Their message was that most of his senior dragoon officers were secret Jacobite sympathizers, and were only waiting for a suitable opportunity to desert to the enemy. Asked for evidence, the man said that he had heard Dundee himself openly assuring the chiefs that the dragoons were ready to join him, and were only waiting for a suitable opportunity. He had also seen him reading letters from his wife telling him the same thing.

Meanwhile, Captain Forbes, hurrying north on his way from the flames of Ruthven, had stumbled on more evidence of treachery, in the form of two dragoon troopers, one of whom, Sergeant Provensal, was dressed, unusually, in blue. They claimed they were on a scouting mission, but, when Forbes reported to the General, it was found that no scout dressed in blue had ever been sent out.

Provensal was in fact on his way to Dundee to pass on messages from the disaffected dragoon officers. The news he brought on 1 June, together with information about the strength and position of Mackay's troops, encouraged Dundee to press ahead and attempt an engagement.

Mackay, outnumbered, judged it wise to retreat. Cut off from the south by Dundee's forces, and the impassable barrier of the Cairngorm mountains, he headed north-east along the Spey valley, seeking the sanctuary of Castle Grant. 'Thus', wrote Philip, 'the hungry fox, seeking in the darkness of night the full sheepfold, turns when he hears the barking of the fierce dogs, and with drooping neck and brush trailing in the mire, he hides his shame under the cover of the woods'. Mackay put it more prosaically: 'Committing to the providence of God (against whom there is no wisdom, nor understanding, nor counsel can succeed), he took his way down the river with hungry horse and men, though resolute ...'.

Dundee guessed Mackay's route correctly and hurried after him, bypassing his camp-site at Culnakyle, and heading for Glenlivet. The pursuit lasted four days, with Dundee gaining steadily. Late on the fourth afternoon, the Highlanders spotted Mackay's troops and gave out a loud hurrah. Some of them cast off their plaids and prepared for battle. But Mackay had no intention of fighting. He had placed the suspect dragoons in the front, and was now marching rapidly on. The sun was setting as Dundee's men closed on the troops that he could see on a hill across the River Spey, but he could not close the final gap before darkness fell. The Highlanders were still eager for action, and wanted to force Mackay to fight. But finally Dundee called a halt. They were within three miles of Strathbogie, a flat stretch where Mackay's cavalry would have had the advantage, and he judged it foolhardy, in the darkness, to carry on. That night, at Edinglassie, a castle on the River Livet, just west of Huntly, he called off the pursuit.

It was here at Edinglassie, on 4 June, that he fell sick. Mackay heard later that he was 'sick of a flux', and it is clear that he had some form of dysentery. Some of the Highlanders, finding themselves in relatively rich country, began to plunder. Dundee's illness 'gave boldness to the disorderly', and some of the clansmen 'thinking themselves masters . . . plundered without distinction wherever they came.'

News about these manœuvres in the Highlands filtered down to Edinburgh, where there was a degree of complacency about events. One newsletter described Dundee 'skipping from one hill to another like wildfire, which at last will vanish of itself for want of fuel.' Another said that the natives 'flock to him in great numbers, not to serve him, but to serve themselves, by stealing baggage, and such other booty as they can lay hold on.' One rumour was that Dundee was fleeing to Ireland, another that he was on the point of surrender.

Mackay knew better. At Suy Hill, he was now joined by Colonel Berkeley's 300 dragoons and Sir James Leslie's 700 foot, which gave him the chance of turning near disaster into a sudden victory. He determined to hit back rapidly at Dundee by mounting a night march and attacking him just when he was resting after the pursuit.

But his plans were betrayed. Word was passed back to Dundee by Sergeant Provensal and his subversive dragoons. Dundee gave immediate orders for a retreat. Marching through the whole day of 5 June, he wasted no time in returning to Cromdale on the Spey, half-way back to Badenoch, though he himself could barely stay on his horse through illness and fatigue.

When Mackay reached Edinglassie later the same day, he found the castle there, owned by the local sheriff, Sir George Gordon, in ruins.

All stores had been destroyed. But he also found some stragglers from Clan Cameron who had stayed behind to plunder, together with two of Livingstone's dragoons. Sheriff Gordon exercised his judicial powers, and took private revenge for the destruction of his house, by hanging the Camerons from the nearest tree.

And Mackay now decided that the time had come to expose the traitors in his ranks. He arrested the suspect dragoons and learned from them of Provensal's role. He also seized the disaffected officers, who included Lieutenant-Colonel Livingstone, and Captain-Lieutenant Creichton, whose later memoirs, as recounted to Swift, give a somewhat dramatized version of events. The officers were court-martialled at Culnakyle and sent down to Edinburgh, where they were committed to prison. Mackay sent a letter to the Duke of Hamilton, recommending that the dragoon officers be executed and Provensal 'put to the torture' along with his confederates. 'If torture be just in any case, it is in this', he wrote. But it was not carried out.

Dundee's retreat was represented to the clansmen as a march to Badenoch, where, they were told, there was a rendezvous with reinforcements. But there was no disguising the change in atmosphere, and some of the Highlanders began to slip away.

Mackay was now closing the gap as he marched back down the Spey to Culnakyle. Sir Thomas Livingstone, who was out ahead of the main force with 200 horse and dragoons, came unexpectedly on a party of Macleans foraging for meal. They were in extended column, and not expecting trouble, when Livingstone attacked. Some of them fled; others were taken prisoner. But about a hundred kept together, and took up a position at the foot of Knockbrecht Hill. They held off their attackers with musket-fire, and, by pitching boulders down the slope at the dragoons, kept them at bay until the morning of 8 June, when they mounted a miniature Highland charge, and broke through Livingstone's troops, routing them and killing their captain before regaining Dundee's camp.

Dundee himself had heard the noise of the engagement and had ridden out in some alarm with his troopers at his back to bring help. But it was not needed. The Macleans, who had helped themselves to helmets, coats, and even horses from the fleeing dragoons, were exultant.

Much encouraged, Dundee's diminishing army marched back to Ruthven. On the way they met Sir Alexander Maclean, who had been engaged in action in Kintyre, but was now ready to bring his 200 or so followers to join the royal standard. They had heard much about

Dundee, and were excited finally to meet him. Something of the mystique that surrounds a leader – so important to the clans – had already begun to form. The Gaelic bards would soon be referring to Dundee as 'Dark John of the Battles'.

Dundee had by now begun to attract considerable attention, and not just from his followers. At one stage during his travels in the Highlands, a serving-maid, called on to serve him with wine, came upon him in his room. What she saw made a distinct impression on her, and years later she recalled what she had seen. Dundee, she said, was 'a swarthy little man, with keen lively eyes, and black hair tinged with grey, which he wore in locks which covered each ear and were rolled upon slips of lead, twisted together at the end'. Clearly, the long flowing hair which shows in all his portraits, required a primitive form of hair-curler to keep it in shape.

But, despite his reputation, Dark John's clan army had begun to melt away with its booty. Food was becoming increasingly scarce. Reports of the enemy's numbers were alarming, and rumours filtering back made it sound ever more formidable. Dundee therefore decided to return to Lochaber and dismiss his army, 'upon their giving assurance that they would be ready to join him upon twenty-four hours advertisement', according to Balhaldie. However, he kept the 200 men brought by Sir Alexander Maclean, recognizing in them a battle-hardened force that had kept together long enough for him to be able to rely on it. Lochiel assured him that 'while there was a cow in Lochaber, neither he nor his men should want.' On 11 June, Dundee returned to his old quarters in Glenroy.

While he was there, other clansmen began to arrive. Sir Donald MacDonald of Sleat, 'illustrious in war beyond his years', as Philip described him, came with 700 men. Balhaldie said that he 'conducted himself according to the strictest rules of religion and morality. He looked upon his clan as children, and upon the King as father of his country.' From Uist came 600 men of Clanranald, with their young chief, known by the ancient title, Captain of Clanranald. He was then only sixteen years old, and with 'the down of youth on his cheeks', still under the tutorship of Donald MacDonald of Benbecula. Despite his age and inexperience, Clanranald was to remain loyal to King James throughout the campaign, and remained so later in exile in France, where he was described as one of the most accomplished gentlemen at court.

Dundee felt more comfortable with allies like this than with men like Keppoch. Even Lochiel, he found, was beginning to revert to type, or rather his men were, without noticeable restraint from their chief. A party of Camerons had decided to make a secret raid into Morayshire, to take revenge for their fellow-clansmen who had been hanged at Edinglassie. The expedition was judged a success in terms of booty, but there had been a skirmish, and amongst those killed in it was a MacDonald, a remote Glengarry relative.

Glengarry was furious at the death of his kinsman, and complained bitterly to Dundee, demanding satisfaction from Lochiel. But Dundee had clearly learned some of the facts of Highland life. In his previous incarnation, as a keen military officer, he would undoubtedly have held a court-martial and punished the erring Camerons for their gross dereliction of duty. Now, however, he listened to the case very much as a chief might have done, and handed down a judgment that would have amazed his fellow-officers back in Galloway.

He said he failed to understand why Glengarry was so upset. 'If there were any injury done, it was to him as General of the King's troops, in so far as they had acted without commission.' As to the deed itself, however, had they been regular troops, regularly paid, then indeed they would have been punished. But, as they were ignorant of military laws, all he was concerned about was preventing unnecessary pillaging of the country. Besides, they had brought back a number of cattle, which were badly needed, and had fairly distributed the booty. As for killing a MacDonald, Dundee professed amazement at Glengarry's concern:

> If such an accident is a just ground for raising disturbance in our small army we shall not dare to engage the King's enemies, lest there may chance to be some of your name and following among them who may happen to be killed.

Dundee had learned a lot during his short time in the Highlands. Furthermore, he had judged his man right. That evening, he sat down to dine with the chiefs, as he always did, with Glengarry amongst the company. And no further mention was made of the matter.

Meanwhile, Mackay, now joined by Colonel Ramsay, had advanced to the edge of Lochaber country. Finding the Highlanders dispersed, he decided on a tactical withdrawal. His troops were exhausted and underfed, and there was still a lack of new grass for the horses. Although it was early June, the ravages of the late winter were still to be felt. He sent Berkeley's regiment to Strathbogie, which belonged to the Duke of Gordon, and where there was enough grass to be found. Ramsay was detailed to Elgin, along with a detachment from three of the 'Dutch' regiments. He himself took the now dependable dragoons, Leslie's 700 foot, 300 men of Leven's and Hastings' regiments, and the 200 Highlanders from Sutherland and Ross, and returned to Inverness, 'where he stayed the matter of a fortnight, to see if the enemy would undertake anything further, and to settle the necessary orders.'

The first stage of an extraordinary campaign had thus come to an end for both sides, with neither having gained a conclusive advantage. Dundee had learned the hard way that his army could only be kept together if there was the promise of immediate military action. Mackay had been frustrated by the territory he was operating in, territory which made conventional tactics impossible.

It was, therefore, a time for reflection, and for regrouping in preparation for the last and conclusive phase of the Highland war.

CHAPTER SIXTEEN
For His Majesty's Service

'All the world will be with us, blessed be God'
Viscount Dundee

News of setbacks in the Highlands caused consternation in Edinburgh. The Privy Council demanded an explanation of what had happened, particularly in Atholl, which was meant to be solidly in Government hands. Mackay sent word from Inverness that he intended to return south.

Meanwhile, efforts continued to force the Duke of Gordon to surrender Edinburgh Castle. He had held on stubbornly for three months, despite the draining of the North Loch to deprive the Castle wells of water. But he was short of ammunition, and had had no communication at all with the King. Dundee sent letters to him through the Countess of Erroll, but these were intercepted, and she was arrested as a collaborator. Thereafter, Gordon heard nothing. On 13 June, with hope and supplies running out, Gordon surrendered, obtaining an indemnity for his small garrison, but none for himself. He was thrown into prison, to be tried later.

From Inverness, meanwhile, Mackay had written to Hamilton telling him that, in his view, present tactics in the Highlands would not work. He said that

> he saw no way to subdue the Highlanders, considering their country was full of mountains, bogs, woods and difficult passes with inaccessible retiring places, where it was impossible to hunt them out, as well as to subsist a fortnight in such barren and desert countries.

Instead, he proposed rebuilding the fort at Inverlochy (later Fort William), backed by a string of other garrisons, and using them as centres of local government, rather as they had been under Cromwell. He asked the Council to give this urgent consideration, and, on 20 June, began moving, with his three regiments of the Scots Brigade, south via Angus.

He gave instructions to the Master of Forbes to seize Braemar Castle, which was held by the notorious outlaw John Farquharson of Iverey, a man known as 'the black colonel'. An attack at dawn was planned, but Forbes arrived late, giving Farquharson and his men a chance to escape 'in their shirts'. They were to return later for revenge, and burn Braemar to the ground.

Mackay, who was surprisingly tolerant of the mistakes made by his subordinates, put Forbes's blunder down to inexperience, and set up another garrison, at Abergeldie, lower down the Dee. But this held him up considerably. He finally arrived in Edinburgh on 12 July, so drained by the illness that had plagued him ever since he landed with William at Torbay, that 'he could not but with great inconveniency keep himself on horseback.' He was also disappointed to find in Edinburgh that no one had done anything about his proposal for a fort at Inverlochy, and there seemed neither men nor materials to build it.

Six days later, on 18 July, the Council issued a proclamation, offering a reward of 18,000 merks for Dundee 'dead or alive', and this was supplemented by another, more generous one of £20,000 sterling, 'which may probably catch him', said Sir John Dalrymple, 'who must be in the power of the clans.

Dundee, however, was safe from that kind of betrayal, as was Charles Edward Stuart in similar circumstances more than fifty years later. He had by now recovered his health, and was seeking to persuade his more uncertain allies to rally to the royal standard. One of those was Duncan Macpherson of Cluny, who had also been subjected to strong pressure from Mackay, with warnings not to 'join with a company of Papists or worse than Papists.'

Cluny, however, sat firmly on the fence, despite a persuasive letter, dated 19 May, from Dundee which counted on 'your constant loyalty, your honour and your conscience', and spoke of an imminent landing of troops from Ireland. Dundee told him not to be put off by stories of James's religious policies:

> There is one thing I forewarn you of, not to be alarmed with the danger they would make you believe the Protestant religion is in. They must make religion the pretext, as it has been in all times, of rebellion. I am as much concerned in the Protestant religion as any man, and will do my endeavours to see it secured.

Dundee was helped, finally, by a communication from James, who was still laying siege to Londonderry. On 22 June, a messenger called Hay arrived in Glenroy, with documents from King James which gave Dundee at long last a commission as Lieutenant-General of James's forces in Scotland, and authority to convene a Convention and proclaim war against Hamilton's Government in Edinburgh. The letter, signed by Melfort, was a copy of a message sent three months earlier, in March, but intercepted.

It promised reinforcements of 5,000 men, though without the cavalry Dundee needed so badly – because it would be 'inconvenient' to ship the horses over – and it asked for Dundee's views on where they should be landed. Commissions for the clan chiefs, left blank for Dundee to fill up, were enclosed, and the letter promised officers, to be dispatched as soon as Dundee gave the word. He was encouraged to hold fast:

> ... assure yourselves, we will stand by you, and, if it shall please God to
> give success to our just cause, we will let the ancient Cavalier party know
> that they are the only true basis the monarchy can rest upon in Scotland:
> and we have found such effects of our mercy in times past, as will make
> us now raise our friends, upon the ruins of our enemies.

The tone was stirring, but the promises came too late, and were by now hopelessly unrealistic. By the time Dundee received James's letter, the siege at Londonderry had degenerated into a sullen stalemate, and only a tiny proportion of the promised troops could be spared.

As soon as he had received this letter, however, he sent off a letter of his own, to Macleod of Macleod in Skye, which reflected the buoyancy of the royal message. He said he had heard that William of Orange was warning the Privy Council of the imminent arrival of fifty-two French men-of-war off the coast of Ireland, with more coming from Brest, bearing 15,000 soldiers; that Londonderry was on the point of capitulation, with horseflesh inside the town being traded for 6d. a pound, and 'for cannon-bullets they were shooting lumps of brick wrapped in pewter plates'; and that James's army was about to land on the west coast of Scotland, and indeed might already have done so. The time had come, therefore, for Macleod to commit himself: 'I shall tell you, that if you hasten not to land your men, I am of the opinion you will have little occasion to do the King great service. For if he land in the west of Scotland you will come too late ...'; Dundee calculated his own potential troop strength as 'about 3,000', and counted on many more when they reached Badenoch, Mar, Atholl, and points south: 'I hope we will be masters of the north, as the King's army will be of the south.' He even had hopes of a Campbell joining up: 'I had almost forgot to tell you of my Lord Breadalbane, who I suppose will now come to the fields.'

This was John Campbell of Glenorchy, first Earl of Breadalbane, with whom Dundee had been in regular correspondence. As a powerful landowner, and a cousin to the Earl of Argyll, Breadalbane would have been an important ally. But he pleaded gout, and retired to his castle of Kilchurn, sitting 'with sore foot at the fireside' and declaring that he would not meddle on either side.

Dundee was more successful with Breadalbane's brother-in-law, Iain Macnaughton of Dunderaw, whom he invited to 'get ready as soon as you can all your name followers and kindly men wherever they are, and march them this way.' Macnaughton duly joined him, but his 'kindly men' were less enthusiastic, and most of them failed to turn up.

Despite confident predictions that clan reinforcements were at hand, the reality, as Dundee knew, was less promising. His frustration at the long silence from Ireland, and his particular dissatisfaction with the Earl of Melfort, James's principal adviser, spilled over in two long and remarkable letters which he wrote to Melfort from Moy in Lochaber on successive days, the 27 and 28 June.

Melfort has justifiably been accused of, effectively, sabotaging King James's cause in Scotland. This was never deliberate, though Dundee's friend Balcarres was one of those who were convinced that he was an *agent provocateur*. Melfort had, rather, a knack for saying and doing the wrong things at the wrong time, an unhappy failing in a diplomat. He possessed, additionally and fatally, an overweening confidence in his own judgment as well as an obsession that every kind of plot was being hatched against him by those whom he considered traitors. He expressed his views in a series of vivid letters which succeeded in alienating friends and enemies alike. He was, as one historian has put it, 'a master of the unforgettable and unforgivable phrase.'

It is, therefore, no surprise to find Dundee, with his painful honesty, blaming Melfort personally for much of the hostility that had grown up towards James, particularly because of his religious views:

> You know what the Church of England is in England; and both there and here they generally say that the King is not disposed to push matters of religion, or force people to do things they scrupled in conscience; but that you, to gain favour with those of that religion, had pressed and

prevailed with him, contrary to his inclination, to do what he did, which has given his enemies occasion to destroy him and the monarchy.

He advised him to stand down as James's Secretary of State, 'that the King's business might go on the smoother', adding: 'I think I have said enough, if not too much, of this.'

Dundee went on to give Melfort a succinct view of his Highland strategy so far. His aim, he said, had been to win time to allow reinforcements to arrive, and to avoid a major encounter with the enemy unless there was a clear chance of victory (shades of Drumclog). But he had suffered from the lack of a commission from James, and from a shortage of money and ammunition. Funds to support his campaign had been a major problem. He had got credit through his sister's husband in the south, and through his wife, but had not been able to raise any himself, since 'nobody durst pay to a traitor.' However, the Queen (Mary of Modena), had sent £2,000 sterling to London, 'to be paid to me for the King's service', with £2,000 more promised. Dundee was touched: 'I did not know the Queen had known anything of our affairs.'

The lack of gunpowder was a serious difficulty. He had started out with only fifty pounds of it in weight, and could not lay his hands on any more. Luckily, however, he enjoyed one advantage: 'the Highlanders will not fire above once, and then take to the broadsword.' But his main complaint was the lack of any communication from James or Melfort during all the time he had been marching up and down the Highlands:

> I wonder, above all things, that in three months I never heard from you; seeing by Mr Hay, I had so earnestly recommended it to you. . . . If you could not have sent expresses, we thought you would at least have hastened the dispatch of these we sent.

Most of his letters, he said, had gone to prospective allies without eliciting much response either. His friend Sir George Mackenzie, 'a very honest man, firm beyond belief', had gone to England; Atholl, 'who did not know what to do', had left too; the Earl of Home, 'who is very frank', was a prisoner in Edinburgh; Breadalbane, who 'pretends the gout', was staying at home; the Earls of Erroll and Aberdeen did likewise. As for the Bishops: 'I know not where they are! They are now the Kirk invisible.'

Dundee was remarkably well-informed about events in Edinburgh. His letter contained a list of notables, with a brisk account of their political sail-trimming or their imprisonment. Tarbat, he said, was 'a great villain', and Douglas, Queensberry's son, was 'a great knave, as well as beast'. Perhaps the saddest figure at this time was his former confederate, Lord Balcarres, who was still in prison and who wrote despairingly that 'death can be no worse to me.'

For Dundee's present allies, however, particularly the stalwart Halyburton 'and many other gentlemen', he had the highest praise. They deserved commissions from the King as well as more troops, 'for they suffer great hardships.' The next step must be to send reinforcements via Inverlochy: 'about five or six thousand as you have convenience of boats', he said optimistically, 'of which as many horse as conveniently can. About six or eight hundred would do well, but rather more.' An alternative landing- place would be further south, on the Mull of Kintyre, where the crossing was shorter. In that case, he would rendezvous with the King's forces and march 'towards the passes of Forth.'

Whether he really believed that all those troops would come is doubtful. He may have been trying to sting Melfort into some kind of action. He may, on the other hand, have been deliberately exaggerating the prospects of support in case the letter fell into enemy hands. He was clearly alive to the possibilities of propaganda. He had been deliberately stressing in all his letters that a landing in the west was imminent, in order to draw Government troops in that direction. One of these communications was amongst the bundle which had been intercepted on its way to Lady Erroll and which had led to her arrest. Dundee plainly felt that these efforts had been successful in drawing Mackay down to Edinburgh, and in leading to all sorts of speculation about possible landing-places in the south and west.

The letter ended with a plea for arms and ammunition. But it had barely been sealed and entrusted to the faithful messenger, Mr Hay, when word reached him that a further letter from Melfort was being delivered. He recalled Hay, and read what the Secretary of State had to say.

Once again, it was a balloon filled with hot Melfort air – false information and querulous complaints. Londonderry, he said, was on the point of falling – which it was not; instead of the promised troops, there were further questions about numbers and landing-places; there was no ammunition sent or promised, instead there were questions about Melfort's reputation, and what Dundee thought of him. In the circumstances, Dundee's reply was surprisingly mild:

I have so often written over all that Derry was ours, that now, say what I like, they hardly believe; and when I talk of relief out of Ireland, they laugh at it … As to yourself, I have told you freely my opinions and am still of the same mind. You desire I may tell you your faults … I must tell you, many of those who have complained of you, have carried themselves so, that they deserve not much to be noticed. However, they have poisoned the generality with prejudice against you, and England will, I am afraid, be uneasier to you than Scotland.

He suggested, bluntly, that, as soon as James had crossed to Scotland, the Secretary of State should resign. But Melfort was deaf to such advice.

Dundee himself, of course, could be equally deaf to other people's advice. A letter sent by Lord Strathnaver from Inverness begged him to call off his campaign. It was a stilted affair ('the courses you take tend inevitably to the ruin of you and yours, if persisted in'), which had been virtually dictated by Sir Thomas Livingstone, who added the postscript: 'The contents of this letter were written by my Lord Strathnaver, upon my desire and by my orders. T. Livingstone.' Dundee replied courteously enough, thanking Strathnaver for his concern, but pointing out that such was the strength of the King's forces, 'I leave you to judge if I or you, your family or mine, be in most danger.'

His confident tone concealed the growing sense of urgency he was beginning to feel. The flow of letters to potential supporters continued, each one stressing the imminence of a royal landing and the rewards of victory. He promised two Robertson chieftains 'a glorious occasion and no great danger', though he held out a clear threat of punishment if they failed to join:

> I am resolved that whoever refuses, in any part of the kingdom, to join the King's standard at my call who have his Majesty's commission and authority to make war, I will hold them as traitor and treat them as enemies.

To Macpherson of Cluny, with whom he corresponded continually, but without effect, almost up to the final battle, he claimed that Londonderry had fallen, that the French fleet was at sea, and that a regiment had arrived from Ireland:

> This I write to you to be communicated to all the gentry of Badenoch; so call them together, for from the head to the foot I will spare none that joins not. The gentry must march first themselves, and I expect 400 men, and no expenses will be allowed.

The reason he was so desperate to persuade Cluny was that Badenoch was still uncertain territory. The whole question of who controlled the land that lay between him and Perth was crucial to any future campaign, and Cluny was one of those whose influence could tilt the balance. While Cluny was important in the raising of the men of Badenoch, Lord Murray, eldest son of the Marquis of Atholl, was an essential ally if the route south was to be secured.

The Murrays were a family divided. The Marquis himself, whom General Mackay despised for his indecision, had prudently retired to Bath to take the waters. Not that the cure had done him much good, for his wife reported on 13 July that 'Since my Lord pumped his head, there is fallen so sad a defluxion on one eye, that since Saturday last he has not been able to look up, eat, drink or sleep.' Three of Atholl's sons were staunch Jacobites. But John, Lord Murray, the eldest son and heir, was far from certain about his own loyalty. That he was not a Jacobite was well known. But whether he was a fervent supporter of King William was unclear. He had a strong moralistic streak, and attempted to reach his decision on purely religious grounds, resisting the pressures from his Presbyterian wife and his father-in-law, the Duke of Hamilton. Writing about his dilemma three years later, he said: 'The want of clearness what was my duty has been the reason of my backwardness in acting either in one side or the other.'

Dundee considered it vital that Lord Murray be persuaded to come out on James's behalf, and bring his well-armed and trained tenants with him, but he predicted shrewdly that even if Murray decided against James, he could no more make the men of Atholl fight against him than the Duke of Hamilton could force the tenants of Strathaven or Lesmahagow to take up arms against their will: 'notwithstanding all the power and interest he has in that country'. On 19 July, he wrote Murray a long and thoughtful letter, laying great stress on the authority vested in the King, and – for he knew his man – stressing the religious tolerance that James stood for.

The tone was diplomatic. He suggested a meeting to 'concert what is fittest to be done for the good of our country and service of our lawful King', and pointed out that he had the King's commission, which carried considerable weight: 'By declaring openly for the liberty of your country and the lawful right of your undoubted Sovereign, you may acquire to yourself and family great honours and rewards; and the everlasting blessing of Almighty God, which is above all.'

He laid great stress on the legality of the King's position, and on his intention 'to secure the Protestant religion as by law established', and to make sure that noble families – like the Murrays – would be secure in their privileges. Nobody was to be persecuted, and James was drawing up an Indemnity which would only exclude 'such as are come from Holland, who are supposed to be chiefly concerned in this usurpation, and those who voted to dethrone the King and get up some other in his place.'

The hatred with which Melfort was viewed was reflected in Dundee's assurances that the Secretary of State could yet be prevailed on to step down:

> He assures me the King will not part with him; but, however, he is resolved to leave him against his will, if he sees that his presence is in any way prejudicial; and that with joy, he says in good earnest, he would resign his office of Secretary for Scotland to any honest man; and bids me give him advice. This by three different letters. . . .

The letter ended with a rallying call: 'The Parliaments of England and Scotland are by the ears, and both nations in a flame. Use the time.'

The plea was met by silence. But Murray's action spoke louder than words, for he sent the letter straight to the Government's new Secretary of State, Lord Melville. Dundee suspected that he might. It was a letter intended as much for propaganda as to win over an uncertain ally, and besides that, he had already taken steps to make the Atholl territory secure for King James. Ten days earlier, he had sent orders to Murray's factor, Patrick Steuart of Ballechin, whose loyalty was unquestioned, to take Blair Castle and hold it while Murray himself was away. Ballechin gained access by pretending that he was strengthening the garrison. Soon afterwards he received from Dundee a commission as colonel.

Murray heard the news in Edinburgh, and prepared to march north. He told General Mackay that he had no hope of persuading the Atholl men to fight for him against Dundee, 'their inclination being more for King James than their Majesties' government', but he promised to try and ensure that they did not join the other side. At least, he said, he would not be denied entry to his own castle. In this, however, he was disappointed. Murray managed to collect some of his tenants together, but, by the time he reached Pitlochry, there was a letter from Ballechin explaining that the castle was not to be surrendered, even to its owner:

> I crave pardon that I cannot wait upon your Lordship at Pitlochry for I have received orders from his Majesty's Lieutenant to defend this place for his Majesty's service, which I resolve, God willing, to do. . . . My Lord, I do not doubt but your Lordship will make up the breach and

declare for King James, which I hope in God will preserve your ancient and noble family.

Murray had by now raised about 1,000 men. He marched them north and proceeded to blockade his own castle. Without cannon, however, he could do little but camp outside.

Dundee still hoped that Murray might change his mind, or was simply waiting for the right time to declare his true loyalties. On 23 July, he sent a further letter, assuring him that

> it was no distrust of your Lordship made me take possession of the Castle of Blair, but that I heard the rebels designed to require you to deliver it up to them, which would have forced you to declare before the time I thought you designed.

But Murray had no intention now of changing sides.

By this time, Dundee had finally received the reinforcements he had been promised. They were a bitter disappointment: there were only 300 men, instead of 5,000. But in the circumstances, he was lucky to receive any at all. In stark contrast to the glowing picture that Melfort had been presenting of the situation in Ireland, James's army, camped outside Londonderry, was weakened and demoralized. Its generals had decided to launch no further attacks, and were now trying, unsuccessfully, to starve the town into submission.

The King could spare no more than 300 men, from one of his regiments, mostly raw Irish troops under a conventional Lowland officer, Colonel Alexander Cannon, who knew little of the Highlands and nothing of clan warfare. There were, however, a number of junior officers in addition. They sailed from Carrickfergus in three French frigates on 10 July, and on the way over encountered two ships of the Scots navy – *The Pelican*, which regularly patrolled the coast, and an escort ship. There was a vicious exchange of fire which killed the captains of both Scottish vessels, but Cannon managed to land with most of his supplies, including thirty-five barrels of powder, ball, match, and flints. Their provisions, however, which were in a ship following them, were delayed and captured, so that, when, some time between 14 and 18 July, Cannon joined Dundee in Glenroy, his men were poorly equipped and fed.

The clans were unimpressed. The new troops were, said Balhaldie, three hundred new-raised, naked, undisciplined Irishmen; which had this bad effect, that the clans, who had been made believe they were to be supported by a powerful army from Ireland, with arms, ammunition and all other provisions, saw themselves miserably disappointed.

The Irishmen could not be compared with those who had served Montrose so well. A Highlander who fought next to them at Killie-crankie said they were brave, but they charged 'like a herd of cattle.'

Dundee made the best of them, and used their arrival to put further pressure on the reluctant Cluny. Cannon had brought a further letter from Melfort, which promised more senior officers when the London-derry siege was over. It was the last letter Dundee ever had from James. It gave him 'our most hearty and royal thanks' and promised to 'make you and your family an instance of our royal bounty and favour to such as serve well.' But it was not what Dundee really wanted, which was trained men and ammunition.

He had already decided to march south, probably in the week beginning Monday 22 July. He told Cluny, in his letter dated 18 July, that he expected him to have raised men by that time, 'and I shall send you word where to join us'. He wanted to move because time was now running short. His intelligence about the enemy – always extremely good – had warned him that Mackay was collecting his troops together, while Argyll was threatening from the west, and, though he was still far short of the 4,000 men he had boasted of having, he knew that the clans would not hold together long without action.

He could count on fewer than 2,000 men at the start. Lochiel had not yet got all his forces together, but Dundee persuaded him to leave the recruiting to his eldest son and bring the 240 men he had under arms. Glengarry came in with 400, and the MacDonalds of Sleat had at last arrived with about the same number, though illness kept their chief, old Sir Donald, at home, and they were led by his son, later known as 'Sir Donald of the Wars'. Others, such as the Clanranald MacDonalds, were well below strength.

There was also some doubt as to where they should go. Lochiel was inclined to head for Strathspey to avenge the clansmen who had been hanged at Edinglassie. Others wanted to march into Argyll, where the Earl was mustering troops, and plunder his lands again. Steuart of Ballechin, now holding Blair, asked if it was still important to hold the castle. But Dundee had already determined that he would go to Blair, and he fixed a rendezvous on 29 July for all those who had not yet joined the standard. He sent Sir Alexander Maclean with 300 men to Braemar to join Farquharson of Inverey, who had fifty men at his disposal. Then, on 22 July, he marched out from Lochaber with some 1,800 Highlanders behind him. There is no surviving account of that day. (The 'Grameid' of James Philip of Almericlose, whose glowing lines would doubtless have done justice to the scene, peters out disappointingly with the embarkation of Cannon.) But at some point, and probably in Lochaber, an episcopalian service was held. The sermon was sufficiently inspiring for it to be repeated at the rising of 1715.

In Edinburgh, General Mackay was now seriously concerned that Atholl was no longer safe territory. Although, as he said himself, he did not 'question the sincerity' of Lord Murray, he knew he could not count on the loyalty of his followers. He calculated that, if that part of the country fell into Dundee's hands, then about 1,500 fighting men might go over to the other side. It would give Dundee effective control over the country north of Perth and allow him time to collect the one commodity he was short of – horses. No campaign, in the General's view, could be sustained for long, or won in the end, without cavalry, and Dundee had barely sixty mounted men. But Perthshire could provide horses, and thus give him a valuable new force.

If, on the other hand, Mackay could seize Blair Castle, then that would not only secure the passes north, but act as a deterrent to the Atholl men. He was still determined to build and secure a fort at Inverlochy, but this plan depended on keeping access to the Highlands open. Murray, still camped outside his own castle, was concerned about a damaging siege, and asked if it might be possible for Mackay to avoid Atholl on his way north. The General retorted that he could not afford to leave Blair in unfriendly hands. He intended to hang Ballechin 'at the gate', and if Murray raised the siege he would ravage his estates.

Speed was of the essence. Mackay's original intention had been to join the Earl of Argyll, who was collecting armed men together in the west. But that plan was now abandoned. Without waiting for the reinforcements of dragoons and of horse which he had been promised, he marched west from Edinburgh on 22 July with fewer than 4,000 foot and two troops of horse. On 24 July, he was in Stirling, where he ordered four petards for the siege he expected at Blair. These were explosive devices which could blow a small hole in a wall, and which Murray would doubtless have hesitated to use on his own castle. Without waiting for them, however, Mackay marched on to Perth, where he arrived on 25 July. There, to his surprise, he heard rumours of the enemy's approach. He wrote to a nearby laird, Robert Menzies of

Weem: 'I do not believe Dundee is so near, though I wish he were.' But at midnight on 26 July, by which time he had reached Dunkeld, he heard the news that Murray had fallen back from Blair, and that Dundee was in Atholl, heading for the castle.

Dundee had done his best to convert Murray before he marched south. On 13 July, he had sent him another letter, which concluded: 'If, after all I have said in my former letters and this, I get no return, my Lord, I must acknowledge I will be very sorry for your sake.' He waited a day for an answer, and then, receiving none, sent two messengers, Major William Graham and Gilbert Ramsay, the advocate-turned-soldier, to make a final plea. The fact that he thought it worth dispatching this one last message shows how much he depended on Murray's support:

> I have tried all that have not already joined Major General Mackay, on this side Tay, who have any command of men; yet, that I leave nothing untried that may free me from blame of what may fall out, I have sent these gentlemen to wait on your Lordship, and receive your positive answer.

But there was none. Murray refused even to see Graham and Ramsay, who returned empty-handed, convinced that he was in league with the enemy. They did, however, have a chance to speak to some of Murray's soldiers, and learned from them about Mackay's movements. They also gathered that the Atholl men were likely to change sides, or at any rate desert, as soon as the opportunity arose.

Dundee set out immediately for Blair. Morale amongst his clansmen was high. As Balhaldie recorded, 'he had gained so upon the affections of his small army, that, though half-starved, they marched forward as cheerfully as if they had not felt the least effects of want.'

On 26 July, they bypassed Loch Laggan and the head-waters of the Spey, making east for Breachachy. There Dundee signed a bond in favour of Cluny for 659 merks, in return for enough provisions for 1,500 men. He then headed through the pass of Drumochter, followed the River Garry east, and camped, before nightfall, just three miles short of Blair Castle where the dour hills of the Grampains begin to slope down to the gentler glens of Perthshire. He had by now been joined again by Sir Alexander Maclean, who, with Farquharson of Inverey, had moved swiftly once again, outmanœuvring the Master of Forbes and laying waste some Gordon land before heading back to the main force.

Murray heard about Dundee's advance while Dundee was still

sixteen miles away. He had already warned Mackay that he would not be able to hold his followers together in the event of an attack, and had been instructed to retreat if there was one. The Atholl men had clearly demonstrated on which side their loyalty lay. In spite of Murray's threats, they had filled their bonnets with water from the river and had defiantly drunk King James's health. On the afternoon of Friday 26 July, without waiting for Dundee's arrival, Murray retreated south through the deep and narrow pass of Killiecrankie, to a place called Moulin, just below it. He left a hundred men behind him to hold the mouth of the pass, but they did not stay there long. Others amongst Murray's followers melted away as well, pleading that they had to protect their cattle from Dundee's marauding clansmen.

Late on the night of 26 July, Dundee entered Blair Castle, and was welcomed by Ballechin. Word had reached him that Mackay was already heading north, and early next morning he called his principal officers together and held a war council. The decision to be made was whether to hold the castle until the other Highland troops arrived at the rendezvous fixed for 29 July, or whether to march straight out and confront the enemy.

There was no question but that they were outnumbered. Dundee's force of around 2,000 was facing an army of nearly 4,000. They had just completed a long march and they were tired and hungry. The Lowland officers, including Cannon, argued that they should wait and recover rather than risk an engagement at this point against an army of disciplined troops under an experienced General.

The Highland chiefs listened in silence, and considered the advice, which sounded persuasive. But then Alasdair Dubh MacDonnell of Glengarry put into words what they all really felt: Highlanders, he said, were different to other troops. Yes, they had suffered hardships, but that did not affect them in the same way as ordinary soldiers, 'who are bred in an easier and more plentiful course of life'; they were ready to engage with the enemy and defeat him; they relished nothing more than 'hardy and adventurous exploits': and it was his view that they should march immediately and attempt to prevent the enemy emerging from the pass, harrying them with 'quick sallies' and 'brisk skirmishes'.

The chiefs agreed, but Dundee waited for Lochiel to give his own opinion: 'For', he said, according to Balhaldie, 'he has not only done great things himself, but has had so much experience, that he cannot miss to make a right judgment of the matter, and, therefore, his shall determine mine.'

Lochiel said that he deferred to Dundee's military knowledge, but his own opinion was straightforward:

> To fight immediately – for our men are in heart; they are so far from being afraid of their enemy that they are eager and keen to engage them, lest they escape their hands as they have so often done. Though we have few men, they are good, and I can venture to assure your Lordship that not one of them will fail you.

He said it was too late to prevent Mackay's soldiers getting through the pass, but they should attack them as soon as possible despite the odds, because the propaganda effect of a victory now would be enormous: 'Their great superiority will give a necessary reputation to our victory.'

Dundee expressed delight at the advice, and the news, which spread quickly outside to the waiting army, was greeted with loud cheers. Before the meeting broke up, however, Lochiel begged Dundee to hold back from the battle himself. If he were killed, the whole campaign would be at risk: 'On your Lordship depends the fate not only of this brave little army, but also of our King and country.' The council agreed, but Dundee refused, saying, as Balhaldie recorded it:

> I am fully sensible that me engaging personally this day may be of some loss if I shall chance to be killed; but I beg leave of you, to allow me to give one 'Shear-darg' [in old Scots, one harvest-day's work] to the King, my master, that I may have an opportunity of convincing the brave clans that I can hazard my life in that service as freely as the meanest of them. You know their temper, gentlemen, and if they do not think I have personal courage enough, they will not esteem me hereafter, nor obey my commands with cheerfulness.

The most he would agree to was to change his red tunic for a dull leather jerkin, of a 'sad' colour, which he wore beneath his breastplate.

There was one disturbing incident. One of the officers who had come over with Cannon, Sir William Wallace, who was Melfort's brother-in-law, produced an order from the Secretary of State saying that he, rather than the Earl of Dunfermline, whom Dundee trusted, should command the cavalry. There was nothing for it but to obey. Not that the cavalry amounted to more than fifty horses; but just as anything Melfort touched turned to dust, so this appointment of Wallace, petty as it must have seemed at the time, was to have a fatal effect that day. Melfort's demotion of Dunfermline was particularly damaging to the cause. As a man of wealth and the owner of a great northern stronghold, in the shape of Fyvie Castle, Dunfermline was not a man to insult.

Dundee's mood, however, could not be dampened. It was reflected in a letter, written the previous evening and dispatched to the ever-reluctant Cluny, in which he urged him to bring his troops within a day, 'if you have a mind to preserve yourself and serve the King'. The letter, signed with a flourish, had ended: 'All the world will be with us, blessed be God.'

CHAPTER SEVENTEEN
One Hour of Dundee

> *No sword was in scabbard and no dirk was in sheath there.*
> *Was there not smashing of skulls and tearing of shoulders,*
> *giving their evening strokes to the red-cassocked folk?*
> Mac Alastair Ruaidh (Angus MacDonald), Bard of
> Glencoe

General Mackay was up at dawn in Dunkeld on the morning of
Saturday 27 July. It had all the makings of a glorious summer's day,
with the sun rising against a clear sky, catching the broad sweep of the
River Tay where it curled past the old cathedral. North lay the open
glen, its tops wooded with pine and birch, leading gently towards the
Grampians and the distant peaks of Beinn Dearg and Beinn a'Ghlo.
Half-way to them, the Tay bends westwards towards Schiehallion and
Ben Lawers, but its tributary the Garry continues north until, eleven
miles on from Dunkeld, past Pitlochry, it finds itself siphoned suddenly through the steep and cramped defile that is the pass of Killiecrankie. Two miles of rocks and bubbling water open out finally to a
broad stretch of open land, dominated by the heights of Ben Vrackie to
the east, and the gentler slope of Creag Eallaich hill.

The troops in Dunkeld were mustered early, the trumpets and pipes
sounding their separate calls for cavalry and foot, and bridles jingled
and feet stamped in the morning air. The three battalions of the Scots
Brigade, in their scarlet uniforms, formed up first, each distinguished
by the red, white or yellow facings on their tunics. They were the best-
drilled and most experienced of all Mackay's soldiers. They had been
with him in Holland and had seen service in the long Flanders
campaign, where siege tactics and regimental manœuvres in fixed
formations had been standard training. Whether these skills could be

easily adapted to rapid and unexpected movements by the enemy in hilly country remained to be seen. These three battalions were much reduced in numbers, because the Dutch soldiers had been removed before they came north, William needing them for his own guard: though Mackay had recruited as hard as he could in Edinburgh, the complement of each was barely 400 men, instead of the 1,200 it should have been.

They carried long smooth-bore flintlocks, the loading and priming of which were more speedy than with the old matchlocks, though it was still a cumbersome process, taking anything up to a minute and a half, which was precious time at the height of battle. Misfires, as the flint scraped and failed to ignite, were common. The pike, that stalwart but clumsy weapon of many centuries' use, had been withdrawn, to be replaced with a short knife on the end of a wooden handle. This, carried at the belt, was the bayonet. It was jammed into the muzzle of the musket after it had been fired and used as a stabbing weapon of defence. It could be deadly at close quarters. But it had the disadvantage that, once it had been inserted, the musket could no longer be used as a firearm.

In command of the 'Dutch' battalions were three officers: Brigadier-General Barthold Balfour was one of those Lowland Scottish Balfours who for generations had sent their sons to see military service on the Continent, and were the backbone of the Scots Brigade. (Barthold, himself a solid and reliable officer, was to have his career cut brutally short that day, when he contemptuously rejected an offer of quarter); Colonel the Honourable George Ramsay, second son of the Earl of Dalhousie, was described by a contemporary as 'a gentleman with a great deal of fire, and very brave'. He was to become Commander-in-Chief of the Scottish army. Finally, at present in command of General Mackay's own battalion, was his brother, Lieutenant-Colonel James Mackay, for whom this day, too, would be his last.

There were three other detachments of infantry, one English, the other two Scottish. The 13th Regiment of Foot (later the Somersetshire Light Infantry), was commanded by the splendidly named Colonel Fernando Hastings. He was later called a 'despicable' officer, and cashiered after it was found that he had dressed his soldiers in the worn-out uniforms of another regiment. But his men were to fight better that day than any of the rest. The impressive-sounding Viscount Kenmure's Regiment of Foot, commanded by the man who had been Dundee's Whig rival from Galloway, consisted, in fact, of a few companies raised barely three months earlier. Finally, 'The Edinburgh

Regiment', as it was known (later the King's Own Scottish Borderers), consisted of soldiers also quite recently levied. It was led by David, Earl of Leven.

There were two troops of horse, Lord Annandale's and Lord Belhaven's. Annandale himself, who had once held a commission in Dundee's regiment, was not there, having pleaded his duties as a member of the Convention, and been reluctantly excused by Mackay. But John Hamilton, second Baron Belhaven, was present at the head of his troop, a 'rough, fat, black, noisy man, more like a butcher than a Lord', as that contemporary observer John Mackay described him. But this was not enough cavalry, in Mackay's opinion, and he had sent back word to Perth to dispatch six more troops of horse.

There was no time to wait for reinforcements, but Mackay did have some artillery, in the form of three 'Sandy Stoups'. These were small cannon, so called after their inventor Alexander Hamilton, made of tin and coated with leather. They were light enough for two of them at a time to be slung across the back of a horse, but they were far from reliable and usually came to pieces after they had been fired for any length of time.

Finally, there were the baggage-horses, upwards of 1,200, weighed down by provisions, slowing the pace of the army, and still only carrying enough for a fortnight's march.

The night before, Mackay had sent forward '200 choice fusiliers' under Lieutenant-Colonel George Lauder to guard the head of the Killiecrankie pass, and join up – or so he planned – with what remained of the Atholl men. The rest marched out as the sun rose above the steep rock of Craig a Barns, which loomed over them to the right. Along the way, at Ballinluig, they were joined by Robert Menzies of Weem, who had brought a hundred of his clansmen over from his estates near Aberfeldy; they were stationed with Leven's men. By ten o'clock, they had reached the little clachan of Moulin, north of Pitlochry, where Lord Murray waited with barely 300 men and a few lame excuses.

Mackay was in charitable mood. He thought Murray's explanations for the absence of most of his soldiers 'reasonable as well as customary to that sort of people', but he took the precaution of putting Hastings' and Annandale's troops behind the baggage just in case the Atholl men should decide to plunder it along the way. Then he gave orders to advance.

Two miles further on, he came on the mouth of the pass, where the glen closes in suddenly, and the light turns to gloom under steep escarpments and thick trees. 'To this day', wrote Balhaldie, 'an army might be stopped in its march by a few resolute men posted at the mouth or issue of it.'

Lauder, who was at the north end of the pass, where, not surprisingly, there was a marked absence of Atholl men, had already sent back word that it was clear. But to lead an army into such a death-trap went against all Mackay's instincts, and he dispatched another 200 men from Leven's regiment forward to join Lauder and send back any intelligence they could about the enemy's movements.

Again word came that there was no sign of Dundee's men. Finally, after his troops had rested for two hours, basking in the morning sun, Mackay gave the order to advance. Balfour's, Ramsay's and Kenmure's battalions went first, spread out and stepping warily by twos and threes along the narrow path of stone and mud. The Garry was in spate, fed by several nights of rain, and it thundered through the chasm as they felt their way up it. Following them came Belhaven, massively astride his horse, with his troop picking their way carefully past rocks and shrubs, carbines at the ready. Leven's and Mackay's own soldiers were next, and then the baggage-horses, with Hastings' and Annandale's men bringing up the rear.

It took nearly two hours for Mackay's long straggling army to clear the pass. There was only one alarm. A lone clansman, said by tradition to have been a Macrae, fired across the stream and killed a trooper. For a moment it seemed as if that might be the prelude to an ambush, but Dundee had held back. The soldiers marched on.

The sun was high in the sky when Mackay emerged from the pass at the point where a little burn tumbles into the Garry at Aldgirnaig. He halted his men in a field of corn beside the river, just short of the house of Raon Ruairidh (now Urrard House), and waited for the baggage to come up.

Though he was now clear of the point at which he had been most vulnerable, he was not in the best of positions. His army, facing northwest, stood on low ground, dominated by the rising slopes of the Creag Eallaich hill to their right, beyond a thicket of trees. On their left, they were hemmed-in by the River Garry, which lay at the bottom of a dip and could be crossed only with difficulty.

Mackay marched the men up from the river, and then stood them at ease. He sent Colonel Lauder forward with his 200 fusiliers, together with one of the troops of horse, along a path which led in the direction of Blair, to scout out the enemy's positions. They had not gone more than half a mile, just short of a small scattering of cottages at Ardclune, when they spotted some armed Highlanders on the other side of the

Clune burn. Lauder alerted Mackay, who immediately gave orders to Brig.-General Balfour to call the men to arms and distribute ammunition. He then galloped up to join Lauder and inspect the ground. Together they watched as a small party of Dundee's men approached slowly along the foot of a hill from the direction of Blair. They were less than a mile away.

Mackay sent orders back to Balfour to bring the infantry up, but then almost at once spotted what looked like the main force of the enemy, now much closer, marching down the open ground above him from left to right. He noted that they were nearing a steep hill covered in trees and shrubs within shot of where he stood, and that, if they took possession of it, they could direct enough musket-fire down on his men to drive them back into the river. Wheeling his horse round, he galloped back towards Balfour and gave the order to the battalions to form a '*Quart de Conversion*' to the right, a rapid move which brought them up, facing the enemy. He then marched them rapidly forwards from the river and up the hill until they came through the trees to some reasonably open ground, 'fair enough to receive the enemy, but not to attack them'.

They were now well clear of the river at their back, above Urrard House, and in full view of Dundee's men, who had claimed the higher ground, and were now looking down from the lower slopes of Creag Eallaich, at a distance of a few hundred yards. Dundee, he saw,

> had his back to a very high hill, which is the ordinary maxim of the Highlanders, who never fight against regular forces upon anything of equal terms, without a sure retreat at their back, particularly if their enemies be provided of horse.

There was no chance of launching a cavalry charge uphill, though Mackay decided that the ground he was on was, at least, defendable. But he was worried about being outflanked on his right and cut off from the pass. He therefore stretched out his battalions three men deep in a long line, each separated from the next by a wide gap, leaving a space in the middle where he placed the two troops of horse. Hastings' battalion, which had only just come up after the baggage, was on the extreme right, Lauder's fusiliers on the left.

Mackay was greatly concerned about the enemy's cavalry. Although less than sixty strong, it was, he believed 'composed all of gentlemen', some of them from Dundee's old regiment (and indeed from the troop he had first raised to patrol the hills of Galloway). Not wanting to expose his own troops of horse to them, he dropped them back a little from the gap in his centre, with the cannon in front of them. Just forward of where they were drawn up was a stretch of marshy ground, which would be treacherous going for the enemy, but which also made communications between his two wings difficult.

The problem with such a long line was controlling it. Mackay had to leave his right flank under the command of Hastings, in whom he did not have much confidence, while he himself, to the right of the central gap, was out of touch with his left flank. He reinforced Hastings' battalion by detaching some infantrymen from each of the others and sending them down to join him. Balfour, he noticed, had advanced too far on the left, so he rode down the line to pull him back, and then turned in order to see that the remaining troops were in line. The busy general, riding up and down his line, soon began to attract some sporadic, long-range firing from the enemy, which wounded one or two of his soldiers. But, to his surprise, there was no immediate charge.

Mackay, therefore, took the opportunity of addressing a few words to his men. It was not an inspiring speech. He stressed the importance of the Protestant religion, and law and order, and he warned his troops not to betray their cause by 'criminal faintheartedness.' If they failed to stand up to the enemy, he said, they would be pursued by naked Highlanders who would certainly outrun them since they were extremely fast. The Atholl men in particular, he said, 'were in arms ready to strip and knock in the head all runaways.' The listening soldiers were not greatly encouraged

The afternoon was hot. The sun shimmered on naked steel and carbine barrels. The horse shifted restlessly behind the line, the men sweated beneath their scarlet uniforms, and the General, who had again taken up his position, waited with mounting impatience. But still Dundee held his men back.

Dundee had tested the discipline of his eager clansmen some time before, by sounding the alarm as they slept. 'The Highlanders instantly were roused, threw away their plaids, seized their arms, and ran to the front of the camp, drew up into order, then calmly stood, expecting the enemy', wrote Balcarres. The exercise was evidence of the drill Dundee had managed to instil in the short weeks that he and the clans had been together. They might never have passed muster on the Continent, but here, in the Perthshire hills, they were a force to be reckoned with. Even Mackay conceded later that 'the Highlanders are absolutely the best untrained men in Scotland, and can be equalled to our new levies though they were better armed.'

Dundee could undoubtedly have taken them down as far as the Killiecrankie pass and launched an ambush as Mackay's army struggled through it. But the council of war at Blair Castle that morning took up valuable time. Dundee was aware that Mackay had sent for more cavalry from Perth, so it was important to attack before they arrived, but the General was given time to get his army out on to the open ground.

It was not, therefore, until mid-afternoon that Dundee made his first move. He sent a small detachment along the road from Blair as a feint. At the same time, he set out with the main army in a circling move over high ground to the east of the castle, keeping above the enemy and out of sight until the last moment. They moved fast, the clansmen taking the rough ground at a run. They crossed the River Tilt and headed round behind the Hill of Lude, where Montrose had raised the standard nearly fifty years before. Then they turned south, down the Clune burn and on to the ridge which ran along the north side of the glen. As they came in sight of Mackay's army, they saw his men jump to their feet, and then, as the General realized the danger and passed on his rapid orders, move up to their new position.

Mackay was not the only one concerned about being outflanked. When Dundee saw the length of the enemy's line, he began to space the Highlanders out along the ridge, keeping each clan well packed, but with wide intervals between them, and a large gap in the centre opposite Mackay's cavalry. But even so he could not match the stretched-out ranks of his opponents.

He placed the Macleans under their chief, the nineteen-year-old Sir John Maclean of Duart, on the extreme right, opposite Balfour's battalion. Next to them were the Irish troops, commanded by Colonel James Purcell, and then the Clanranald MacDonalds under their student chief, with the Tutor of Clanranald in attendance. To their left, the tall dark Glengarry chief with his brother, Donald Gorm, formed up his MacDonald clansmen, alongside the smaller detachment of Glencoe men, under their formidable chief, Alasdair MacIain, and then came the Grants of Glenmoriston.

In the centre was a wide gap, behind which Dundee placed his cavalry under Sir William Wallace. Then came Lochiel and 180 of his Camerons, and Sir Alexander Maclean with his experienced men, together with smaller groups of MacNeils from Barra and MacDonalds of Kintyre under John MacDonald of Largie. Finally, on the extreme

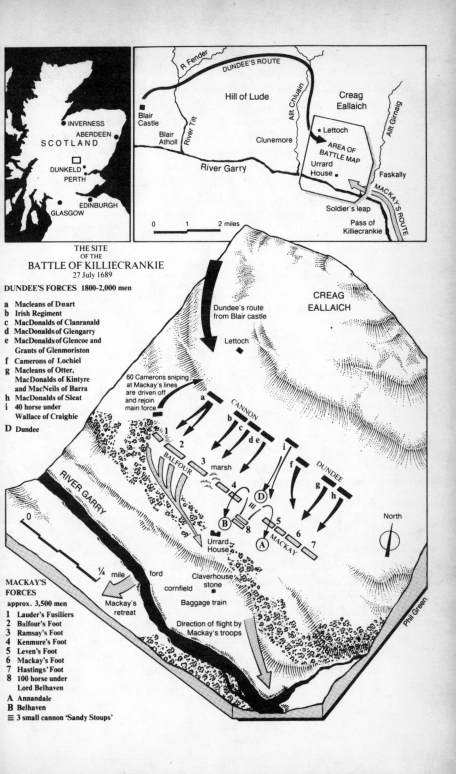

INVERNESS
ABERDEEN
SCOTLAND
DUNKELD
PERTH
EDINBURGH
GLASGOW

R Fender
DUNDEE'S ROUTE
Hill of Lude
Allt Chluain
Creag Eallaich
Blair Castle
River Tilt
Blair Atholl
Clunemore
Lettoch
AREA OF BATTLE MAP
Urrard House
Allt Girnaig
Faskally
River Garry
MACKAY'S ROUTE
Soldier's leap
Pass of Killiecrankie

0   1   2 miles

THE SITE
OF THE
BATTLE OF KILLIECRANKIE
27 July 1689

DUNDEE'S FORCES 1800-2,000 men

a   Macleans of Duart
b   Irish Regiment
c   MacDonalds of Clanranald
d   MacDonalds of Glengarry
e   MacDonalds of Glencoe and
    Grants of Glenmoriston
f   Camerons of Lochiel
g   Macleans of Otter,
    MacDonalds of Kintyre
    and MacNeils of Barra
h   MacDonalds of Sleat
i   40 horse under
    Wallace of Craighie
D   Dundee

CREAG EALLAICH

Dundee's route from Blair castle

Lettoch

60 Camerons sniping at Mackay's lines are driven off and rejoin main force

CANNON

BALFOUR

marsh

DUNDEE

RIVER GARRY

Urrard House

North

MACKAY'S FORCES

approx. 3,500 men

1   Lauder's Fusiliers
2   Balfour's Foot
3   Ramsay's Foot
4   Kenmure's Foot
5   Leven's Foot
6   Mackay's Foot
7   Hastings' Foot
8   100 horse under
    Lord Belhaven
A   Annandale
B   Belhaven
≡   3 small cannon 'Sandy Stoups'

¼ mile   ford
0

Claverhouse stone
cornfield
Baggage train
Mackay's retreat
Direction of flight by Mackay's troops

Phil Green

left were the MacDonalds of Sleat, again commanded by a young chief, Sir Donald MacDonald, who wore a red coat, and was accompanied by Sir George Barclay, one of the officers James had sent over.

Apart from Lochiel and Alasdair MacIain, the chiefs were young – two of them, at least, teenagers. So Dundee lacked experience amongst his commanders. He was also far short of his ideal strength. Because the rendezvous he had set was still two days away, he was deprived of the bulk of his fighting force – possible two-thirds of those he counted on were not there, including the Keppoch MacDonalds, and most of the Camerons, who were being brought over by Lochiel's son. Lochiel had further detached sixty soldiers to guard a house overlooking the enemy lines. Nevertheless, each clan was assigned one of Mackay's battalions as a target to aim for.

Dundee put the right flank under the general command of Colonel Cannon, and placed himself on the left, next to the Camerons. With him were some of his most loyal friends: David Halyburton of Pitcur, described by one of Dundee's officers as 'like a moving castle in the shape of a man'; William, Earl of Buchan, and Lewis, Viscount Frendraught, whom one witness noticed wearing a black cravat; The Lords Dunfermline and Dunkeld; Gilbert Ramsay, the soldier-advocate, and James Philip of Almericlose, who must surely have described the scene in the most heroic of all his verses, though these particular ones have never been found.

Dundee is said to have delivered a speech which was later printed and doubtless polished in the process. If the document we have, whose authenticity has been much disputed, caught the general sense of what he said, his speech was certainly a great deal more eloquent than Mackay's. For he spoke of king, religion and country, and reminded the Highlanders that they were fighting a usurper, and might expect 'the reward of a gracious King' if they won. He told them of 'the honour of dying in our duty, and as becomes true men of valour and conscience.' The slogan he chose for the battle that day was 'King James and the Church of Scotland.'

Dundee, for all his agreement to dress in a 'sad' cloth, was hardly inconspicuous as he rode up and down his line. One of the Gaelic bards said that he wore a 'white helmet', which may have meant the kind of white plume he was said to have had at Seneffe, and, since the enemy were watching him from what Mackay called a musket-shot away, he would, like the General himself, have been marked out from the start.

Taking advantage of the lull, Mackay ordered his four leather-bound cannon to open up. They created much noise and smoke, but they were singularly ineffective, and one at least of them broke up almost as soon as it had begun firing. Meanwhile the detachment which had been sent from Blair were proving effective enough snipers for Mackay to send his brother up with a party to dislodge them, which they did after a skirmish, driving the clansmen back to join the main force.

The General hoped this might provoke an attack, for he was worried that Dundee would wait for twilight, and rely on the 'fright and disorder' that charging Highlanders in the darkness might induce in his troops. But Dundee was watching the sun, which was now shining directly into the eyes of his soldiers, and, though a desultory fusillade wounded one or two of his men, which made the rest impatient for action, he held them back until the sun had moved below the hills. Lochiel then encouraged his followers to give a great shout, which echoed round the glen. Though there was an answering cry from below it was generally held to be a feeble response. Finally, as the sun began to drop below Beinn Dearg in the distance, at about eight o'clock, Dundee gave the order to charge.

Uttering a great roar, the clansmen set off down the slope, pouring over the ridge in a breaking wave of Highland fervour. They had thrown aside their plaids, which left them for the most part dressed only in shirts. Many were bare-footed, as they ran over the springy turf, clutching their muskets, and screaming their battle-cries. They came down the hill, holding their musket-fire until the last moment. They were sustained, as they charged, by the momentum the ground gave them and the unleashing of their pent-up ferocity.

Seen by the nervous soldiers from below, the Highland charge was an awesome sight. What they were watching was one of the most formidable weapons of war the century had seen; one that had broken trained armies and superior numbers as much by sheer terror as by the force of arms; one that stemmed back to the first time a marauding clan poured over a hilltop to snatch a neighbour's cattle. It was a military phenomenon that had been noted as early as the sixteenth century, when, at the battle of Rymenant, the Highlanders tied their shirts around their waists, and 'came on naked among the armed men', as one observer described them. And it had been developed formidably, under Montrose, whose Irish soldiers led by the redoubtable Alasdair MacColla, had used it to deadly effect.

The clans came down the front slope of Creag Eallaich 'like one great clap of thunder', as Balhaldie described it. The left wing, mainly MacDonalds and Camerons, helped by the steeper slope, were fastest, the contour bringing them together so that they converged on Mackay's regiment immediately below them. The musketeers waited for their command, given by Mackay's brother, the Lieutenant-Colonel, and then fired three withering volleys in platoon order which tore through the charging clansmen.

The shots opened gaps in the line, but the main body came together and continued the charge. Their orders were to wait before firing until they were 'one barrel's length' from the enemy. But they let off their muskets too early, causing little damage. Then, however, throwing aside their firearms and drawing their broadswords, they raged on down the hill, 'in great confusion' according to General Mackay, but with terrible effect. As the infantry struggled to insert their bayonets into the muzzles of their muskets, which, fired once, were now useless, the Highlanders hit them with the force of a tidal wave. The battalion splintered and broke. It became clear, too late, that a line only three deep was far too fragile to take the shock of the charge.

Lieutenant-Colonel Mackay and a few of his officers stood their ground and were killed, the rest turned and fled, 'in the twinkling of an eye', as the General saw it. Such was the force of the attack that the Highlanders charged straight through the lines, missing most of Leven's regiment to their right. As they passed, Leven's musketeers loosed off a devastating round of fire into their flank, inflicting huge damage on the Camerons, who should have met them face on. But Lochiel had swerved too far to the left, and, with Sir Alexander's men and the MacDonalds of Sleat, swept through the now fleeing ranks of Mackay's soldiers, taking with them only the left-hand edge of Hastings' infantry. Colonel Hastings wheeled the remainder of his battalion round, and then watched as the MacDonalds poured past him, pursuing the fugitive soldiers down towards the pass.

On Dundee's right wing, Glengarry's men ran straight down on to Kenmure's battalion. The Lowland soldiers, though inexperienced, loosed off at least one volley which caused much slaughter, bringing down Glengarry's brother Donald amongst many others, before the clansmen were on to them, swinging their broadswords, and knocking aside muskets with their targes.

Balhaldie described the strange silence of the battle after the shooting had ceased: 'The noise seemed hushed; and the firing ceasing on both sides, nothing was heard for some few moments but the sullen and hollow clashes of broadswords, with the dismal groans and cries of dying and wounded men.'

The Highland swords caused great damage, splitting skulls, cleaving through necks and shoulders, splintering bones. The infantry found that the thick buff belts they wore across their shoulders were scant protection against the cutting-edge of the blades, with slashing forward- and back-strokes strong enough to shear off pike-heads and even the blades of swords at their hilts.

Kenmure's men might have stood their ground longer, but, as they engaged with the enemy, they found themselves dealing with their own fleeing cavalry, for Belhaven's troop of horse, ordered forward by Mackay to attack Glengarry in the flank, wheeled suddenly left, panicked, and careered back on to Kenmure's men, scattering them as they galloped through the ranks. The combination of Glengarry's charge and the thundering horses was enough to break the battalion, which turned and ran. At the same time, Annandale's troop of horse, without their commander, wheeled right to attack Lochiel, and then also scattered, taking part of Leven's battalion with them.

Mackay himself, watching these things happen, called on the cavalry officers to turn and follow him. He spurred his own horse forward through the enemy and passed by the running Highlanders quite unharmed, though his attendant's horse was shot from beneath him. Looking round, he realized that no one had followed him. The scene below was now one of confusion. On the left of the line, Balfour's regiment, which had faced the charging Macleans, had broken almost at once and began to escape downhill towards the river, running round behind Urrard House in the direction of Killiecrankie. The Macleans followed them hard, causing much slaughter at the mouth of the pass, where the soldiers were jammed together on the narrow path. One of them, finding himself trapped on a rock, leapt over a yawning chasm to escape, a seemingly impossible feat. Those who were not so lucky piled up, dead and wounded, in the roaring torrent of the Garry.

Ramsay's regiment, which took the force of the Irish soldiers and Clanranald, held its ground a little longer, but then it too broke. And even Colonel Lauder's 200 fusiliers, 'the choice of our army', as Mackay said later, who were posted on a 'little hill wreathed with trees' on the extreme left of the line, turned and ran. Quite why, the General could not see, though, as he noted, 'resolution and presence of mind in battle being certainly a singular mercy of God, he denieth and giveth it when and to whom he will, for there are seasons and occasions, that the most firm and stout-hearted do quake and shake for fear.' Mackay could see nothing in the centre, which was by now wreathed in smoke, but there the battle was decided, and there tragedy for the Highland army had already struck.

Dundee himself had waited briefly on the ridge as the clans set off, watching the first wave as it neared the enemy's guns. Then he spurred his horse downhill, heading straight for the centre of Mackay's line, where the cavalry and the cannon were, with Colonel Wallace and his troop behind him.

Mackay had been right to worry about Dundee's cavalry. Small as the force was, it was a formidable sight as it advanced down the slope towards the marshy ground at the bottom. It may well have been the sight of its flying banners and glittering armour as it headed for them that caused Belhaven's troop to swerve violently to its left and gallop back through Kenmure's startled men. And almost simultaneously, Annandale's troop turned right to avoid the charge.

But then, as Wallace's troop reached the foot of the hill, something happened which caused Wallace to pull up and swing round to his left, away from the action, taking the troop with him. Whether his courage failed him, as Balhaldie suggested, whether he saw the marshy ground ahead, or whether he decided suddenly to follow the diagonal line the Camerons had taken, is unknown, but his action opened a fatal gap behind Dundee. And it may have led to his death.

Dundee, 'intent on the action, and carried on by the impetuosity of his courage', as Balhaldie put it, did not see what had happened until he was about to enter the smoke that hid the combat in front of Mackay's line. Seeing their leader galloping ahead, a small band of horsemen, comprising Dunfermline, Pitcur, and fourteen of his other mounted companions, spurred their mounts onwards to join him, leaving the rest of Wallace's troop behind. Dunfermline noticed Dundee's horse swerve suddenly to the right, perhaps to avoid the marshy ground, at which point Dundee looked round and saw, for the first time, that the cavalry were not behind him. Rising in the saddle, he waved to Wallace's men to come up and join him. At that point he was lost to sight in a cloud of smoke. There was still ragged fire from his left, where the Macdonalds of Sleat were engaged with part of Hastings' regiment, and he may have turned his horse towards the action to join them. Some of Mackay's men, according to the General, were still holding their ground and firing their muskets.

It was then, with the battle barely begun, that a bullet struck Dundee. Whether it hit him as he raised his arm to signal, or whether it struck as he turned to his left, is not known, probably the former, for Balhaldie says that he was hit on the left side 'about two hand's-breadth within his armour', which might have risen up as he waved. Balcarres, who says he had a vision of Dundee's death as he lay in prison in Edinburgh, wrote that the wound was on the right side, but gave no detail. The Gaelic bard Iain Lom, talked of Dundee's being hit 'beneath the skirt of [his] tunic'.

Either way, Dundee fell from his horse, for the moment unseen by his followers, who charged on, driving the enemy cavalry headlong away from the battle, and capturing the little leather cannon which stood in the centre of what had once been Mackay's line.

Behind them, on the battlefield, at least one battalion, Leven's, stood almost intact, while to the right, where Hastings had wheeled his men around to allow the MacDonalds through, half of that battalion still remained in place. When Dunfermline and his sixteen men returned from seeing off the enemy cavalry, they were amazed to find the enemy's foot-soldiers still drawn up in rank. Wallace's troop of horse was nowhere to be seen, so Dunfermline tried to gather together some fifty or sixty Highlanders who were still on the field. Helped by Lochiel's son-in-law, who talked to them in Gaelic, he collected enough to mount an attack on Hastings' men. But as he did so, Leven's soldiers advanced to attack them, and the Highlanders, who were, according to Lochiel's memoirs, 'rather followers of the army than soldiers', rapidly dispersed.

As Dunfermline retreated along the line, he saw his commander, Viscount Dundee, lying on the ground. He was not yet dead, and was being tended by a soldier called Johnston. But just as Dunfermline and his little group of horsemen came to his aid, Leven's men opened fire. Dunfermline had his horse shot under him, and Pitcur was mortally wounded, though he disguised the seriousness of his injury, and only succumbed two days later. Gilbert Ramsay, the soldier-advocate, was also killed, fulfilling a premonition he had had the night before of his own death. The rest drew back to regroup. Once again, they collected together some Highlanders, this time under one or two of the chiefs. They took possession of a house – almost certainly Urrard – and exchanged fire with the enemy.

By now it was twilight. Mackay's casualties, though heavy, were considerably less than they might have been. By pursuing his soldiers down the pass, or stopping to plunder the baggage, the Highlanders had left whole troops virtually intact. General Mackay himself, who had watched most of the action from higher ground, now gathered Leven's men together and marched them across what had once been his battle-line to join Hastings, most of whose troops were still together on the right wing. He sent a nephew of his, a captain who had been badly wounded in a sword attack but was still on horseback, to round up as many officers as he could, then looked for a piece of defendable ground. His first thought was the garden behind Urrard House, but he soon realized that it was a potential death-trap. He was still debating the matter when his nephew returned with news that most of the officers had already fled, and none were prepared to come back and fight.

Through the gathering darkness, Mackay could see some soldiers on the edge of the wood beyond Urrard, where Balfour's and Lauder's men had been. Ordering his regrouped battalion to prepare for an attack, he set out towards the dim figures, only to discover that they were not soldiers from his army, but enemy clansmen. Quickly wheeling his horse round, he rode back to his men, and ordered them to retreat as quietly as they could. He led them down the slope and across to the other side of the River Garry, where he was joined by Lord Belhaven, and a lieutenant and cornet from the Earl of Annandale's troop. Avoiding the pass of Killiecrankie, they set off into the hills towards Strathtay. By the early hours of the morning, they had reached the home of Mackay's Perthshire ally Robert Menzies of Weem, and there they spent the rest of the night.

Back on the battlefield, Dundee was dying. His last words were reported later by a Lieutenant John Nisbet of Kenmure's regiment, who was taken prisoner and heard, at Blair Castle, what had happened.

The soldier, Johnston, had caught Dundee as he fell from his horse, and stayed with him until the end. Since Dundee had no idea what was happening around him, he asked Johnston:

'How goes the day?'

'Well for the King', replied Johnston, 'but I am sorry for your Lordship.'

'It is the less matter for me', said Dundee, 'seeing that the day goes well for my Master'.

Later, a letter was concocted and sent to James, purporting to be Dundee's last message to the King. 'My wounds forbid me to enlarge to your Majesty at this time, though they tell me they are not mortal', ran the letter, which contained an account of the battle and the losses on both sides. But it is certainly bogus. Dundee died in agony in the gathering darkness, not dictating a letter to an attendant scribe.

During the night his body was stripped (probably by some Camerons) of its armour and most of its clothes. The robbing of corpses on the battlefield was not unusual, and the clansmen may not have known who he was. But that it happened is certain. Balcarres says that the virtually naked body was found in the morning by one of his officers, who wrapped him in a plaid. And Iain Lom, whose poem addresses

Dundee in person, wrote: 'your naked body lies white and shameless, and all unclothed.'

As soon as it was found, the body was taken to the church at Blair, where it was placed in a rough coffin, ready for burial. (When Pitcur died later, his body was placed alongside his leader's.) The interment, as Nisbet was told, took place next day, though in early September some of Mackay's officers claimed to have seen the body, still lying in a vault in the church. His armour and some of his clothes were later recovered by his brother, David Graham, who retrieved them from the Camerons. Today, the breast-plate can be seen at Blair, with a fake hole drilled in the centre of it on the instructions of the fourth Duke of Atholl, 'to improve its warlike appearance'. A tablet marking the site of Dundee's eventual burial was put up in the church on the bicentenary of his death.

The casualties on both sides had been terrible. On the Government side, Mackay lost up to a third of his force, perhaps 1,200 men, though Dunfermline thought it was more. There were prisoners taken too, the Atholl men bringing in 400–500 of them. Most of the soldiers were released, without having to swear an oath for King James, but the officers were held. They were treated well, according to John Nisbet. Only three senior officers were killed: Brigadier-General Balfour, who angrily refused quarter when pinned down by attacking clansmen, Lieutenant-Colonel Mackay, and a Colonel Fergusson of Kenmure's regiment.

The same was not true on the other side. Although the losses were smaller – perhaps 700 dead and 200 wounded –, the chiefs and their officers, who charged at the head of their clans, suffered proportionately more – 'lost with their elbows to the field', as Iain Lom described it. The Camerons, whose flank had been exposed to the raking fire of Leven's regiment, lost half of their 240 men, and Lochiel himself, who had stopped to take off his shoes before running to catch up and lead his men into the final assault, was wounded. 'Great's the pity for King James that you're not yourself as you were', wrote Angus MacDonald, the Glencoe bard, who called the battle 'a Pyrrhic victory'.

Those on the extreme left, the MacDonalds of Glengarry and Sleat, suffered worst. Archibald MacDonald of Largie was carried back to Blair, mortally wounded, and his Tutor too was killed – 'gone down like the bracken', – leaving, as the Glencoe bard pointed out, no direct heirs to succeed him. Young Sir Donald MacDonald of Sleat, who had taken over command from his elderly father, was killed: 'You were young to be put to the test', said the bard, 'and many a woman mourns you between Trotternish and Sleat.' Five of his relatives were also lost, and the poet complained that a physician, brought with them to tend the wounded, failed to do so – 'no healer stayed to heal' –, so that more MacDonalds died on the field than need have done. The Macleans, who were also on that wing, suffered many casualties.

Some measure of the scale of losses can be made by comparing the figures of Killiecrankie with those of the much larger Battle of the Boyne in the following year, when James's forces were defeated by William. There, the number of participants was 69,000 and the total losses 1,300. At Killiecrankie, there were some 4,300 participants, and 1,900 dead. Thus, at the Boyne about one man in fifty fell, while at Killiecrankie over a third died.

But the Glencoe bard, in the end, was celebrating a victory as well as lamenting the dead, and he summed up the battle in a fine flourish of Gaelic pride:

The Highlanders cast off their plaids above the gate of Raon Ruairidh, no sword was in the scabbard and no dirk was in sheath there. Was there not smashing of skulls and tearing of shoulders, giving their evening strokes to the red-cassocked folk?

Whatever the losses, a victory, he stressed, was a victory. And those who heard of it next day from Perth to Edinburgh were fully aware of it. News of Killiecrankie preceded word of Dundee's death. Mackay, hurrying across the hills towards the safety of Stirling, was convinced that the victor would run him down with his cavalry, and chose his escape route with that in mind, crossing ground which was unfriendly to pursuing horse. He found all the country round Perth 'in favour of the rebels'.

In Edinburgh, there was alarm. Hamilton wrote to the Secretary of State, Lord Melville, that Dundee was 'master of all the other side of Forth', and asked for reinforcements from the west and from North-umberland. Sir John Lanier, who was in charge of the Edinburgh garrison, was ordered to Stirling to take command. 'In this confusion and disorder we are in here,' Hamilton told Melville, ' ... all I can further say is that I beg you may haste down the King's commands, in this unhappy juncture, to your Lordship's most humble servant.' Sir John Dalrymple was equally concerned: 'I think the other side of the Tay is lost', he wrote to Melville, 'and Fife is in very ill tune. The Lord help us.' While Sir William Lockhart believed 'we have nothing to hinder Dundee to overrun the whole country'.

But within a few days, it had been firmly established that Dundee was dead and that Mackay had survived. Hamilton gave Melville the reassuring news on 30 July, and added that Mackay, with most of his senior officers, had arrived in Stirling. Word had reached him also that Colonel Cannon had taken over the Highland army, and the significance of that was not lost on him, nor on any who heard it.

With the death of their commander, the Highland army had suffered a fatal setback. The force of Dundee's personality, his achievements, and his inspiration, which counted far more with the clans than military experience, had moulded a disparate army, and had held it together against all the odds. 'They say Colonel Cannon commands now the Highlanders, since Dundee is gone', wrote Hamilton, 'by whose death I think they have little reason to brag of the victory.'

Mackay agreed, for, although he could not bring himself to say a good word for Dundee personally, he realized that Dundee's successor was quite unable to command the respect of an army in the same way. Mackay was particularly scathing about Cannon, who was held in low esteem by the clansmen, 'for he and Dunfermline do nothing but drink acquavity, as I'm informed.

As for the Highlanders themselves, the spirit that had sustained them through the campaign and the battle vanished almost overnight with the death of the man whom they knew as 'the terror of the Whigs, the supporter of King James and the glory of his country', and of whom Lochiel said: 'He seemed formed by Heaven for great undertakings.' As Balhaldie wrote: 'The next morning after the battle, the Highland army had more the air of the shattered remains of broken troops than of conquerors, for here it was literally true, that "The vanquished triumphed and the victors mourned."'

The Gaelic poets felt themselves bereft by the loss of Dundee, and in Edinburgh even Dalrymple conceded that he had qualities which had not been seen in the Highlands since the famous Graham who had preceded him: 'He had ever before his eyes ideas of glory, the duty of a soldier, and the example of the Great Montrose.'

Within a few weeks of his death, an Edinburgh contemporary, Dr Archibald Pitcairn, had composed an elegy in Latin, which John Dryden immediately translated:

> Oh last and best of Scots, who didst maintain
> Thy country's freedom from a foreign reign,
> New people fill the land now thou art gone,
> New Gods the temples, and new Kings the throne.
> Scotland and thou didst in each other live,

Nor wouldst thou her nor could she thee survive.
Farewell, who dying didst support the State,
And could not fall but with thy Country's fate.

A less literary contribution, also contemporary, first introduced the name by which Dundee would romantically be remembered:

> *Bonny Dundee*
> O Scotland lament the loss of thy Friend
> who loving hath gained thee bith Honour and Fame
> His valour was such he might justly pretend
> The greatest of heroes to merit the name
> But alas! a sad fate put a stop to that hand,
> which had been sufficient to conquer alone;
> Now Scotland thou'rt under another command,
> For Bonny Dundee's gone to his long home.

Some twenty-six years later, at the Battle of Sheriffmuir, as the Highland ranks were breaking, a soldier, turning away in grief and frustration, is said to have exclaimed: 'Oh, for an hour of Dundee'.

It is a phrase that might stand as an eloquent coda to the whole Jacobite movement. For, alone amongst those who were to champion the doomed cause of the Stuarts over the next sixty years, John Graham, Viscount Dundee, was the one who showed, however briefly, the twin qualities of unwavering loyalty and true leadership.

EPILOGUE

What might have happened had Dundee survived? Would he have swept on to Edinburgh, shaking William III's hold on his northern kingdom? Might he even have threatened William's still-disputed claim to the English throne? Or would his campaign have deteriorated, as so many others did, into clan wrangling, troop defections, and ultimate defeat in the face of superior military odds?

Most historians have pointed to the latter as the likeliest outcome. But it is important to remember how fragile William's cause was at this early stage. Both in Edinburgh and in London, there were still deep misgivings over the means by which William and Mary had secured the throne, and there were enough supporters of King James within the army to make an uprising a genuine threat (one regiment in England had mutinied rather than go over to William, and there were said to be more Roman Catholics in his army than amongst the forces commanded by King James).

Dundee would, of course, have faced eventually the army of General Schomberg, then assembling to take on the Jacobite forces in Ireland, and Schomberg would have won massive support from the Presbyterians in the west. But by then Dundee, not only sustained by the mounting numbers that victory would have brought him, but reinforced by the French naval support he had for so long been counting on, would have been a formidable opponent. And, by drawing Schomberg north, he would have relieved the pressure on James's army in Ireland. The Battle of the Boyne might never have taken place.

Lord Balcarres was in no doubt himself. He told James that, if Dundee had survived, 'the Prince of Orange could neither have gone nor sent into Ireland; by which your Majesty would have been entire

Master of the Kingdom, and in condition to have landed what forces you pleased in Scotland. . . .'

That, however, is as far as speculation can reasonably go. In the event, Hamilton's and Mackay's predictions about Dundee's successor, Colonel Cannon, proved accurate. Within days of Killiecrankie, there were disputes about tactics. The clans who had come in after the battle began to drift home again (the Keppoch MacDonalds, for example, were with the army for little more than two weeks). After raiding in Aberdeenshire, and drawing Mackay's forces north, Cannon marched south again, and arrived at Dunkeld in August 1689, to find the town held by a regiment of Cameronians, raised by the Earl of Angus, and commanded by William Cleland, the soldier-poet who, as a very young man, had fought against Graham of Claverhouse at Drumclog. He and the preacher Alexander Shields had held the regiment of about 800 men together despite much of the quarrelling so familiar to Covenanters, and they had been ordered to guard the little cathedral town against the clan army, then estimated at more than 3,000 strong.

On 21 August, the Highlanders attacked Dunkeld in four places at once, helped by cannon-fire. But the famous charge was useless in the narrow streets and against well-defended houses, and the Cameronians fought doggedly, retreating to the Cathedral and Dunkeld House as the dead piled up outside. They melted the lead off the roofs to supply bullets, while the Highlanders gradually ran short of ammunition. At the height of the battle, Cleland himself was killed near Dunkeld House, but his men still held out amidst burning buildings and corpse-strewn streets. The Cameronians were on the point of defeat when the Highlanders, short of ammunition and demoralized by their losses, pulled back. Cannon, who had led his men from behind, later claimed Dunkeld as a victory.

After that, the clans dispersed for the harvest, many of them taking the opportunity to plunder on their way home. They agreed to reassemble in September, but, though the campaign continued through the autumn, it was not until the following year that an army of any strength was gathered, under an experienced officer, Major-General Thomas Buchan. On 1 May 1690, however, Buchan was surprised while in camp near the Spey at the Haughs of Cromdale. Sir Thomas Livingstone's troops attacked at dawn and routed the Highlanders, inflicting a swift and bloody defeat. The Keppoch MacDonalds, who were by this time with the clans, escaped the action altogether, and Keppoch himself, 'who was ever keen for plunder, but never once fought for his King', quietly retreated, and shortly afterwards began negotiating with the Government.

The Highland war was, for the time being, effectively over. Although Buchan and Cannon continued to campaign, with small forces, throughout the following year, the defeat of James at the Battle of the Boyne meant that support from Ireland, so long promised but never delivered, would now not arrive at all. Mackay's plans for garrisoning Inverlochy were put into effect, and the Earl of Breadalbane began peace negotiations with the clans on behalf of the new Secretary of State, Sir John Dalrymple, Earl of Stair.

The threat to William's government from the disaffected north had never fully disappeared, however, and as Breadalbane's negotiations, involving large-scale offers of money to the clan chiefs, came to nothing, the seeds were planted for a plan to eliminate Highland opposition altogether. Stair, who referred derisively to the Highlanders as 'the Killiecrankies', proposed a scheme for mass extermination. In the end it came down to a small but bloody, and never to be forgiven massacre inflicted on the MacDonalds of Glencoe in February 1692.

For the family of Dundee, reprisals for his rebellion were inevitable. The title had, on his death, passed to his infant son, James, but in early December the child died, and Dundee's brother David succeeded to the Viscountcy. David had been taken prisoner in September 1689, and, though released later that year, he was stripped of the Dudhope estates and the title, and in July 1690, a process of forfeiture was pronounced against him by the Privy Council. The Claverhouse properties were bestowed instead on the Marquis of Douglas.

Dundee's widow, Lady Jean, having left Dudhope to stay with her Cochrane relations in the west, returned to Edinburgh. There she became a regular visitor to the prison where the dragoon officers under Colonel William Livingstone of Kilsyth, who had attempted to defect to Dundee during the campaign against Mackay, were held. In September 1693, she married Livingstone following his release from prison, and shortly afterwards the couple sailed for exile in Holland. They had one child, a boy, born in June 1695.

In October that year, the Livingstones were staying in an inn at Utrecht called the 'Castle of Antwerp', where they were visited by various Scottish exiles, including a number of Dundee's loyal officers who had stayed together on the Continent, fighting as a troop in the French army. On the night of 15 October 1695, the ceiling of the inn collapsed under the weight of the 300 tons of peat that had been stacked under the roof. Jean and her baby son were killed instantly, while Livingstone himself escaped unhurt. The bodies of both mother and child were embalmed, and were brought back to Scotland in March 1696. They were buried in the Livingstones' family churchyard at Kilsyth by an episcopalian minister.

Almost a hundred years later, in July 1795, a group of young people exploring the graveyard opened up a lead coffin in the Livingstone vault, and found the bodies of his wife and her baby son, perfectly preserved. They were reburied, and, in 1850, a small memorial was erected, placing on record that the last Livingstone of Kilsyth had died in 1733, and that 'without surviving issue this noble family became extinct'.

BIBLIOGRAPHY

Any assessment of the career of John Graham of Claverhouse has to begin with the three-volume account of his life by Mark Napier published in 1859. Discursive, rancorous and opinionated it nevertheless brought together for the first time most of the letters written by Claverhouse to Queensberry, Linlithgow and others, and produced the earliest 'apologia' for his subject. This was closely followed by equally sympathetic, if shorter, works by Louis Barbé and Mowbray Morris (for full titles of all these, see below). The scholarly life by Professor C. Sanford Terry (1905) filled many gaps, and correctly dated the year of Claverhouse's birth, but was less reliable on Killiecrankie. Michael Barrington's biography in 1911 was strongest on the military background. There was then a gap until, in 1937, Gordon Daviot wrote a colourful and entertaining account of the Claverhouse story, closely followed by another biography by Alistair and Henrietta Tayler in 1939. Since then, nothing. In the meantime, great strides in understanding the military struggles of the seventeenth century in Scotland have been made by modern Scottish historians. Bruce Lenman's *The Jacobite Risings in Britain*, David Stevenson's *Alasdair MacColla and the Highland Problem in the 17th Century*, Paul Hopkins' *Glencoe and the End of the Highland War* and John Prebble's *Glencoe* are among several works that have broken new ground and proved immensely helpful.

To understand Claverhouse's early career in the west of Scotland, it is necessary to understand the Covenanters, and no source can ever hope to outstrip the massive four-volume *History of the Sufferings of the Church of Scotland* by the Revd Robert Wodrow. A work of unashamed Presbyterian propaganda, it is nevertheless a treasure-chest of documents, proclamations, and Government orders, all printed verbatim, many of them no longer to be found. The Revd James Kirkton's *Secret and True History of the Church of Scotland*, William Aiton's *History of the Rencounter at Drumclog and Battle at Bothwell Bridge*, the Memoirs of William Veitch, Howie's *Scots Worthies*, and J. King Hewison's two-volume history of the Covenanters, together with the more extreme anti-episcopalian diatribes give one the flavour of the Covenanting legend, though in varying degrees all have to be treated with caution since they contain few traces of balance. The best modern work is Ian Cowan's *The Scottish Covenanters*.

The account of Archbishop Sharp's murder, and his career, comes from the various contemporary documents and depositions describing it, from his own writings, and from Dr Julia Buckroyd's excellent Life of Sharp. Sir George Mackenzie's *Memoirs of the Affairs of Scotland*, and Andrew Lang's *Life of Mackenzie*, shed fascinating light on one of Claverhouse's lifelong friends. Old General Dalyell emerges from various works, including the Dalyell papers, but the best description of him is by Captain Creichton, whose memoirs were adapted by Jonathan Swift. The extraordinary affair of Claverhouse's three-year courtship of Helen Graham is mostly to be found in the Red Book of Menteith. Fountainhall's *Historical Notices* and Dalrymple's *Memoirs of Great Britain and Ireland* are essential reading on the political situation in Scotland at the time. Military details come from various sources, including Sir James Turner's military essays, but the most authoritative we found to be Charles Dalton's *The Scots Army*, and the papers on the Scots Brigade edited by James Ferguson.

Few of the biographies of James VII give much space to his Scottish life, and fewer still have much good to say about him. But Malcolm Hay's interesting *Enigma of James II* is worth studying for an alternative view. We have drawn on Professor Gordon Donaldson's *Scotland. James V to James VII* for passages on the law in Chapter Nine.

There are virtually no references in English sources to Claverhouse at court in London, Windsor or at Newmarket, which is curious, given the time he spent there. But the memoirs of his greatest friend, Colin, Earl of Balcarres, provides a moving account of the final period of his life in the form of a long letter to James VII, full of might-have-beens. The Memoirs of Lochiel, written by Drummond of Balhaldie, who was almost certainly Lochiel's grandson, give the richest, albeit highly coloured, material on Dundee's Highland campaign. The *Grameid* by James Philip of Almerieclose is as useful for the accompanying notes of the Revd A. D. Murdoch, who translated and edited it in 1888, as for the verse itself. The *Memoirs of Major-General Hugh Mackay of*

Scourie, by himself, provide a punctilious commentary on his campaign and the final battle, as does the Marchioness of Tullibardine's *Military History of Perthshire*.

On Dundee himself, the Memoirs, a slim volume by 'An Officer of the Army', while sketchy, are an important skeleton of work, but nothing can compare to his own letters. Those to Linlithgow are to be found in the Bannatyne Club edition of 1826, which also contains the ones written to Hamilton, Murray and Melfort; the letters to Queensberry, which are in the family papers of the Duke of Buccleuch, were all published by Napier; seven others come from the Cluny papers; and there is a small miscellaneous collection amongst manuscripts held by the National Library of Scotland.

We are indebted to Ronnie Black, lecturer in Celtic Studies, for his translations of various Gaelic poems about Killiecrankie, some not, to our knowledge, drawn on before. The most accessible source is the late Annie MacKenzie's *Orain Iain Luim: Songs of John Macdonald, Bard of Keppoch* in the Scottish Gaelic Texts Society Series (1964). Other sources are in Gaelic only. They include one by Iain Lom's son, in Peter Turner's collection of 1813. The poem attributed to the Glencoe bard is in Ronald MacDonald's so-called 'Eigg collection' of 1776, in Peter Turner's revised edition of 1809, and in a longer version in A. and A. MacDonald's collection of Gaelic Poetry (1911). An anonymous poem on the battle comes from Duncan MacRae's 'The Fernaig Manuscript' (Ed. 1923).

Primary Sources (Unpublished)

The Queensberry MSS. From material in the archives of the Duke of Buccleuch and Queensberry:
Vol. 113
Vol. 121: Letters to the M of Queensberry 1677–1693
Vol. 122: Letters to the M of Q, Lord Stair and others 1680–1690
Vol. 123: Letters to the M of Queensberry 1678–1680
Vol. 126: On the Treaty of Union and State Affairs 1684–1707
Bundle 559
Bundle 1135: 70 Letters from the Earl of Rothes, etc.
Bundle 1153: 15 Letters from King to Queensberry
Vol. 110: Privy Council warrants relative to the Kingdom of Scotland 1663–1684

The National Library of Scotland MSS department:
The Wodrow Collection

Denmilne Collection
Balcarres Papers

Archives of the Catholic Diocese of Westminster:
The Browne MSS

Primary Sources (Printed)

Acts of the Parliament of Scotland
Register of the Privy Council of Scotland
Calendar of State Papers Domestic

Bannatyne Club:
Balcarres Memoirs (1841)
Letters and Journals of Robert Baillie 1637–1662, 3 vols (1841–1842)
Memoirs of his own Life and Times by Sir James Turner 1632–1670, ed. T. Thomson
Diary by John Nicoll 1650–1667, ed. D. Laing (1836)
History of the Church of Scotland by John Spottiswood, ed. M. Russell and M. Napier, 3 vols (1847–1851)
Letters of John Grahame of Claverhouse, Viscount of Dundee
Fountainhall, Sir John Lauder of (Lord), *Historical Notices of Scottish Affairs 1661–1688* (printed 1848)
Fountainhall, *Historical Observes etc., October 1680 to April 1686* (printed 1840)
Letters from Argyll to Lauderdale (1829)
Leven and Melville Papers 1689–1691 (1843)
Mackay, Maj.-Gen. Hugh, of Scourie, *Memoirs of the War carried on in Scotland and Ireland 1689–1691* (Bannatyne Club, 1833). (A Short Relation is appended to the *Memoirs*. Some supplementary letters in HMC, rep. 6, appendix.)

Scottish History Society:
Charles II and Scotland in 1650 Ed. by S. R. Gardiner
Journals of Sir John Lauder of Fountainhall (1900)
The Graemeid by James Philip of Almericlose (trans. by the Revd Alex Murdoch, 1888)
Papers on the History of the Scots Brigade in the United Netherlands 1572–1782, ed. James Fergusson, 3 vols (1899)
Jaffray, Alexander, *Diary*
Erskine, The Hon. John, of Carnock, *Journals of 1683–1687* (1893)

Atholl, *Chronicles of the Atholl and Tullibardine Families, arr. by the 7th Duke* (Edinburgh, 1896)
Aberdeen, George, Earl of, *Letters 1681–1684* (Spalding Club, 1851)
Burnet, Gilbert, *History of His Own Times*, 2 vols (London, 1724–34).

Clarendon, Earl of, *History of the Rebellion*, ed. W. Dunn Mackray, 6 vols (Clarendon Press, 1888)

Clarke, Revd J. S., *Life of James II* (from the original Stuart MSS), 2 vols (London, 1816)

Shields, Revd Alexander, *A Hind Let Loose* (1687)

Annals of the Viscount and 1st and 2nd Earls of Stair, by J. Murray Graham, 2 vols (Blackwood & Sons, 1875)

A Short History of the Life and Times of Major John Bernardi (London 1729)

The Military Memoirs of Capt. George Carleton (London, 1728)

Memoirs of Capt. John Creichton written by himself (printed 1731)

Fountainhall, Sir John Lauder of, *Chronological Notes of Scottish Affairs from 1680 to 1701* (Edinburgh, 1822)

Fountainhall, *The Decisions of the Lords of Council and Sessions etc.* (Edinburgh 1761)

Dalrymple, Sir John, of Cranstoun, *Memoirs of Great Britain and Ireland etc.*, 3 vols (London, 1790)

Drummond, John, of Balhaldie, *Memoirs of Sir Ewan Cameron of Lochiel* (Abbotsford Club, 1842)

The Lauderdale Papers, ed. Osmond Airy, 3 vols (Camden Society, 1884)

The Red Book of Menteith, by Sir William Fraser, 2 vols

The Red Book of Grantully, by Sir William Fraser, 2 vols (1868)

Mackenzie, Sir George, of Rosehaugh, *Jus Regium or the Just and Solid Foundations of Monarchy* (London, 1684)

Mackenzie, Sir George, *A Vindication of the Government in Scotland During the Reign of King Charles II etc.* (London, 1691)

Mackenzie, Sir George, *Memoirs of the Affairs of Scotland from the Restoration of Charles II* (Edinburgh, 1821)

Mackenzie, Sir George, *The Laws and Customs of Scotland in Matters Criminal etc.* (1678)

Mackenzie, Sir George, *The Right of the Succession Defended etc.* (London, 1684)

Macpherson, James, *Original Papers Containing the Secret History of Great Britain from the Restoration to the Accession of the House of Hanover etc.*, 2 vols (London, 1775)

Napier, Mark, *Memorials and Letters Illustrative of the Life and Times of John Grahame of Claverhouse, Viscount Dundee*. 3 vols (1859–62)

Mackay, John, of Rockfield, *Life of Lt.-Gen. Hugh Mackay of Scoury, C-in-C of the Forces in Scotland 1689–1690 etc.* (Edinburgh, 1836)

Memoirs of the Lord Viscount Dundee, the Highland Clans and the massacre of Glenco, With an account of Dundee's officers after they went to France by an Officer of the Army (London, 1714)

Deeds of Montrose, by George Wishart, trans. by the Revd A. Murdoch and H. F. Morland Simpson (1893)

Morer, Revd Thomas, *A Short Account of Scotland. Being a description of the nature of that Kingdom and what the Constitution of it is in Church and State etc.* (London, 1702)

Bibliography

Peterkin, Alex. *Records of the Kirk in Scotland* (1838)
Letters and Sermons of Samuel Rutherford, ed. J. Cyril Downes (London, 1955)
Memoirs of Revd John Blackader, written by himself when a prisoner on the Bass, ed. Andrew Crichton (Edinburgh, 1823)
Kirkton, James, *Secret and True History of Scotland from the Restoration to the year 1678*, ed. C. Kirkpatrick Sharpe (1817)
Stewart, James, of Goodtrees, *Jus Populi Vindicatum or the People's Right to defend themselves and their Covenanted Religion Vindicated etc.* (secretly printed 1669, burnt by the hangman 1670)
Stewart, James, of Goodtrees (and the Revd James Stirling), *Naphthali. The Wrestlings of the Church of Scotland for the Kingdom of Christ from the beginning of the Reformation until 1667 etc.* (2nd edition 1680)
Wodrow, Revd Robert, *Sufferings of the Church of Scotland from the Restoration to the Revolution etc.*, 4 vols (Glasgow, 1836)
Wodrow, Revd Robert, *Analecta*, 4 vols (Maitland Club, 1842)
A Cloud of Witnesses (for the Royal Prerogatives of Jesus Christ), ed. the Revd John Thomson (Johnstone Hunter & Co., 1871)
Calderwood, David, *History of the Kirk*, ed. T. Thomson and D. Laing, 9 vols (Wodrow Society)
Life of Robert Blair, ed. T. McCrie
Aiton, William, *A History of the Rencounter at Drumclog and the Battle of Bothwell Bridge etc.* (printed by Borthwick & Co., Hamilton, 1821)
Burt, Captain E., *Letters from a Gentleman in the North of Scotland to his friend in London etc.*, 2 vols (London, 1818)
Scottish Diaries and Memoirs 1550–1746 by J. G. Fyfe Mackay (Stirling, 1928)
Dalyell, Sir Thomas, *The Binns Papers 1320–1864*, ed. Sir J. Dalyell (1938)

Historical Manuscripts Commission
The HMC provides a wide range of material on the Scottish families which played a leading part in Restoration Scotland and consequently in the life of Dundee. This includes some of the Buccleuch MSS.

Secondary Sources

Barbé, Louis, *Viscount Dundee* (1903)
Barrington, Michael, *Graham of Claverhouse, Viscount Dundee* (Martin Secker, 1911)
Buchan, John, *Montrose*, (Thos Nelson, 1928)
Buckroyd, Julia, *Church and State in Scotland* (1980)
Buckroyd, Julia, *Life of James Sharp* (1987)
Cant, R. G., *The University of St Andrews* (1970)
Childs, John, *The Army, James II and the Glorious Revolution* (1980)
Cowan, Ian, *The Scottish Covenanters* (1976)

Cowan, Edward J., *Montrose: For Covenant and King* (Weidenfeld and Nicolson, 1977)

Cullen, L. M., and Smout, T. C., *Comparative Aspects of Scottish and Irish Economic and Social History 1600–1900* (John Donald)

Dalton, Charles, *The Scots Army 1661–1688* (London, 1909)

Daviot, Gordon, *Graham of Claverhouse* (1937)

Dickinson, W. C., and Donaldson, G., *A Source Book of Scottish History*, 3 vols, (1961)

Dictionary of National Biography

Donaldson, G., *Scotland. James V to James VII*, Edinburgh, Oliver Boyd, (1965).

Douglas, R., *The Peerage of Scotland* (1784)

Dow, E. F., *Cromwellian Scotland* (1979)

Drummond Norie, W., *Loyal Locaber* (Glasgow, 1898)

Dwyer, J., Mason, R. A., and Murdoch, A., (eds.) *New Perspectives in the Politics and Culture of Early Modern Scotland*, Edinburgh, 1982.

Elder, John R., *The Highland Host of 1678* (Jas. Maclehose and Son, 1914)

Fergusson, Lt.-Col. Alexander, *The Laird of Lag. A Life Sketch* (Printed for David Douglas, 1885)

Fortesque, Hon. J. W., *History of the British Army* (Macmillan, 1899)

Fraser, Charles Ian, *Clan Cameron* (1953)

Fraser, Robin, *A Pattern of Landownership in Scotland* (Haugheud Publications, 1987)

Fraser, Sir Wm., *History of the Carnegies etc* (1867)

Gilfillan, Revd George, *Martyrs and Heroes of the Scottish Covenant* 10th ed. (Gall and Inglis, Edinburgh)

Gordon, Patrick, of Ruthven, *A Short Abridgement of Britane's Distemper*

Graham, Louise G., *Or and Sable. A Book on the Graemes and Grahams* (Edinburgh, 1903)

Haswell, Jock, *James II, Soldier and Sailor* (1972)

Hay, Malcolm V., *The Enigma of James II* (London, 1938)

Hewison, James King, *The Covenanters*, 2 vols (John Smith and Son, 1913)

Hill, James Michael, *Celtic Warfare 1593–1763* (John Donald, 1986)

Hopkins, Paul, *Glencoe and the end of the Highland War* (1986)

Lang, A., *History of Scotland*, 4 vols (Wm. Blackwood and Son, 1909)

Lang, A., *Sir George MacKenzie. His Life and Times* (1909)

Lenman, Bruce, *An Economic History of Modern Scotland* (1977)

Lawson, Cecil C. P., *A History of the Uniforms of the British Army* (Peter Davies)

Makey, Walter, *The Church of the Covenant 1637–1651* (John Donald, 1979)

McCrie, Revd Thos., *Sketches of Scottish Church History* (John Johnstone, Edinburgh, 1844)

MacKenzie, W. C., *The Life and Times of John Maitland, Duke of Lauderdale 1616–1682* (Kegan Paul, 1923)

McNeill, P. G. B., *Jurisdiction of the Scottish Privy Council 1532–1708* (Glasgow, unpublished PhD, 1961)

Macpherson, Hector, *The Cameronian Philosopher, Alexander Shields* (Wm Blackwood and Sons, 1932)

Marshall, R. K., *The House of Hamilton in its Anglo-Scottish Setting in the Seventeenth Century*, (Edinburgh, unpublished PhD).

Mathew, David, *Scotland Under Charles I* (Eyre and Spottiswoode, 1955)

Mitchison, Rosalind, *Lordship to Patronage*. (The New History of Scotland, 1983)

Moncreiffe, Sir Iain of that Ilk, *The Highland Clans* (1967)

Money-Barnes, Maj. R., in collaboration with C. Kennedy *The Uniforms and History of the Scottish Regiments* (Allen, 1956)

Morris Mowbray, *Claverhouse* (1887)

Napier, Mark, *Memoirs of the Marquis of Montrose* (Edinburgh, 1856)

Parker, K., *My Lady Dundie* (Hodder and Stoughton, 1962)

Paul, Sir. J. B., *The Scots Peerage*, 9 vols (1904–14)

Peterkin, Alex. (ed.), *Records of the Kirk of Scotland*

Petrie, Sir Charles, *The Marshal Duke of Berwick*

Ramsay, A. A. W., *Challenge to the Highlander* (John Murray, 1933)

Robb Nesca, A., *William of Orange* (1982)

Robertson, J. Logie, *The Political Works of Sir Walter Scott* (1904)

Ross, Andrew, *Old Scottish Regimental Colours* (Wm Blackwood and Sons, Edinburgh, 1885)

Smellie, Alexander, *Men of the Covenant* (1909)

Smout, T. C., *A History of the Scottish People* (1969)

Southern, A., *Clavers, The Despots' Champion* (1889)

Stevenson, David, *Alasdair MacColla and the Highland Problem* (1980)

Stevenson, David, *Scottish Covenanters and Irish Confederates* (Ulster Historical Foundation, 1891)

Stevenson, David, *The Scottish Revolution* (1973)

Stewart, Col. David, *Sketches of the Highlanders of Scotland*, 2 vols (John Donald, 1977)

Tayler, Alistair and Henrietta, *John Graham of Claverhouse* (1939)

Terry, C. Sanford, *John Graham of Claverhouse, Viscount of Dundee 1648–1689* (1905)

Terry, C. Sanford, *The Pentland Rising and Rullion Green*, Maclehose & Sons (1905).

Thompson. J. H., Hutcheson, Mathew, (eds.), *The Martyr Graves of Scotland* (Oliphant, Anderson and Ferrier, Edinburgh)

Trevor, Meriol, *The Shadow of a Crown* (Constable, 1988)

Tullibardine, The Marchioness of, *A Military History of Perthshire 1660–1902* (R. A. and J. Hay, Perth, 1908)

Turner, F. C., *James II* (Eyre and Spottiswoode, 1948)

Veitch, Andrew, *Richard Cameron, The Lion of the Covenant* (1948)

Walton, Col. Clifford, *History of the British Standing Army 1660–1700*

The Wigtown Martyrs, RSCHS, ix, (1947).

Wilcock, John, *A Scots Earl ... Archibald, 9th Earl of Argyll 1629–1685* (Edinburgh, 1907)

Wormald, Jenny, *Court, Kirk and Community: Scotland 1470–1625* (The New History of Scotland, 1983)

INDEX

Index

Claypotts Castle 12–13
Cleland, William 32, 43–7, 226
'clickys' 75
Cluny, see Macpherson, Duncan, of
    Cluny
Cochrane, Honourable Jean, Lady
    Dundee, marries Claverhouse 107–10;
    son, James Graham, born 152, 164;
    death of 227–8; marries William
    Livingstone 227–8
Cochrane, Sir John, of Ochiltree 101,
    107, 109, 110, 134–6
Cochrane, William 166
cock-fighting 89, 93
coinage debased 93–4
Colchester, Lord 165–6
Coll of the Cows 169
Colmonell churchyard 132–3
Colyear, David, First Earl of Portmore 25
Commonwealth, Grahams and 17
Condé, Louis, Prince de 8, 22–3
Constable of Dundee 110, 114
conventicles, beginnings of 4; 'outed'
    preachers 6–7; Claverhouse breaking
    up 33–4, 71–2; punishment for
    attendance at 36; marriages and
    baptisms in the fields 70; Claverhouse
    searching for 71–2; on Claverhouse's
    wedding day 110–11; at Black Loch 111
Convention of Estates 152–8
Cornewall, Captain Henry 51
coronation, of Charles II 29
court manoeuvres 90–106
Covenanters, beginnings 4; signing of the
    National Covenant 14–16; Charles II
    and 16, 28–9; reform of St Andrews
    University 18; regarded James Sharp as
    a betrayer 19; Restoration and 29;
    figureheads of 30–1; illegal ministry
    30–1; defeated at the battle of Rullion
    Green 31; at Rutherglen 41; at Loudon
    Hill 43; defeat of Claverhouse at
    Drumclog 43–8; defeated at Bothwell
    Bridge 52–5; indemnity offered 64; Earl
    of Argyll 65, 69–70, 134–6; Richard
    Cameron; 'Lion of the Covenant' 66;
    Test Act and 68–70; imprisoned on
    Bass Rock Island 74–5; James, Duke of
    York's policy of toleration 78–9;
    Dundonald family 108; beginning of
    'killing time' 114; graveyards of
    'martyrs' 120; see also conventicles;
    execution and hanging
Covenanters in Glasgow 49–51
Crawford, Corporal 46
Creichton, Captain John 73, 147, 186

Crichton, John 42
Crichton, Thomas 172
Cromwell, Oliver 3, 17, 20

Dalrymple, Sir James, Viscount Stair
    83–5, 142
Dalrymple, Sir John, Earl of Stair
    72, 83–5, 140, 142, 191, 222, 227
Dalyell, Lieutenant John 43
Dalyell, General Sir Thomas, of the
    Binns, defeats Covenanters at the battle
    of Rullion Green; Bothwell Bridge and
    55; appointed Commander-in-Chief
    63; interrogates Hackston 67; eccentric
    looks and long beard 73; annoyed with
    Claverhouse 97–8, 112; court
    manoeuvres 102–6; death of 131
dancing 79
'Dark John of the Battles' 187
Declarations, of Arbroath 15; of
    Independence 66; of Indulgence 140,
    142; of Rights 149–50
Defoe, Daniel 130
'De'il o' Drumlanrig' 36
Delamere, Lord 149
Denmark, George, Prince of 146
Dingwall, William, in Caddam 5, 46–7
dissenters, see Covenanters
dissidents, see Covenanters
Divine Right of Kings and the National
    Covenant 15
Douglas, Archibald, 4th Earl of 21
Douglas, Colonel James 122–3, 130, 133,
    141, 144
Douglas, James, preacher 43
Douglas, Thomas 41
Douglas, Lord William 131
Drumclog, battle of 9, 43–8
Druminnor Castle 167, 168
Drumlanrig 71
Drumlanrig, James Lord 115, 122, 131
Drummond, Alexander, of Balhadie 161
Drummond, John, of Balhaldie 169,
    177–79
Drummond, Lord George 123, 127, 132
Dryden, John 223–4
Dudhope Castle 12, 94, 110, 114, 151
Dumbarton, Lord George Douglas, 1st
    Earl of, 130–1, 135, 136
Dumfries, Claverhouse at 5, 8, 33
Dunachton Castle 183
Dunbar, battle of 11, 17
Dundas, Elizabeth 89
Dundee, James, 2nd Viscount 152, 159,
    164, 227
Dundee, Lady, see Cochrane,

239

Index